Before Nature Dies

Books by Jean Dorst

THE MIGRATIONS OF BIRDS

BEFORE NATURE DIES

Before Nature Dies

JEAN DORST

Curator of the Division of Mammals and Birds
The National Museum of Natural History, Paris

Translated by
CONSTANCE D. SHERMAN

With a Preface by Prince Bernhard
President of the World Wildlife Fund

ILLUSTRATED

Houghton Mifflin Company Boston
1970

TO ELAINE

Contents

Colour Plates

Black-and-White Illustrations

Preface

by H R H Prince Bernhard

PRESIDENT OF THE WORLD WILDLIFE FUND

The modern world is seriously out of balance because of man's tendency to exterminate wildlife and to upset the harmony of his whole environment. Natural resources are endangered at a time when human populations are expanding with increasing speed and needs are daily greater. Some of our activities seem to contain the germs of destruction of the human race.

The number of animals and wild plants which are disappearing or becoming exceedingly rare continues to grow. Careless hunting, deliberate vandalism and, above all, destruction of habitats are responsible for these ravages. Man is injuring the earth by poor soil management, scattering pesticides heedlessly and poisoning the planet with the waste products of his technical civilization. Marine resources are pillaged by gross over-exploitation of some of the oceans.

This book deals with the grave dangers threatening man and nature in the modern world and proposes a rational management of the earth. The establishment of reserves, to be treated as sanctuaries, the administration of land with a view to its use, and the preservation of a balance similar to that of nature are all to be advocated.

Man must realize that he has neither the moral right nor any material interest in hounding an animal or vegetable species to extinction. A true reconciliation of man and nature is desirable so that mankind may live in accordance with the natural laws from which he can never be completely liberated.

The primary duty of modern man is thus the preservation of his natural capital, and this is the goal of the *World Wildlife Fund*, an international foundation to preserve nature. For this reason I am anxious to express the hope that this book, with its comprehensive discussion of natural resources and all the problems involved in the preservation of nature, may find a place not only in scientific institutions but also on the desks of the relevant authorities and, above all, in the libraries of those who love nature and are aware that much must be done, and soon, before nature dies.

Bernhard,
Prince of the Netherlands

Foreword

Man and Nature at odds

*We have become rich through the lavish use of our natural resources and
we have just reason to be proud of our growth. But the time has come to
inquire seriously what will happen when our forests are gone, when the
coal, the iron, the oil and the gas are exhausted, when the soil has been
further impoverished and washed into the streams, polluting the rivers,
denuding the fields and obstructing navigation.*

> Theodore Roosevelt
> Conference on the Conservation of
> Natural Resources, 1908.

Conservation of nature and rational exploitation of its resources
are problems which go back to man's first appearance on this earth.
Human beings have always exerted a far greater influence on their
habitat than any other species of animal and, even in the remote past,
they upset the balance of nature to their own detriment.

In the eyes of biologists the history of man assumes the same
importance as the great cataclysms on the geological scale, or
Cuvier's 'revolutions', during which the flora and fauna of the
entire world were transformed in both composition and balance.
The rapid changes in animal and plant populations revealed by
palaeontology are no more important than the 'revolution' that has
occurred since man appeared on earth. And this is unequalled in
speed and scope if we consider the brief span during which our
species has been active.

Even if 'human time' is taken as a scale, tremendous modifications
have been produced during a very short period. If we condense the
total history of man since the Stone Age to a twelve-month year.

the Christian era would begin early in December, and the American Declaration of Independence would be signed on the 29th of the month. The energy then at man's disposal was still limited to his own muscle and that of draught animals. The whole 'mechanical' history of humanity is encompassed in the last two days, and it is during this short period—a fraction of a second on the geological scale—that man has modified the face of the earth most profoundly; at times this has been to his real benefit, but often he has disfigured it shamefully, causing devastation and catastrophes in the eyes of both naturalists and economists.

Some forms of damaging nature go back to ancient times. Primitive man had at his disposal a weapon whose power was out of proportion to his feeble technical skill: namely, fire. The civilizations of classical antiquity laid waste the Mediterranean world. Later the discoverers of the sixteenth and subsequent centuries pillaged and massacred. At the present time the situation is more serious than ever before. Industrial civilization is the order of the day and we are witnessing a population explosion unparalleled in human history. Yet natural resources are wasted with a disconcerting prodigality that may lead to the extermination of the human race. We have absolute confidence in recently developed techniques. Progress in physics and chemistry has increased the power of our tools so fantastically that people believe technique can solve all our problems without the help of our environment. The old pact uniting man and nature has been broken, for man now thinks he is powerful enough to free himself from the vast biological complex of which he has always been part. For, beyond the species forming the animal and vegetable kingdoms, there exists a much larger entity, an organism constituting the life of the entire planet. Ecology is the science which deals with the relationships of living beings with each other and with their physical environment. This tells us that biological communities, the animal and plant populations within a certain habitat, have a life of their own and function as definite entities whose evolution is governed by laws. There can be no doubt about the functional unity of the living world. These vast communities, forming a thin layer on the surface of the earth, are governed by complex laws as strict as the physiological ones controlling a man's various organs.

A study of the troubles from which we are suffering and a

'A grove of giant redwoods or sequoias should be kept just as we keep a great or beautiful cathedral' (Theodore Roosevelt): Sequoia National Park, California

Hunting mosaic in the Hippone Museum, Algeria. This work, dating from the end of the 4th century, contains lions, panthers, hartebeests, oryx, wild asses and ostriches, all of which have vanished from North Africa: hunting methods are clearly shown (nets, traps, beaters on horseback, and groomsmen surrounding the animals and blinding them with flaming torches). A great many animals were required for circus games

detailed analysis of their causes reveal that man has broken certain laws. His activity has tended to simplify the ecosystems, to channel their productions in a purely human direction and often to slow down the conversion cycle of living substances. It has tended to separate the multiple elements that produce rich natural habitats—for example, salt water, fresh water and land in the coastal marshes, which are some of the most productive areas in the world. Man has thus seriously injured certain habitats, and the global balance sheet shows a deficit.

It is, however, true that man cannot be a simple element in a truly natural habitat once he has crossed a certain threshold of civilization—once the hunter and berry-gatherer have become shepherd and farmer—because of his intellect. As the earth in its primitive state is not adapted to our expansion, man must shackle it to fulfil human destiny. In order to satisfy our elementary needs, especially for food, we have to transform certain habitats to increase their productivity directly or indirectly.

This does not mean that man should use the recipe indiscriminately, transforming the entire earth's surface for his immediate profit. He has succeeded in domesticating some wild animals and modifying them to a certain degree. But he cannot go beyond this point lest they perish. The same is true of those vast living organisms forming biological communities. Man can enslave them, domesticate them, transform them until they are monsters in the eyes of a biologist. But he can do this in only a small part of the world; he must respect a certain balance in nature and submit to laws that are really part of the constitution of living matter.

Man will doubtless always require bodies of protoplasm containing chlorophyll and embedded in a plant cell. At this level living matter is synthetized by solar energy and converted into the chemical energy from which food chains are derived. A food chain is a series of species, each of which lives at the expense (as a predator or parasite) of its predecessor. Food chains form ecological associations, so man will always be an integral part of the natural system. Yet frequently he has forgotten the fundamental laws of nature in the belief that they are no longer applicable to his species.

Human activities, when carried to the extreme, seem to contain the germs of our destruction, like the excesses observed in the course of the evolution of some animal groups. A characteristic may become so developed and magnified as to be positively harmful to the species. Many lines have thus disappeared during geological times because of some exaggerated development. Although man's technical civilization has enabled him to attain a high standard of living, the excess may prove fatal. Fraser Darling humorously calls this 'Irish-elkism' in a comparison with the evolution of the large Irish deer, which produced larger and larger horns until this monstrosity contributed to its extinction. Similar cases occur in the evolution of many living organisms, also in the evolution of races and human populations, as the writer recalls in connection with ancient Mexican civilizations (*Pelican in the Wilderness*, New York, 1956).

It is symptomatic, moreover, that man is spending more and more of his energy and resources protecting himself from his own activities and their harmful effects. Thus we seem to live in an absurd universe because we have circumvented certain laws that govern the whole world.

We must also observe that the impact of man on nature will never be comparable to that of any other zoological species, since, in addition to the instinctive biological behaviour common to all animals, man has cultural traditions and beliefs capable of modifying his simple actions and reactions.

Here it is appropriate to contrast Oriental philosophies with our own Western conceptions. Shri Ramakrishna said: 'God is immanent in all creatures. He exists even in the ant; the difference is only in the manifestation.' The tenets of Taoism, which proclaim the unity of all existences, prescribe a respect for life in all its forms, except, in case of absolute necessity, for human beings. The farmer, for example, who has cut thousands of flowers in mowing hay for his cattle, must not break off a single one on the edge of the road for pleasure, because this act is contrary to his ethics. We find considerations of this kind in the *Book of Rewards and Punishments*, an eleventh-century Chinese miscellany containing a large number of precepts about the protection man must give even the most humble animals and plants. Oriental philosophies and religions, particularly Buddhism and Hinduism, are full of such reflections. As all forms of life proceed directly from God or can be identified as part of

Him, man is metaphysically part of a complex of which he is only one element.

On the other hand western philosophies emphasize the supremacy of man over the rest of creation, which exists only to serve him.

A passage from the Scriptures is revealing: 'And God blessed them: and God said unto them, Be fruitful, and multiply, and replenish the earth, and subdue it; and have dominion over the fish of the sea, and over the birds of the heavens, and over every living thing that moveth upon the earth. And God said, Behold, I have given you every herb yielding seed, which is upon the face of all the earth, and every tree, in which is the fruit of a tree yielding seed; to you it shall be for food.' (Genesis I: 28–29). Even the most materialistic philosophers regard man as the supreme being to whom everything should be subject. Descartes, who said we should be masters and possessors of nature (*Discourse on Method*), considered animals as machines unworthy of our sympathy, and Kant thought that man has no responsibilities save to himself. There is therefore nothing astonishing in the fact that the protection of animals and plants received no support from the European philosophy whence our technical civilization was derived.

But whatever our opinions may be on this moral plane, if man is to rule the earth for his own benefit he must do it as effectively as possible. All biologists are convinced that this requires the observation of certain natural laws and the maintenance of a balance which cannot be modified beyond a certain point.

The problem of the conservation of nature has reached a dangerous point; moreover its essential aspects have changed. At the close of the past century, when naturalists were frightened by the extent of the destruction wrought by people who believed natural resources inexhaustible, they envisaged only the protection of certain animals and plants threatened with extinction. Sanctuaries were created, which made it possible to save a large number of species and to protect large sections of primitive habitats.

The problem to-day is no longer the same. We still have to struggle to save the last vestiges of the wild. But it is far more essential to preserve the natural resources of the whole world and to guarantee man an income which will permit him to survive. While saving humanity we shall also assure the safety of the living creatures of the world. The conservation of nature thus assumes several aspects which, although closely connected, at first appear very different. Naturalists, of course, continue to work for the protection of all species in the animal and plant kingdoms, as well as for the preservation of a representative sampling of all natural habitats. A study of natural environments sheltered in 'living museums' is indispensable to an understanding of the evolution of areas transformed by man.

But conservation of nature implies conservation of natural resources as a whole, beginning with those of water, air, and, especially, soil, on which we depend for life. It also requires the protection of landscapes as a harmonious setting for man's life and his activities. All too often we have disfigured whole regions by poorly planned industrial units and agricultural projects. Man needs balance and beauty, and those who think they have no interest whatsoever in aesthetics are often much more sensitive to it than they realize.

We need to study these different problems to-day and to achieve a rational management of the earth's surface. Plans for development should ascertain for what purpose the land is best suited, and, especially in marginal zones, they should set aside large areas where natural habitats can be preserved. The old antagonism between the 'protectors of nature' and the planners should cease. The former must learn that the survival of man requires intensive agriculture and a complete transformation of certain areas; they must abandon a number of sentimental prejudices, some of which have done serious harm to the cause they are defending.

On the other side, the technocrats must admit that man cannot free himself from certain biological laws, and that a rational exploitation of natural resources does not involve transforming habitats automatically and completely. They must understand that the preservation of natural areas constitutes land-use quite as much as their modification. A realistic agreement between economists and biologists can and must lead to reasonable solutions and assure the rational development of humanity in a setting in harmony with natural laws.

Those who deal with conservation often have a curiously guilty conscience. They seem to be apologizing for withdrawing certain areas of the globe from human influence and depriving man of a fair profit. They must abandon this attitude, for their opinions are quite as defensible as those of engineers charged with the transformation of a region. Like them, and with them, they must contribute to the total improvement of a territory, which implies maintaining some natural habitats in their original state. The preservation of rare species is only the best-known of the multiple reasons for this.

We must, then, strike a balance between man and nature. To some people the term 'natural balance' has a romantic connotation, but to biologists it is a realistic goal. They admit that man must transform part of the earth's surface for his own good, but they deny that he has the right to transform the entire surface of the world, since this would be against his own interests. Thus man will be the first to benefit from a reconciliation with nature.

A book dealing with such a large number of subjects could not be written without the assistance of specialists in many different fields. I am particularly grateful to Professor Roger Heim, Member of the Institut de France and former Director of the National Museum of Natural History. It was he who suggested this book.

My thanks go also to those who read certain chapters and gave me the benefit of their criticism, particularly Messrs F. Bourlière, M. Blanc, K. Curry-Lindahl, P. Ducourtial, R. D. Etchécopar, F. Fournier, Mrs S. C. Hixson, Messrs. D. J. Kuenen, R. C. Murphy, K. Scott and G. Tendron.

The essential documentation was made available by a number of people. Although I cannot name them all, I should like to express my gratitude to Messrs J. R. Aubry, J. G. Baer, J. H. Baker, C. L. Boyle, R. C. Clement, J. H. Calaby, G. W. Douglas, R. G. Fontaine, E. H. Graham, L. Hoffmann, Mrs R. H. McConnell, Miss J. Mignon, Messrs R. R. Miller, R. H. Pough, H. Siriez, the late Professor V. Van Straelen, Sir George Taylor and Mr E. B. Worthington.

I have knocked at many doors in order to collect the photographs which appear as illustrations. Those to whom I am particularly indebted are: Mr A. G. Bannikov, Miss Phyllis Barclay-Smith, Messrs M. Cowie, I. Eibl-Eibesfeldt, R. A. Falla, E. P. Gee, W. Meijer, P. Molloy, P. Pfeffer, F. Roux, Peter Scott, R. M. Warnecke and Prince Yamashina, as well as the National Audubon

Society, the Inter-African Bureau for Soils, the US Department of Agriculture, Forest Service and Soil Conservation Service, and the Kansas State Historical Society.

The drawings were done by my talented friend Paul Barruel, the maps and diagrams by Mr J. Brouillet. Miss Odile Jachiet prepared the manuscript.

Finally, I express my appreciation to Dr Constance D. Sherman, who translated the book. I am deeply grateful for her accurate rendering of the original text and for her work in bringing much of the statistical content up-to-date.

Paris, January 1968
J.D.

YESTERDAY

1 Pre-industrial Man and his impact on Nature

Man's impact on biological balances dates from his appearance on earth. If it is possible to regard man at that distant time as a natural element like any other animal, it was a purely temporary condition. The history of humanity may be envisaged partly as the struggle of our species against its environment, involving a progressive liberation from certain natural laws, and the gradual enslavement of the world, its soil, plants and animals by man's inventions. For a long time man's influence was negligible because populations were small and technical equipment modest. This situation prevailed until modern times in certain parts of the world. If we examine all past civilizations, it is apparent that some attained very great perfection intellectually while lagging behind technically. Hence their impact on nature was, on the whole, relatively slight.

This does not mean that ancient man did not exert a dominant influence on his environment, an influence often prejudicial to his own interests. Unlike most other animal species, man is capable of destroying his habitat long before feeling the effects of this wantonness. When a herbivore multiplies beyond the capacity of its habitat and starts to destroy it, populations decrease rapidly and pressure on the habitat immediately drops. When a predator multiplies to such a point that its prey is exterminated or considerably reduced, predator populations diminish. Man knows no short-term limiting factors because of his intelligence, his resistance to unfavourable environmental conditions and his ecological flexibility. The natural biological balance between man and nature disappeared as soon as the hunter became a shepherd, and certainly by the time he began to farm. Problems of conservation have existed since the dawn of human history. Some parts of the world which formed the cradle of ancient cultures were ruined long before 'modern' civilization penetrated them. Natives in Africa and America had ravaged large areas before any Europeans arrived. And in Asia the strong population pressure and a certain contempt for nature in the wild had already caused irreparable damage.

In other areas man maintained a balance with his environment until the white man came. A glance at the situation prevailing before European expansion and the rise of 'western' civilization will clarify this.

1 THE HUNTER AND FISHERMAN

At first man lived on fruits, plants and animals that were easy to capture. Then he invented various types of weapons which enabled him to hunt and fish. At this stage, reached in the lower Paleolithic Age, man was completely dependent on his natural environment. The fluctuations of this environment, affecting the quantity of food available, obliged him to adapt himself or to seek his requirements elsewhere. Although these men felled trees to feed their fires and make clearings for camps, the habitats were scarcely modified. Furthermore, depredations were limited, for there was an auto-regulation of predator-prey relationships similar to the one found throughout the animal kingdom.

This situation can be studied to-day among primitive tribes, such as the Australian aborigines, who live by fishing, hunting and gathering. Gathering implies conservation practices, notably the burial of fragments of plants destined to produce a new crop (*Ipomea*, *Dioscorea*). It should, however, be observed that these Australians when hunting may set fire to 30 or 50 square miles of savanna in order to catch or locate their prey (Meggitt, 1963).

Tribes more devoted to hunting are ruled by laws that are partly religious, partly ethical, but basically ecological since they reflect a harmonious relationship between man and his environment. No predator wishes to exterminate his prey, and primitive man is no exception to this rule. Accordingly, these hunting tribes have developed legislative codes recalling the basic ecological principles governing the predator-prey balance. The Mbuti Pygmies in the Ituri Forest of the north-eastern Congo live chiefly on game (various kinds of antelope, occasionally elephants, okapis and monkeys), small prey (terrestrial mollusks, larvae, termites), and plant products (roots, tubercles, berries). These 'children of the forest' (*bamili nde ndura*) are completely adjusted to their surroundings, which supply them with food and shelter, and which they do not attempt to modify. The nature of the terrain, seasonal movements of game, the ripening of fruit, and hunting practices have shaped the rhythm of their life quite as much as the social and political organization of their tribes (Turnbull, 1963). Indians in the Amazon forest live in much the same fashion; they have strict rules to protect game, yet permit its rational exploitation.

More advanced tribes of hunters have, however, exerted a much greater influence on the natural balance of their environment because they set fires to help them capture frightened herds. Some prehistorians think that man played a part in causing the disappearance of some of the larger and more gregarious mammals, especially the cave bear (*Ursus spelaeus*). Brush fires have been—and still are—lit in Africa to the detriment of plant associations. Thus primitive man already possessed a weapon of sufficient power to modify natural habitats, opening the way to accelerated erosion and devastation. Layers of ash, carbonized debris, and even burned tree trunks prove that fires ravaged large areas on the northern plains of Germany and Belgium during the Mesolithic Age. Some authors are inclined to believe that the sudden disappearance of conifers and birches is partially due to man, who, by means of fire, could have changed the natural balance in vast regions (Narr, 1956).

This influence becomes even more apparent among tribes which have developed techniques for a kind of wild pastoralism. The best example is that of the North American Indians, who were responsible for extending prairies across the great plains in the centre of the North American continent. Their favourite prey was the bison, on which they depended for food and clothing and to which they were mystically attached. Although the Indians made no attempt to domesticate these large herbivores, daily contact had given them a thorough knowledge of the animals' habits. As the bison liked open habitats, the Indians deliberately set fire to the forest so as to enlarge the grassy plains. Climatic conditions do not explain this extension of the North American prairies, which otherwise should be partially forested.

On the whole, hunting tribes have caused very little change on the face of the globe. Spread over large areas, they are still an integral part of their surroundings. In primitive societies the method of preserving meat by smoking and salting was unsatisfactory as a basis for trade, but the development of more advanced techniques threatened the natural balance.

2 THE SHEPHERD

In the next stage men gradually became shepherds. In the Near East herbivores were domesticated 7000 or 8000 years ago, thus permitting man to draw a profit from the otherwise unproductive green cover consisting especially of Gramineae. Aside from llamas and alpacas, all the mammals now domesticated originated in the warm or cold temperate zones of the Old World. Since that remote period man has not attempted to domesticate any other animals, but has improved initial stocks by artificial selection and scattered them around the world.

The impact of shepherds on their habitats was far more extensive than that of the hunters. It consisted essentially in a regression of closed habitats (forests) and an increase of open ones (savannas, steppes). The usual procedure was to burn trees, bushes and, in general, all living species, which were then replaced by annual herbaceous plants. The use of fire—which was pre-industrial man's best weapon for transforming habitats—is still practised by shepherds in tropical Africa. But farmers also set fires after a hasty clearing of the fields; so the two worked together to destroy the forest and replace it by open habitats. The landscape was thus completely transformed, erosion accelerated, and rivers and even the climate affected.

Transformation of habitats is made worse since man often tends to increase the number of domestic animals, causing overgrazing with disastrous consequences to the balance of both the soil and the biological communities. This occurs frequently because, among many pastoral societies such as the Masaï of East Africa, cattle are not only a source of food but a symbol of wealth and power. We should also emphasize the mystic links that have existed since time immemorial between shepherds and their flocks. These are extremely important. The classical example is in India, where, especially in the Indo-Ganges plains, cows are held sacred. This religious tradition goes back to ancient times when vanished tribes of shepherds made it a law. According to the Manava-Dharma-Çastra in the Manu Code, traditionally attributed to the first Manu and dating from a period between the second century BC and the second century AD, it is more serious to kill a cow than a Brahmin. The effect of such beliefs on overgrazing speaks for itself.

Shepherds were largely responsible for destroying vast areas of the world, especially in the Mediterranean region and the Near East, long before industrial civilization began its ravages. Although numerous wars forced abandonment of conservation practices and intelligent land management, it was the shepherd who played the dominant role in the degradation of the Mediterranean world. Here many deserts are man-made, since the vegetation does not correspond to either the environment or the climate. Contrary to the opinion of certain writers, particularly Ellsworth Huntington, the Mediterranean climate seems to have undergone no perceptible change during historic times. According to Reifenberg's formula, 'the nomad is less the "son of the desert" than its father' (The struggle between the 'desert and the sown,' *Proc. Int. Symp. Desert Res.*, Jerusalem, 1952 (1953): 378–89). The magnificent effort which the Israelis are now making to restore the soil proves that the land of Canaan 'flowing with milk and honey' is not a totally lost paradise. In Africa also invading shepherds transformed large areas in the savannas and continued the destruction wrought by farmers in the forests.

Finally we should not close this discussion of the origin of pastoral economy without mentioning the sort of competition that seems to exist between domesticated animals and their savage ancestors. This has led to the almost complete extinction of domestic animals in their native state. The aurochs, ancestor of the ox, has vanished, and so has the unknown progenitor of the dog, while survivors of the species that have given birth to our horses, asses, camels, sheep and goats are all in a highly precarious state.

Some people believe that domestication saved species destined to disappear naturally, but their disappearance seems rather to have been due to competition with domesticated breeds. There is no proof, however, of either hypothesis.

3 THE FARMER

The passage from a pastoral to an agricultural economy cannot be outlined simply, for numerous conflicts arose between these activities. The story of Cain and Abel, for instance, relates how the shepherd yielded to the farmer. This new form of economy involved an even greater transformation of natural habitats, particularly large-scale deforestation which is the first step in soil deterioration.

Many authors believe that agriculture began more than 5,000 years BC in the 'Fertile Crescent' of the Near East bordering the plains of Mesopotamia. It spread towards the Mediterranean basin and Europe, changing according to the nature of the environment. Each technical improvement made possible an extension of cultivated areas. Thus the invention of the iron plough opened rich, heavy soil to agriculture, which, until that time, had been confined to light soil. The enlargement of cultivated areas led to an increase in human population.

In the Mediterranean region the natural balance was ruptured and the soil degraded at a very early period (Fries, 1959). Although soil fertility was not immediately reduced everywhere, the changes wrought by man were rapid and basic. There have been lively discussions about the causes of agricultural decline in the Mediterranean basin. Some (especially Huntington, 1915) attribute it to a change in climate which became progressively more arid; others believe that man is solely responsible. The latter seem to be right, and it appears that man ruined a region where the natural balance was much more fragile than in other areas, such as central Europe (see Hyams, 1952, and Monod, 1959).

Although Mediterranean plains were doubtless never forested, the trees on the mountain slopes and hills were burned in antiquity, especially by shepherds, and irrationally exploited (Heichelheim, 1956). The classic example is the famous cedars of Lebanon, which were chopped down to build Phoenician ships, the palaces of Achemenides (the beams of Persepolis came from Lebanon) and the temple in Jerusalem. 'And Solomon sent to Hiram (King of Tyre) saying . . . command thou that they cut me the cedar trees out of Lebanon . . . When he heard the words of Solomon, Hiram rejoiced greatly and said . . . I will do all thy desire concerning timber of cedar and concerning timber of cypress.' (I Kings: 5). These two sovereigns did not suspect they were ruining their kingdoms. When Strabo, born about 60 BC, was alive, the forest mantle was still large enough to enable shipyards in Italy and Spain to obtain excellent timber in areas that are now deforested. During the Middle Ages this devastation continued at an even faster tempo.

Central and northern Europe, which were originally heavily forested, were first ravaged during the Neolithic period, four and three thousand years BC, in an immense zone extending from Hungary and the southern part of the great German and Polish plains to Belgium. Men belonging to the Danube culture used the hoe to cultivate barley and a primitive kind of wheat, besides other plants. Their use of fire to make clearings was the first step in a progressive deforestation which was, however, restricted by the smallness of the population and by the fact that these forests, being denser and having a greater regenerative power than those in the Mediterranean area, were transformed more slowly by man.

It would also be wrong to believe that intertropical regions remained intact until the Europeans came. A progressive destruction of original forest dates from the first settlement of farmers and shepherds in the tropics. One of the basic principles of primitive culture in these areas is the 'shifting cultivation' practised by nomads. As soils become unproductive, so people are frequently forced to move on.

At the beginning of the dry season, a man clears a sector of forest, chops down the bushes but leaves the trees. The sun dries out any remaining plants, which are then burned to ashes. The ground is planted, and crops ripen during or at the end of the next rainy season. This ground does not remain fertile for any length of time, and after one or two harvests the farmer may move to begin the same cycle elsewhere. Vegetation reappears in the deserted area in accordance with climatic conditions; at first it consists only of bushes but later there is secondary forest. When the soil regains its former fertility, a new cycle can begin. As the ground may need to lie fallow 20 or 30 years, large tracts of land are required to assure a satisfactory rotation.

This shifting cultivation was the pattern everywhere, and it is still practised by natives in many intertropical regions. As soon as populations increase, they cause serious damage to nature with their brush fires in the clearings and the open habitats of wooded and grassy savannas. In Africa destruction of vegetation has been accelerated, particularly in rain-forest, since the European penetration and the development of manufacturing, but the green blanket which formerly covered the entire continent, except in areas with particular soil conditions, has been ravaged since prehistoric times. According to Aubréville (1949), Africa was originally covered with dense forests; in a wet climate they were rain-forests: elsewhere they were mostly dry. Savanna existed only in zones near the desert, and there it was very restricted.

Long before he made iron tools or thought of agriculture, primitive man set fire to the vegetation so that he could circulate and hunt more easily. Dense dry forests thus evolved into the modern more or less wooded savanna, where the predominant plants are sun-loving and fire-resistant. When the modern African farmers arrived, they settled in dry forest and later in rain-forest. The use of clearings for shifting cultivation hastened regression of the forest and the creation of savannas, by cutting paths through fire resistant rain-forests. The transformation of Africa shows that primitive man could leave his mark on an entire continent long before he had powerful tools at his disposal.

Similar events occurred elsewhere, especially in Madagascar, where an extraordinary variety of biological environments created a continent in miniature. Most of the island, except the south-west, must have been almost entirely covered with forest. Long before any Europeans came, the eastern forests were felled in accordance with the *tavy* method (the local name for shifting cultivation) to make clearings which produced only one or two harvests before they were abandoned for secondary growth (*savoka*). The low areas of the west were burned to such an extent that to-day few vestiges of primitive associations remain. Long before the arrival of Europeans, Madagascar was one of the most devastated parts of the globe (Humbert, 1927).

In many parts of Asia shifting cultivation ravaged primitive forests. On the high plateaus of Vietnam the *ray*, which had a three-year rotation, caused yearly destruction of woods valued at about 30 million dollars. In the Philippines the practice of *kaingin* has long been responsible for forest destruction, extension of savannas

Examples of North American animals reduced to a remnant
population:
above Pronghorn: *below* Alaska grizzly

The rarity of these
American species is
largely due to man's
destruction of their
habitats:

Ivory-billed
woodpecker:
male at the entrance
to his nest

California condor

Prairie chicken

(especially *Imperata* savannas) and secondary associations with little economic value.

In the New World the classic example of devastation by pre-industrial man is the Mayan Empire. The disappearance of this civilization, one of the most highly developed in Central America, was chiefly caused by deforestation, shifting cultivation—the *milpa* —and fires that were set to transform habitats. Cities whose monuments attest their power and splendour are dead because of the imprudent cultural practices of short-sighted man. (See C. W. Cooke, *Journ. Wash. Acad. Sci.* 21, No. 13: 283-7, 1941.) We must hope that Professor Roger Heim was too pessimistic when he wrote: 'The collapse of the Mayan empire forecast that of world civilization in a forthcoming century' (*Un naturaliste autour du monde*).

At first man submitted to the imperatives of his natural habitat, as primitive tribes still do, but this period was relatively short. Soon he counter-attacked in a manner unique in the history of animals. In assuring his survival, he destroyed his habitat. It has sometimes been claimed that the destruction of nature really began with the expansion of the white man. His destructive economy and ravages are contrasted with the conservative methods of all races of natives, who are less harmful than Europeans because of their lack of technical equipment. This is a serious error. Primitive, pre-industrial societies had already gravely injured a number of natural habitats, and some animals doubtless vanished during this period. The ravages were, of course, limited, but humanity already possessed the germs of self-destruction which developed dramatically during subsequent phases of its history.

2 Man against Nature

A continent ages quickly once we come.

Ernest Hemingway, *Green Hills of Africa*

We have seen how the primitive balance of nature was upset as soon as man acquired the necessary tools and populations increased. The Mediterranean basin, South-east Asia and certain areas of the New World were transformed a long time ago, but a large part of the globe was practically intact at the time of the Great Discoveries. At this point man became truly aware of the world, which hitherto had been divided into sectors having little or no contact with each other. After the first circumnavigations of the globe, Europeans awoke to the wealth of hitherto unexploited areas. At the same time a technical civilization developed which prepared the way for the industrial revolution of succeeding centuries.

During this accelerated expansion waves of Europeans set out to win global treasure, each one bringing new bands of colonists determined to exploit virgin or undeveloped lands. North America was settled by the white race in the 18th century; then came Australia and finally Africa, the last continent to be devastated together with South America.

It is these three continents which have suffered most and have the largest toll of extinct or rare species. This is due to the brutality of men equipped with powerful weapons, who have mishandled areas that were once virgin or where nature was still more or less in balance with primitive man. It is true that certain animal or plant species have also been exterminated in Europe and Asia and that natural balances have changed there. But these transformations occurred in stages, permitting the flora and fauna to find refuges and become progressively adapted to humanity. The evolution which required centuries in Europe and Asia was condensed into a few decades in America and Africa. It was a devastating explosion rather than a slow development.

There are numerous causes for these disasters. Some come from man's voluntary or involuntary destruction of an animal or plant species for his immediate profit, but indirect causes are often even more serious. Large-scale deforestation or systematic drainage of swamps may lead to the destruction of whole areas. The destiny of these habitats determines the fate of a large number of plants and animals that often have strict ecological requirements. The entire flora and fauna thus vanish together, and we may be sure that man destroyed numerous very small animals and plants before he had even learned of their existence.

We shall sketch the principal ravages of man since the era of the discoveries, with particular emphasis on birds and mammals. A large number of historical accounts make it possible to trace their spectacular decrease. (See the important works of Allen (1942), Harper (1945) and Greenway (1958)). No less than 120 forms of mammals and about 150 bird forms have vanished. It is estimated that about ten forms (species and subspecies) of birds became extinct before 1700: about 20 in the 18th century: about 20 from 1800 to 1850: about 50 between 1851 and 1900 and another 50 since 1901. There has been an average loss of one avian form a year during the past century. The same facts could be recorded for a number of small creatures of the plant and animal world which had a place in the balance of nature often out of proportion to their size, but whose disappearance is in many ways as serious as that of the large fauna.

We shall trace man's assault on nature by continents, listing them in the chronological order of their devastation. This assault reveals the thoughtless pillage of a world exploited by men who were dazzled by wealth and foolish enough to consider it inexhaustible.

1 EUROPE

Europe and Asia were the first continents to suffer from man. Although almost all the original habitats have disappeared, the most striking change has been the destruction of forest cover, which once extended over most of the continent. Around the

Mediterranean the scattered forest, consisting chiefly of evergreen oaks and pines, has relatively slight regenerative power. Furthermore, it was destroyed at a much earlier date than other regions: Attica was entirely deforested in the 5th century BC. This process was continued during the Middle Ages when forests gave way to fields or pasture, and to supply the needs of industry and ship-building, which flourished during the heyday of Genoa and Venice. In vast areas the Mediterranean forest was replaced by wasteland and scrub, many modified surfaces were eroded, and some species, such as the conifers *Abies nebrodensis* in Sicily and *Abies pinsapo* in southern Spain, became very rare.

In other parts of Europe the forest consisted chiefly of oaks and deciduous trees, notably beeches, which gave way to conifers in the north. They formed a dense, almost continuous, forest zone, as revealed in place names all over Europe. Suffixes indicating forests occur in place names that are to-day far from any wooded area: for example, *ham*, *cote* and *hurst* in English; *wald* and *holz* in German; *drewa* in Slavic. The components *sart* in English and French, *rode*, *schwend* and *han* in German, and *trebynja* in Slavic indicate clearings. French names have preserved numerous references to forests, such as 'bois', 'bosc', or those recalling a species of tree.

Deforestation did not really begin until the Middle Ages; then it gradually spread from south to north and from west to east as populations became settled (*fig* 1). Deforestation was, moreover, essential to man's way of thinking, for forest was identified with savagery. This kind of psychosis, which had a sound economic and social basis, corresponds to what took place many centuries later in other parts of the world and what is happening to-day in some newly developing countries. Charlemagne granted parts of the forest to all men strong enough to clear them. During the Carolingian era two-fifths of France was cultivated after an intensive period of clearing. For a long time the only restraint was exercised by the great feudal lords, who wanted to preserve enormous forests for hunting. Pasturage was also responsible for deforestation, because cattle were taken to the forest during warm weather. The ox, sheep and pig progressively ravaged closed associations.

After a rapid decrease in the size of the forests from the 7th to the middle of the 9th century, followed by a slowing down of the process in the 10th century, deforestation was accelerated in western

Europe under the monasteries' influence. In France, first the Bene-
dictines, then the Cistercians, sought to establish communities in
the forests; there were 500 monasteries at the end of the 12th and
750 in the 15th century. These formed clearings which continued
to grow, first in the west and then in the western-central part of
the continent. In western Germany the Harz, Eifel, Thuringian and
Black Forest mountains resembled large islands in the midst of
cultivated zones.

Starting in the 12th century, deforestation progressed eastward
with the Germanic tribes. Simultaneously Slavic peoples undertook
a similar task in Poland and eastern Europe. There was no continuous, systematic deforestation, since wars, epidemics and various
economic conditions would bring the process to a temporary halt,
but the phenomenon continued, and, by the 16th century, wood
became scarce just as enormous quantities of wood products were
required for the developing industries—glass, construction of mine
galleries, smelting of minerals and refining of metals. The danger
was understood by some, and in 1715 it was proposed that the King
of France limit the number of forges to let the forests recover. But
nothing could be done to halt the process of industrialization, while
shipyards were destroying some of the finest timber forests. It has
been said that English forests never recovered from the wars against
France, and certain French and Baltic forests suffered severely. In
1862 the Battle of Hampton Roads proved the superiority of metal
vessels, but by that time some of the most beautiful European
forests had vanished.

Some large wooded areas remain, but they have been cut up
into small sectors with greatly modified ecological conditions.
Furthermore, as foresters have endeavoured to transform them for
economic reasons, a forest map does not reveal the true picture.
The progressive destruction of forest cover has also been accompanied by drainage of swampy areas and numerous other changes that
follow an increase in human population.

Evolution of the wild flora and fauna is dominated by these
factors. Relatively slow change permitted many species to become
adapted to new conditions as they sought refuge in reduced but
unmodified zones. Small animals are able to live there, although
their numbers have dwindled as they are restricted to certain
narrowly circumscribed areas. Large mammals suffered, because

Fig. 1
Extent of forest in central Europe about 900 and in 1900.

they were unable to live when their habitats were transformed
and subdivided. Some have disappeared, although none in recent
times.

The first animal to become extinct in Europe was the aurochs
(*Bos primigenius*), which was still abundant in Germany at the time
of Julius Caesar. In the 6th century Gregory of Tours described
hunting aurochs in the Vosges and even in western France near
Maine. In the 9th century Charlemagne pursued it near Aix-la-
Chapelle. Hunting and the clearing of forests eliminated the aurochs
from western Europe and, by the beginning of the 15th century,
it survived only in Russia and Poland in the Jaktorowka Forest
in Mazovia. The last one died there in 1627, despite the efforts of
Polish kings to save this ancestor of our domestic cattle. Various
attempts were made to revive the species artificially, but none have
been very successful.

The European bison (*Bison bonasus*) met a similar fate. Its original

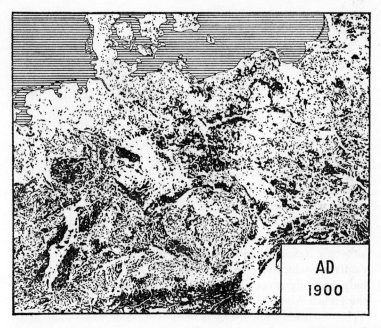

AD
1900

habitat extended over a vast zone from the Caucasus to France and Belgium. Like the aurochs, the bison disappeared gradually from west to east as forests were felled. Little by little its numbers dwindled in eastern Europe, until it was found only in the Bialowieza region, on the border between Poland and Russia. By 1892 only 375 remained, and the herd showed signs of degeneracy. Wars, especially the First World War, threatened the survival of the species, which was saved from extinction only by the strictest measures. The Caucasian bison, classed by mammalogists as a distinct race (*Bison b. caucasicus*), had completely disappeared in the wild state, although some hybrids were preserved in zoological gardens; it has recently been reintroduced in the Caucasus.

While other European herbivores suffered less than the aurochs and the bison, their numbers have dwindled at an alarming rate. The ibex (*Capra ibex*), found only in the mountains from Spain to the Caucasus, has been hunted until certain races restricted to Spain and Portugal have disappeared. The form *lusitanica* has been considered extinct since 1892. By the 16th century the ibex was rare in Switzerland; later it disappeared but was reintroduced in

1911. In Italy the population had shrunk to several dozen by 1821 (Couturier, 1962).

The chamois (*Rupicapra rupicapra*) also suffered from hunting. Prince Augustus of Saxe Coburg, for instance, shot 3412 of them, mostly in Upper Styria, and the Swiss G. M. Colani killed 2700 in the Engadine. The species has also suffered from a reduction of mountain forests, but it was never threatened with extinction.

Large carnivores have paid a heavy toll. It is very difficult for them to live in areas transformed by agriculture and grazing, where their predations arouse the ire of the inhabitants. The lion (*Panthera leo*) was the first to disappear from Europe. That it was still fairly common in antiquity is evident from the accounts of Greek historians who describe its exploits in Thrace and Macedonia, but the species vanished from Europe during the first century AD.

The bear (*Ursus arctos*) has survived in a large part of its habitat, although it has abandoned districts transformed by man. This carnivore, which used to live in all parts of France, is now found only in the Pyrenees. Couturier (1954) reports that the last bear in the French Alps was killed in 1921 in Savoy, and the last one in Vercors was observed in 1937. Its numbers are declining there, as in Spain. The bear has disappeared from Switzerland, where it inhabited Grisons until the beginning of the 20th century. It has vanished in Austria and Germany, but a good many still survive in Jugoslavia and eastern Europe, except in Poland.

The fate of the wolf has been very similar to that of the bear. It was still abundant in 19th century France, where systematic hunting aimed at exterminating it. In 1883 1300 wolves were killed in France, the majority by poisoned bait. In most areas the animals vanished between 1880 and 1920, although a few survive in the wildest regions of the Massif Central and in the Landes. The wolf is, however, still abundant in Spain, the Balkans and Russia; it thus survives in areas that have preserved extensive original habitats. The wolf is a real menace to cattle-breeders, who have no choice but to exterminate it.

Birds have also suffered, especially large ones. Some disappeared for mysterious reasons, like the waldrapp (*Comatibis eremita*), which was in Switzerland in Gesner's time but now occurs only in North Africa. Others like the capercaillie, which were hunted mercilessly, have sought refuge in mountain ranges.

Whooping crane: its long migratory route has made it peculiarly
susceptible to shooting

Slaughter of bison by travellers on the Kansas Pacific Railroad: from a woodcut of 1871

Above Bison slaughtered for their hide: from a photograph taken in 1872, *below* Bison remains collected in Dodge City, Kansas, in 1874

Above Caribous migrating in northern Canada: *below* Caribous
slaughtered at a river-crossing

Large birds of prey have become much scarcer in Europe. Eagles (several species of the genus *Aquila*) are now rare everywhere, and vultures have been victims of hunting and radical changes in pastoral methods. The lammergeier (*Gypaetus barbatus*) has also disappeared from a large part of its former habitat, especially in the Alps. As the chief nourishment of this bird consists of bones of animals killed by wolves and other large carnivores it is extremely sensitive to any change in the natural balance, and thus is in danger of disappearing with the carnivores.

The extent of human influence in Europe is evident from these examples. Nowhere else, save in the United States, has man so changed the natural balance for his own benefit. Such transformations are all the more serious since Europe is one of the most densely populated parts of the globe. Although hunting is directly responsible for the disappearance or scarcity of large animals, the modification of habitats is even more harmful.

Paradoxically, fewer species have become extinct in Europe than anywhere else. Since the continent developed over a period of twenty centuries, the fauna and flora had time to adapt to changes as they occurred. This was impossible in other parts of the world, notably in North America, where man irrupted explosively. The speed at which natural habitats are transformed is a highly important factor in everything dealing with the protection of nature.

2 NORTH AMERICA

The North American continent was in an almost primitive condition when Europeans settled it at the beginning of the 17th century. They found a widely scattered population living harmoniously with its habitat. Devastation began at once and accelerated as the population increased and spread from east to west. Changes that had required centuries in Europe were wrought on a much larger scale within some two hundred years. The slow modification of European habitats was replaced by brutal transformation wrought by men who thought natural resources were inexhaustible. In 1949 Fairfield Osborn called the United States the 'country of the great illusion'. He said: 'the story of our nation in the last century as regards the use of forests, grasslands, wildlife and water sources is the most violent and the most destructive of any written in the long history of civilization. The velocity of events is unparalleled and we to-day are still so near to it that it is almost impossible to realize what has happened or, far more important, what is still happening. Actually it is the story of human energy unthinking and uncontrolled.'

When the white man arrived, the east coast of the United States and Canada was covered with dense forest extending from the Atlantic almost to the Mississippi Valley. Deforestation was relatively rapid. It is estimated that of the original 420 million wooded acres only 17 or 20 million remain, and doubtless only a fraction of these represent primitive forest associations. Most primitive areas are in the west, and less than 7% of the whole United States is now forested. Clearing began in the valleys, but during the 19th century even the hills were deprived of their forest crowns. In 1754 there were 24 acres of forest for every inhabitant of Massachusetts; in 1800 the number had decreased to 10·8 and in 1830 there were only 8 acres per person. Soon the entire north-east was cultivated, and by 1830 the most fertile land east of the Mississippi had been occupied. The rich areas of the southern states, planted with tobacco and cotton, began to show serious signs of erosion.

Then came the vast migration which colonized first the great grassy plains of the central United States and later the west. The plains were dedicated to an extensive cultivation of wheat and corn, to the detriment of the original habitats and the wild flora and fauna, especially large mammals and birds. Beyond the Great Plains mountain chains offer more diversified habitats, from the luxuriant forests of Washington and Oregon to the arid deserts of Nevada and California. There again man has exerted a considerable influence, less marked than in the east save in one respect. In the east, a wide variety of trees was selectively eliminated, species by species, whereas in the west pure crops of single species were wiped out at once.

As in Europe, the devastation of nature has profoundly modified the original landscape. The east lost its forest cover, the central prairie was transformed into an agricultural zone, and only the most arid regions of the west retained something of their original aspect. Grassy regions were converted into an extensive grazing area, which in turn became rapidly overpastured.

Fig. 2
Passenger pigeon, Ectopistes migratorius.

The transformation of primitive habitats caused a rapid decrease in birds and mammals unable to adapt to the changes. But there was also a will to destroy, to eradicate wildlife, which has no equivalent in European history. It is therefore not surprising that several North American animals have vanished.

The most pitiful example of the destruction of a species is that of the passenger pigeon (*Ectopistes migratorius*) (*fig* 2). This bird, called *tourte* by the French Canadians, nested in enormous flocks throughout the forests of the eastern United States, southern Canada (Manitoba, Ontario and Quebec) and in Virginia and Mississippi. It formed large colonies especially in associations of oaks, beeches and maples. Occasionally trees collapsed under their weight. Some observers estimated that at least 136 million birds nested in an area of 569 square miles in Wisconsin until 1871. In 1810 Wilson (*in* Greenway, 1958) conjectured that one flock contained 2,230,272,000 birds.

The migrations of this pigeon were rather irregular. Although a fraction of the population wintered in Pennsylvania and Massachusetts, the majority flew to states bordering the Gulf of Mexico. When the flocks settled on trees, branches broke under their weight. The passenger pigeon was certainly the most plentiful bird in the eastern part of the American continent.

Although Indians had long been accustomed to taking a certain number of pigeons for food, the species was flourishing when the white man arrived. But the picture soon changed. Thousands of hunters decimated the migrant birds, shooting at random and killing many they did not even bother to pick up. During the nesting season collecting parties were organized. When other methods failed, hunters would fell the trees to get at the plump nestlings.

By 1870 the great nesting colonies had vanished everywhere except around the Great Lakes. Small flocks of pigeons were observed until about 1880, and the last wild bird was seen in 1899. A reward of 1500 dollars was offered in vain in 1909 to anyone who could supply information about a nesting pair. The last survivor died in captivity in the Cincinnati Zoo on 1st September, 1914. Massive destruction of young and adult birds is to blame for the elimination of a very abundant species; transformation of the habitat was a contributing factor, but the disappearance of the passenger pigeon was an inevitable corollary of deforestation in the eastern part of North America.

Man is also responsible for the disappearance of the Carolina parakeet (*Conuropsis carolinensis*), a bird with a long pointed tail, green plumage and an orange-yellow hood, which inhabited the south-eastern part of the United States from southern Virginia and Nebraska to the Gulf of Mexico (*fig* 3). These little parakeets nested in hollow trees in wooded areas. Their numbers dwindled rapidly, and, as in the case of the passenger pigeon, the last known survivor died in 1914 in the Cincinnati Zoo. It has been suggested that the birds were victims of epidemics, but this seems highly doubtful, and there is evidence to prove that populations declined as colonization advanced westwards and transformed the landscape. Since Carolina parakeets were reputed to be injurious to crops, it is not surprising that they vanished in a relatively short time.

The ivory-billed woodpecker (*Campephilus principalis*) has also disappeared from the south-east where it lived in dense forests along river banks. There is no doubt that the destruction of its habitat by man was largely responsible for its extermination, though a few may still be left.

When the Great Plains were transformed they too lost several characteristic birds, while others, such as the prairie chicken (*Tympanuchus cupido*), dwindled very rapidly as their habitats were

Fig. 3
Carolina parakeets, Conuropsis carolinensis.

divided (*fig.* 4). Hunting expeditions organized to supply large city markets were partly to blame, but transformation of the habitats had even more serious consequences; the elimination of certain plants that constituted the prairie chicken's diet made it impossible for this bird to survive.

The Central Plains are on the routes of numerous migrants which come south in the autumn to their winter quarters along the Gulf of Mexico or in tropical regions of South America. Two of these birds have practically disappeared. The first is the Eskimo curlew (*Numenius borealis*), which nested on the tundras of northern Canada and wintered on the humid Argentine pampas. Its southward flight followed the Atlantic coasts and crossed part of the ocean, but on the return trip the bird took a more continental route, up through the central part of the United States. The flocks used to be large but hunting, coupled with cyclones, which caught the birds on their autumn flight southward over the Atlantic, caused serious losses. Since 1945 only a few birds have been observed each year.

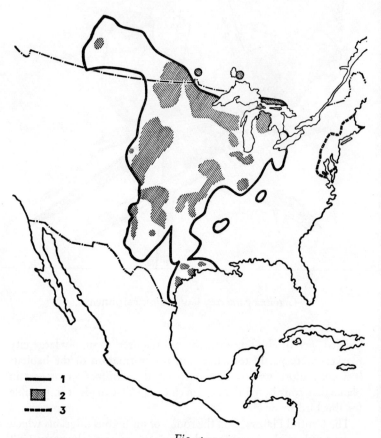

Fig. 4

Reduction of the territory of the prairie chicken, Tympanuchus cupido

1 *distribution at the beginning of European colonization*

2 *distribution today* (T.c. pinnatus, attwateri *and* pallidicinctus)

3 *boundary of distribution of the eastern subspecies* (T.c. cupido), *now extinct*

From J.W. Aldrich and A. J. Duvall, Fish and Wildlife Circ. *no. 34* 1955

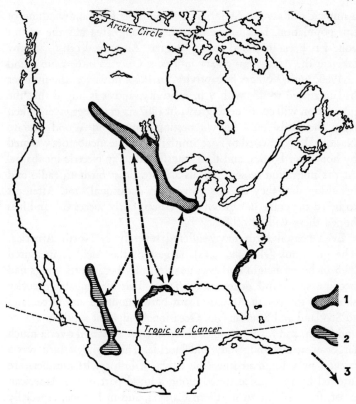

Fig. 5
Area of original distribution of the whooping crane
   1 breeding area   2 wintering area   3 migratory routes
The wintering area of this crane is now restricted to a small strip bordering the Gulf of Mexico.
From R. P. Allen The Whooping Crane *New York 1952.*

The same is true of the whooping crane (*Grus americana*), whose nesting area extends over a vast area in north-western Canada, from Slave River to the United States, especially to Iowa and Illinois. It winters along the Gulf of Mexico, where coastal lagoons supply the bird's ecological requirements (*fig* 5). The length of these migrations makes it extremely difficult, if not impossible, to protect the whooping crane, and many biologists believe that only a miracle can save it. Shooting is responsible for the dwindling of this population, because neither the nesting area nor the winter zone has been modified to any degree. An annual census is now taken at the Aransas sanctuary in Texas. Only 33 birds were found in 1963, with 7 others in captivity. In 1966, however, the number had increased to 43, with 9 in captivity, and it is hoped that the population will continue to grow. In 1967 six crane eggs were taken from the birds' only known nesting grounds in Wood Buffalo National Park, carried to Fort Smith in portable incubators warmed by hot water bottles, and then transferred to an electric incubator. At the migration season appeals are broadcast on both radio and television, but they do not prevent an occasional shot. Attempts to breed the crane in captivity have been fairly successful, and it is hoped there will be others.

Even coastal birds have suffered severely in North America. The great auk (*Alca impennis*), largest of the Alcidae, measured 29·5 inches in height and was unable to fly because its wings had become small and degenerate (*fig* 6). This bird inhabited rocky shores of the North Atlantic from Newfoundland and Greenland to Scotland and Scandinavia. Occasionally it went south to France and Spain, and fossil or subfossil remains are scattered over a much larger area, including Italy and Florida. This flightless bird was a natural prey for man since the dawn of history. Its numbers are attested by remains scattered along a good part of the American coast, from Maine to northern Canada, and in Europe, especially Norway where it seems to have been used as food by Neolithic tribes.

Many historical documents mention this defenceless bird. In 1590, for example, an Icelander filled a whole boat with great auks collected on the eastern shore of Greenland, and numerous other accounts describe their exploitation. Even at this period it appears that populations had shrunk and the 18th and 19th centuries saw the disappearance of most of the large nesting colonies, notably the one on Funk Island, off the east coast of Newfoundland, where the largest colony of all was ravaged by fishermen. When the Norwegian Stuwitz landed there in 1841, he found only piles of bones, some mummified birds and fragments of shells. Other colonies survived for a time nearby but the birds were killed by sailors and fishermen for bait. The last colony seems to have been

Above Brush fire in Central Africa
Below Ruins of Ramrod, the former Ram Chahrestan: the city disappeared beneath the sand in the 10th century

Galapagos land tortoise: Santa Cruz Island. It was from this animal that the islands derived their Spanish name

Fig. 6
Great auk, Alca impennis.

at Eldey Rock off the east coast of Iceland, and the last surviving bird was collected there in 1844.

The great auk is another example of a flourishing species exterminated by man. No other cause is to blame for the disappearance of a bird scattered over too vast an area to be menaced by natural dangers. Few specimens are preserved in European and American museums, and the eggs are so rare that they bring 30 times their weight in gold.

The list of threatened North American birds is, unfortunately, still not closed. The California condor (*Gymnogyps californianus*) is similar to, if not identical with, a fossil species widespread in North America. It is now found in only a few areas in southern California. Fifty-one condors existed there in 1966, 13 more than in 1965, and these included many immatures. Man is completely to blame for the rarity of a species which has no natural enemies.

Among mammals, the most spectacular case of destruction is the American bison (*Bison bison*). The domain of this large **bovine** extended over the Great Plains from Lake Erie to Louisiana and Texas. Within this vast territory bison migrated seasonally along fixed routes to satisfy their food requirements. It is estimated that there were originally some 40 million of them on the plains, 30 million on the prairies, and 5 million in the wooded areas, making a total of 75 million. This seems incredible in view of the fact that an old male could weigh 2000 pounds. The large herds had no natural enemies except coyotes, which occasionally captured some of the young.

Early explorers were tremendously impressed by these herds. But then the slaughter began, continuing, especially after the American Revolution, as colonists moved west. Organized massacres are more to blame than transformation of habitats for the decline of the bison. There were two distinct phases of this destruction. The first, from about 1730 to 1840, was relatively limited and justified, at least in part, by the transformation of virgin lands into fields and the demand for leather and hides. Constantly migrating herds of this size are obviously incompatible with land cultivation, as we shall see elsewhere, especially in Africa.

So far, however, hunters merely wished to limit the number and exploit the herds effectively. The second phase, which began about 1830, was much more deadly, for it aimed at total eradication of the bison. The animals were slaughtered in the northern part of their habitat to starve the Sioux and other Indian tribes whom the whites were fighting. But hunting was also a game. Railway brochures promised travellers they could shoot bison without leaving their seats. Often only the tongue, which was considered a great delicacy, was taken, and the rest of the carcass abandoned. Whole armies were mobilized, with officers and chaplains, to destroy the bison systematically. The famous 'Buffalo Bill', W. F. Cody, who was hired to provide food for workmen building a railroad, shot 4280 bison in 18 months.

During the 1872-3 hunting season 200,000 animals were killed in the State of Kansas alone, so we can estimate that between 1870 and 1875 2·5 millions were slaughtered annually on the Great Plains. Their bones were collected after a time for manure or animal charcoal. Teams were organized to bring them to a point near the railroads, and records show that there were 20,000 skeletons on some of the piles. The famous Santa Fé Railroad transported

10,793,350 pounds of bison bones between 1872 and 1874. It is not surprising, therefore, that by 1868 the bison had practically disappeared from the south-western United States. There were probably still a few roving herds, but they were so small that hunters lost interest and there was no more 'exploitation' after this period.

The herds of bison in the northern United States had also declined, when, about 1880, the final assault came from some Indian tribes. It is claimed that one hunter slew between one and two thousand bison in a single hunting season (from November to February). The animals became so rare that hunting stories of 1880-5 all tell of the 'last' bison in various districts (*fig* 7). Hunters in the north-western United States thought for a long time that the bison had emigrated to Canada but would soon return in numbers. In fact Canadian bison had been practically exterminated, and this led to famine and very high mortality among Indian tribes during the year 1886-7.

Although the almost total destruction of bison is the most tragic episode in the history of man's relations with the New World fauna, other mammals also suffered severely. The wapiti (*Cervus canadensis*), for example, which originally roamed from southern Canada to northern Alabama, has vanished from the eastern United States, along with the forests which formed its habitat.

In northern Canada the numbers of barren grounds caribou *Rangifer tarandus arcticus*) and woodland caribou (*Rangifer tarandus caribou*) declined as their territories grew smaller. The former, once thought to number 100 million, were reduced to 30 million in 1911, 2·5 million in 1938, and 200,000 in 1960. This regression has seriously affected the economy of the Eskimos and the Indians of northern Canada.

The pronghorn (*Antilocapra americana*) is the last survivor of a group that has left many fossils in North America. When the whites arrived, this animal was found from Manitoba and Alberta in Canada to the Mexican plateaus, and from the grassy plains to California. Its characteristic habitat was the large, semi-arid plains, where it numbered between 30 and 40 million (*fig* 8).

The grizzly bear (*Ursus horribilis*) was the most dangerous of North American animals. It inhabited the west from the edge of the Great Plains to the Pacific, going north to Alaska and south to

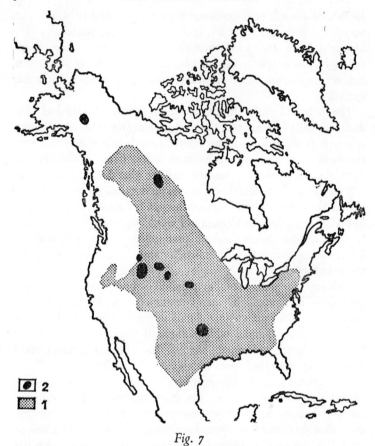

Fig. 7
Reduction in the territory of the American bison
  1 distribution at the beginning of European colonization
  2 distribution today
From Petrides, 1961.

Mexico. Largely exterminated throughout this habitat, it now numbers only five to six hundred in the United States, Alaska excluded.

Examples could be multiplied. On the whole, populations of all North American animals have greatly declined. The east and Central Plains have suffered particularly because of cultivation and rapid

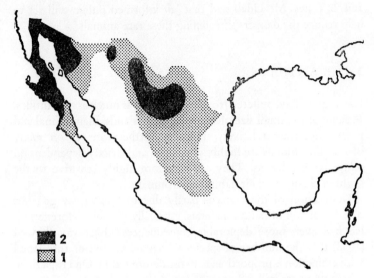

Fig. 8
Reduction in the territory of the pronghorn, Antilocapra americana, *in Mexico*
  1 distribution at the beginning of colonization
  2 distribution today
From A. S. Leopold, 1947.

industrialization, with a constant increase in human population. The west, which remained wilder because of its mountainous relief and more arid climate, has also undergone profound changes. By the end of the 19th century the natural balance was upset everywhere; most representatives of the large fauna were nearly extinct, many habitats permanently spoiled, and many species of the flora and small fauna defunct.

North America affords one of the most tragic examples of the destruction of an entire natural complex under the brutal influence of so-called 'civilized' man. On 11th March, 1967, Secretary of the Interior Stewart L. Udall designated 78 species of mammals, birds, reptiles and fishes in the US threatened with extinction. This list, the first to be issued under the Endangered Species Preservation Act of 1966, includes 14 mammals, 36 birds, 6 reptiles and amphibians and 22 fishes. Mr Udall said that 'an informed public will act to help reduce the dangers threatening these rare animals.'

3 THE ANTILLES

Few regions have suffered from colonization as much as the Antilles. Because of the small size of many of these islands, their animal and plant species are relatively unstable. Furthermore, as on many islands, the animals are highly developed and strictly dependent on particular conditions. They are therefore highly sensitive to the slightest change in their natural environment.

Destruction of the fauna is partly due to human ravages, but transformation of natural habitats, especially massive deforestation, has had even more deplorable consequences. Greenway showed (1958) that the number of species which are extinct or threatened with extinction is proportionate to the deforestation. On Hispaniola, where there are still 5·8 acres of forest per inhabitant, not a single bird has vanished; but in some of the Lesser Antilles, where there is now less than one acre of forest per inhabitant, between two and four bird forms have disappeared.

Domesticated animals have wrought havoc too. Rats were brought accidentally by ships, but mongooses were introduced deliberately about 1870 to combat snakes, particularly the deadly fer-de-lance. These carnivores spread rapidly and began to slaughter the birds and terrestrial mammals, which had never known such a predator.

The very limited number of mammals included bats which had come to the islands from the continent at different times, and several highly differentiated forms, particularly solenodons. These insect-eaters, about the size of a cat, had no apparent relatives except the tenrecs of Madagascar and the African potamogales. One species lived on Hispaniola (*Solenodon paradoxus*), the other in Cuba (*S. cubanus*) (*fig* 9). These primitive animals were considered extinct until Hyatt Verrill rediscovered them in 1907 in wild areas of north-eastern Hispaniola and eastern Cuba. They are, however, in a precarious state.

Among rodents, the large Antillean agoutis (*Dasyprocta albida*), which resemble little antelopes, have almost disappeared. Seven-

Fig. 9
Cuba solenodon, Solenodon cubanus.

teenth-century travellers, including Father du Tertre, praised their delicate meat and told about hunting them with dogs. They were direct victims of such chases, as were other rodents with a more or less spiny coat. Distantly related to porcupines, hutias of the family Echimyidae included several distinct genera—*Boromys, Capromys, Plagiodontia.* Most of them have disappeared, and some are known only from bones discovered in grottoes in Cuba or Hispaniola, where they may have served as food for the aborigines. Several species are still represented by small populations, especially in Jamaica and eastern Cuba.

Birds of the Antilles have also suffered severely. The most spectacular disappearance is that of the Cuban macaw (*Ara tricolor*), which was observed for the last time about 1885 in swampy areas of the southern part of the island. This rather small, predominantly red and yellow bird (*fig* 10) is the only macaw of its group identified in this region, although other species may have lived there. Old accounts are highly confused; furthermore, it is quite possible that some of the macaws mentioned by the discoverers, especially Ferdinand Colomb, were imported by Caribs, who kept them in captivity. Several birds belonging to other groups have also been exterminated, notably the Guadeloupe aratinga and several amazones. This is all the more regrettable, since they were among the most beautiful and interesting members of the parrot family.

Several species of rails and goatsuckers have also disappeared or are

Fig. 10
Cuban macaw, Ara tricolor.

threatened. Since the former cannot fly and the latter nest on the ground, they are an easy prey for mongooses and rats.

Animals of the Antilles, especially birds, have been reduced to skeletal, often highly localized, populations. The cahow, a petrel (*Pterodroma cahow*), nests only in Bermuda. Once thought to be extinct it was rediscovered after the last war but is still definitely in danger. The present population is probably only 50 or 60 birds. A glance at the list of birds shows that the area of distribution of some forms is restricted to 75 or 100 acres. Under such conditions the slightest change can add new victims to the long list of vanished species.

4 SOUTH AMERICA

As South America is just beginning to develop economically, this continent had, until very recently, suffered less than the rest of the world. The forests stretching from the foot of the Andes to the mouths of the Amazon are essentially intact and cultivated areas are small. Brazil, for example, with an area of 3,287,195 square miles, had only 31% of the land surface under cultivation in 1960. This does not imply that the rest of the country has preserved its original plant cover. Forests in eastern Brazil have been ravaged since colonial days, and, since South America is rapidly becoming industrialized, the whole picture may change radically in the near future.

White egret – a victim of plume hunters

Leadbeater opossum: considered extinct, it was rediscovered in 1961 in Cumberland Valley, Victoria, Australia

Potoroo, a rat-kangaroo which has been a prey of foxes: it is now found in only a few parts of its old territory, which extended from southern Australia to Queensland

Rock wallaby: hunting and destruction of the habitat have caused its population to dwindle

Colony of marine iguanas: Galapagos Islands

Although most of the South American flora and fauna have not yet been seriously threatened, some species are in danger. The delicate grey fur of the chinchilla (*Chinchilla laniger*) has been sought by trappers for a century (*fig* 11). These rodents, resembling little rabbits, were native to the high Andes of Peru, Bolivia and Chile and never came down below 9000 feet in the northern part of their habitat. Travellers used to see thousands of them on the plateaus, but to-day they have almost vanished, even in northern Argentina,

Fig. 11
Chinchilla, Chinchilla laniger.

where they were still relatively abundant at the beginning of the 20th century. At Coquimbo, which was the centre of the industry in Chile, 18,153 dozen pelts were sold in 1905. This figure was cut by half in 1907 and again a year later. In 1909 only 2328 dozen were sold, and to-day the business no longer exists. Chinchillas are now being raised on farms. This has made it possible to preserve the species, which is now practically extinct in the wild save in Bolivia (Sajama) and northern Argentina.

The highly specialized vicuñas (*Lama vicugna*) and guanacos (*Lama huanacus*) of the upper Andes have dwindled alarmingly. Although fairly large flocks remain in some regions, both animals are hunted despite protective laws. They also suffer from competition with livestock, particularly sheep, which have been introduced on the high plateaus.

If the South American continent has preserved large natural

habitats, the islands adjoining it were not so fortunate. The Juan Fernandez Islands were pillaged by man and introduced species, particularly goats. Magnificent forests have been reduced until they are now found only in the most secluded spots. The last sandalwood (*Santalum fernandezianum*), a valuable native species, fell before the axe at the beginning of the 19th century. Philippi's fur seal (*Arctocephalus ph. philippii*) was once so abundant that when Dampier visited the islands in 1683 he claimed there was no bay or rock that was not full of them. Originally estimated at between two and three million, the population numbered between 500,000 and 800,000 in 1798; by 1891 it had shrunk to about 400, and the species is now considered extinct. There is only one related subspecies, the Guadalupe fur seal (*A. ph. townsendi*) which has survived in a small colony on Guadalupe Island, off Lower California.

The devastation was even more tragic on the Galapagos Islands. This archipelago constitutes a natural laboratory where evolutionary phenomena are perceptible in the development of the flora and fauna. Charles Darwin formed some of his famous theories on his visit to the Galapagos on the 'Beagle' in 1835. The islands are formed by the peaks of a vast volcanic mass that rose from the sea about 600 miles off the South American coast in the Pacific just below the Equator. They are purely 'oceanic' and have never been connected to the continent. Their animal population has therefore arrived by flying, swimming or on gigantic plant rafts, like those still carried towards the sea on great tropical rivers.

The Galapagos are still in the Reptilian Age, since no mammals have succeeded in reaching them except for several rodents, two sea lions and a bat. They are essentially the domain of the gigantic land tortoises from which the islands derived their Spanish name, creatures with a shell which alone measures up to 4·7 feet across. The archipelago also has several large iguanas, especially marine iguanas (*Amblyrhynchus cristatus*), the only lizards that do all their feeding in the sea.

The avian fauna is just as strange. The most paradoxical sea birds are the penguins (*Spheniscus mendiculus*), members of an antarctic group that reached equatorial latitudes by following the cold currents along the coasts of Chile and Peru. The flightless cormorants (*Phalacrocorax harrisi*) are an interesting case of insular winglessness, apparently linked to the absence of predators.

This remarkable fauna includes many native species, of which birds comprise 70%. Nature was intact when the islands were discovered by the Spaniards in the 16th century. The first arrivals were corsairs and pirates, who were followed during the 19th century by mutineers and prisoners. Attempts to colonize the islands continued until the close of the century. Man's influence on the fauna was immediate and calamitous, especially as the animals showed no fear. First to suffer were the defenceless giant tortoises, which provided excellent meat and fat. Soon a tortoise industry was established, with ships (especially whalers) calling at the islands and scouring the area. Teams collected the fat, melted it down and obtained from $3\frac{1}{2}$ to 10 quarts of fine oil from each tortoise. By studying logs of whaleboats, the biologist Townsend found that 105 ships captured more than 15,000 tortoises between 1811 and 1844. These figures are, of course, by no means complete, since they deal with only a fraction of the vessels that took part in the hunt. According to the same author, American whalers collected 100,000 tortoises after 1830, and Bauer estimates that ten million tortoises have been massacred on the Galapagos. It is not surprising, therefore, that they have disappeared on several islands and are quite rare on most of the others.

Introduction of domestic animals wrought havoc among reptiles as well. The first goats were brought to the Galapagos by corsairs in the 17th century. They multiplied rapidly and soon began to destroy plant cover, competing with the tortoises which were less agile and unable to fend for themselves. The Spaniards then introduced dogs to destroy the goats, but they preferred to chase young tortoises and iguanas, which were easier to capture. Cattle, pigs, rats and mice also helped destroy the plant cover and eliminate native animals. Pigs were among the worst offenders, as they dug up tortoise and iguana eggs buried under a thin layer of sand. To-day it is estimated that only one egg out of 10,000 will produce a tortoise that can grow to a length of twelve inches. At this size it is safe from all enemies save man.

Birds have suffered dreadfully, particularly the flightless cormorant and the penguin. Since they are now restricted to one small part of the coast, it is likely that they will perish.

The Galapagos are one of the zones where nature is most gravely menaced. And this is all the more serious since these islands are a unique complex where study may eventually help to explain some mysterious biological phenomena.

5 ASIA AND MALAYSIA

The northern part of the Asiatic continental mass should be distinguished from the tropical zone with its natural prolongation, the Malay peninsula. As tropical Asia covers no less than 14 million square miles, the flora and fauna have been able to take refuge in still relatively untouched areas despite the fact that this part of the globe has been the home of large populations since our history began. Cultivated areas represent only a fraction of the total. In India, for example, only 30% of the country is farmed. Efforts have been made to improve the yield rather than to extend agricultural districts into unsuitable marginal zones.

Furthermore, natural habitats have been adapted so slowly that the fauna could take refuge in relatively untouched mountain ranges, which are often wooded or covered with jungle. Finally, the religious respect for life in all its forms shown by some Asiatic peoples provides excellent protection for wild fauna, especially in India.

The human population is denser in parts of Asia than anywhere else in the world. Such overpopulation led to large-scale devastation, particularly deforestation, on the Chinese plains, in Java and some parts of the Philippines. Bad agricultural practices, notably shifting cultivation, ruined certain zones, and a large number of Malay savannas are secondary man-made creations in countries where the climax is forest.

Overhunting and over-intensive transformation of habitats have reduced numerous animal populations to the point of extinction. The chief sufferer has been the rhinoceros, which was slaughtered to satisfy the demands of Chinese pharmacists, as rhinoceros horn is famous for its alleged aphrodisiac properties. High prices (up to half its weight in gold) caused the massacre of this unfortunate animal, and to-day all Asiatic rhinoceroses are rare, while some species are represented by only a few score survivors.

The Indian rhinoceros (*Rhinoceros unicornis*) has now disappeared from a vast area stretching from northwestern India to the Indo-

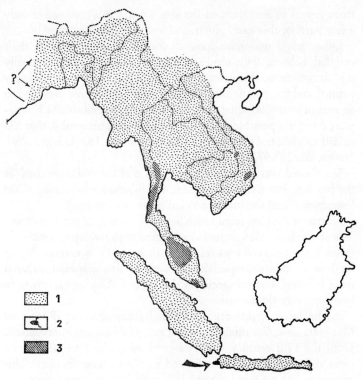

Fig. 12
Reduction in the territory of the Javan rhinoceros, Rhinoceros sondaicus
  1 distribution about 1850
  2 distribution today (Udjung Kulon Reserve)
  3 Regions where the species has been sighted, according to unconfirmed
reports; a few animals probably remain there (especially in Malacca)
From L. M. Talbot, 1959-60.

Chinese Peninsula, except for about 625 in Nepal and Assam. The Javan rhinoceros (*Rhinoceros sondaicus*) is now the rarest of all large mammals. It used to range from Bengal and the Indo-Chinese Peninsula to Java. To-day it is known only in western Java, although there may be a few survivors in Burma (*fig* 12). The Sumatran rhinoceros (*Didermocerus sumatrensis*), the only Asiatic rhinoceros which, like its African relatives, has two horns, was also distributed from Assam to Sumatra and Borneo. To-day it is confined to only a few parts of this vast habitat, and less than 200 now remain.

Other large mammals have dwindled in most parts of their original habitat. The elephant (*Elephas maximus*) has gradually withdrawn from cultivated areas, the Indian leopard is probably extinct, and the Asiatic lion (*Panthera leo persica*) is now confined to an area of some 500 square miles on the Indian peninsula of Kathiawar; there it is possible, I learnt from Dharmakumarsinhji, that 250 to 290 survive, but the number may be less than 150 (Ullrich, *Zool. Garten*, 26: 287-97, 1962) (*fig* 13).

We should also mention several birds that are in danger, such as the Japanese ibis (*Nipponia nippon*), the Siberian white crane (*Grus leucogeranus*) and the Indian bustard (*Choriotis nigriceps*).

Northern Asia has fared much better because until recently it was almost uninhabited; vast surfaces covered with swampy, coniferous forest were reservoirs where fauna thrived. To a certain degree fur-bearing animals, especially the sable (*Martes zibellina*), suffered from hunting, but no species in this part of Asia appears to have been seriously threatened.

In the large steppe area extending from southern Russia to Mongolia most mammals have been victims of human intervention. Until the 17th century the saiga antelope (*Saiga tatarica*) roamed from the steppes of eastern Poland to the Chinese frontier. This enormous habitat receded until 1920, when there were only a few hundred, perhaps a thousand, animals surviving. Natural causes doubtless help explain the decline of a species sensitive to snowstorms and frozen soil, but overhunting, coupled with cultivation of part of the saiga's habitat, is the chief cause of its decline. Herds of saigas were driven into vast enclosures with a 'funnel' opening three miles in width. The interior of this corral bristled with sharp points on which horsemen drove the frightened animals. The survivors were then slaughtered at the rate of 12,000 a day. They were killed for food and for their horns, which the Chinese used in pharmaceutical preparations. To-day, however, thanks to recent measures the species is flourishing again.

This zone was also the domain of the wild horse (*Equus caballus przewalskii*), formerly common in western Mongolia and Dzungaria, and the wild camel (*Camelus bactrianus*), which extended from Mongolia to Chinese Turkestan. These populations have been so

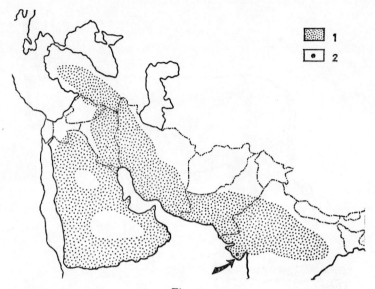

1 distribution about 1800
2 distribution to-day (Gir Forest, on the Kathiawar Peninsula)

Fig. 13
Reduction in the territory of the Asiatic lion, Panthera leo persica
  1 *distribution about 1800*
  2 *distribution to-day (Gir Forest, on the Kathiawar Peninsula)*
The Asiatic lion is now reduced to an area of about 500 square miles.
From L. M. Talbot, 1959-60.

greatly reduced by hunting that they are now found only in very small numbers in pocket-sized areas. Furthermore, there is no certainty that the survivors are pureblooded, for they may be the offspring of domestic animals that have returned to their wild state.

Several large mammals of the Near East and the Asiatic Southwest have also suffered from hunting. Characteristic of the region are certain Equidae, intermediaries between horses and asses, such as the Syrian wild ass (*Equus hemippus*) and the onager (*E. onager*) (*fig* 14). Hunted since ancient times, they were almost exterminated by nomad Arabs equipped with modern weapons. The Arabian oryx (*Oryx leucoryx*), which was formerly found throughout much of the Middle East, now inhabits only Saudi Arabia. The poor animal is threatened with extinction by motorised parties, when as many as sixty cars take part in the hunt.

Fig. 14
Persian onager, Equus hemionus onager.

6 THE PACIFIC

The Pacific is dotted with numerous islands inhabited by animals whose ancestors came chiefly from Asia. Since they have had time to evolve slowly, there is a large proportion of species peculiar to the region. Most of the oceanic islands have no native mammals; New Zealand was reached only by bats.

These islands have suffered heavily from man, in particular from Europeans. Hunting, the introduction of rats and domestic animals which have gone wild, transformation of habitats and, above all, deforestation have destroyed animal populations and ravaged plant associations. Modern civilization has affected a large number of native species which were in balance with their natural environment but highly sensitive to external influences. Most of the animals have become rare and some have vanished.

Birds—many of them unique to the region—were the first to suffer. Among the extinct forms is the Stephen Island wren (*Xenicus*

Flightless cormorant and Galapagos penguins: Fernandina
Island

Galapagos land iguana: Barrington Island

Above Great Indian rhinoceros: Kaziranga, Assam
Below Gaurs grazing in Kanha National Park, Madhya Pradesh, in central India

lyalli) of Stephen Island in Cook Strait. Although related to the surviving New Zealand species, the bird was well differentiated. The population was small and it is not surprising that the lighthouse keeper's cat succeeded in exterminating this semi-nocturnal song-bird in a single year (1894). The few specimens preserved in museums were all 'collected' by this cat. Once again the introduction of predators is shown to be harmful to faunas that developed far from such pests.

Among the most spectacular New Zealand birds were the moas or Dinornis(*fig* 15), a family of swift ground birds distantly related to ostriches, with some species 11 feet 4 inches in height. The largest,

Fig. 15
Moa or Dinornis.

Dinornis maximus, could have the femur 16·5 inches, the tibia 39 inches and the metatarsus 21 inches in length. Fossils have been found from the Miocene and Lower Pliocene periods. It is possible that the Dinornis represent a primitive survival which had completed its evolution by the time man appeared, but he certainly contributed to the extinction of these living fossils. Remains of at least six of the 27 species have been found near man-made hearths, and an analysis of carbon 14 shows that these are not more than 700 years old. The Maoris, who invaded New Zealand 600 years ago, hunted moas in the swamps and on the savannas. They set fire to the brush to speed the hunt and also destroyed the birds' nests and eggs.

Fig. 16

Kakapo or owl parrot, Strigops habroptilus, *a New Zealand terrestrial parakeet. Formerly widely distributed, this highly specialised bird is now confined to the forests on South Island. Deforestation and the introduction of mammals are responsible for its decline. Its total population is probably less than 200.*

Since New Zealand had no flesh-eating animals, birds lost the ability to fly and lived on the ground. Once introduced, dogs and stray cats ran amuck. The highly specialized kiwi or apteryx and the strigops, a curious nocturnal parrot (*fig* 16), have all had their numbers greatly reduced (see Williams, 1962).

Rails with vestigial wings, like those which formerly inhabited Auckland (*Rallus muelleri*), Wake (*R. wakensis*), Tahiti (*R. pacificus*), Chatham (*R. dieffenbachi, R. modestus*), Fiji (*Rallina poeciloptera*), Laysan (*Porzanula palmeri*), Hawaii (*Pennula sandwichensis*), and Samoa (*Pareudiastes pacificus*), are virtually extinct because pigs and rats devoured their eggs and young, goats trampled their nests and disturbed their habitat, and dogs, cats, and occasionally mongooses pursued the adults. The kagu (*Rhinochetus jubatus*) of New Caledonia is threatened by imported predators. Most of these birds vanished

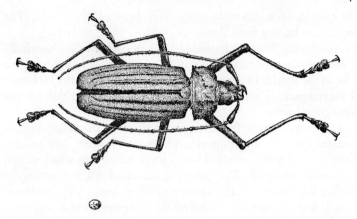

Fig. 17

Xixuthrus heros. *Prionid coleopter of the Fiji Islands; a lady-bird*
Coccinella septempunctata *shows its size. The population of this
gigantic insect has dwindled considerably due to the devastation of its
forest habitats.*

during the past century, with a few exceptions, notably the Wake
Island rail (*Rallus wakensis*) which was exterminated by starving
Japanese troops during the last war.

From time to time there are happy surprises, particularly on
large islands where animals can find refuge. The famous takahe or
notornis (*Porphyrio mantelli*), which is closely related to the swamp
hen or blue coot, formerly inhabited all the moist prairies and
borders of ponds in New Zealand. For fifty years this bird was
considered extinct before it was rediscovered in 1948 in several
remote valleys of the Murchison Mountains. Although the population is not declining, in certain ways the species appears to have
reached the end of its natural evolution, for it seems 'senile' in
comparison to other swamp hens. The fertility rate for instance is
lower.

Examples of devastation could be cited for every island in this
region (*fig* 17). The Hawaiian Islands have suffered severely.
Zimmerman (1948) estimated that at least a third of the insects
have been exterminated by man's destruction of habitats, the
dwindling supply of native plants and the introduction of predators
and competitors. *Carelia*, the largest land mollusk on the islands, has

29 species, of which only seven have been collected alive. The others are known from shells.

Among the 70 native species of birds on the Hawaiian Islands, 27 have become extinct. Of the rest, 42 of which are found nowhere else in the world, 19 are in danger. Among these are the Hawaiian honeycreepers, a family of 22 birds that cannot withstand any change in habitat.

Native to Hawaii, the perching songbirds of the family Drepanididae (*fig* 18) are of great evolutionary interest. Within this family an adaptive radiation led to some bird forms which at first appeared unrelated. The offspring occupied all the ecological niches left vacant by the absence of other birds. This evolution recalls that of Darwin's finches on the Galapagos, but it was more fundamental as the group showed a higher degree of differentiation than the latter. The bill was slender and pointed in some cases, strong and globular in others, according to the bird's diet.

These birds with their bright yellow, red or orange plumage were hunted as adornments for royalty. The feathers were stitched on cloaks or gigantic headdresses reserved for chieftains. This reduced the population but several species were still relatively common when the practice was abandoned, and it does not therefore, by itself, seem responsible for the extermination of any of the Drepanididae.

European colonization alone is to blame for the decline and loss of these birds. Massive deforestation, especially in low-lying areas, was a major factor, for most of the birds were accustomed to a special diet and disappeared with the plants from which they obtained food. Rats also caused harm by climbing trees and preying on native birds. However, several Drepanididae once thought to be extinct have been rediscovered. Four species (*Palmeria dolei, Pseudonestor xanthophrys*, which had not been seen since 1890, *Psittirostra psittacea, Ps. bailleui*) were found between 1940 and 1950, and others doubtless survive (Richards and Baldwin, *Condor*, 55: 221-2, 1953). Moreover, all the forest birds known from the island of Kauai have been found in remaining forest (Richardson and Bowles, *ibid.*, 63: 179-80, 1961). These authors stress the absolute necessity of preserving the native forests without which the species would vanish.

Intensive hunting, transformation of natural habitats and pre-

Fig. 18
Drepanis pacifica,
the Hawaiian 'Mamo'.
Endemic in forests
on the island of
Hawaii, this bird
was exterminated by
plume hunters and
colonists. The last
individual was observed
in 1898.

dation by imported mammals almost destroyed the nene or Hawaiian goose (*Branta sandvicensis*), a species peculiar to the Hawaiian Islands but related to the North American barnacle goose. This web-footed bird formerly spread over all the open habitats of the island of Hawaii but declined until only about 30 birds were left in 1951. Only breeding in captivity saved this species from extinction.

Plume hunting has also been highly injurious to the birds of the Pacific. The Japanese organized collecting expeditions which massacred on a grand scale. The most tragic example is Steller's albatross (*Diomedea albatrus*) which roamed over much of the Pacific but nested in a small number of colonies on some islets of the Seven Islands' archipelagoes and Bonin. On Torishima Japanese collectors used sticks to strike the nesting birds on the ground and collected between 100 and 200 a day. It is estimated that between 1887 and 1903 more than 500,000 albatrosses were slaughtered for their plumes. The collectors were victims of a volcanic eruption in 1903, but others replaced them, and as late as 1932 more than 3,000 albatrosses were massacred on this islet. The population dwindled until only 63 birds were seen here in March 1965. Then, in October, the staff of the Meteorological Station was evacuated because the Torishima Volcano was threatening, and since that time the island has been deserted. In 1966, 23 birds were counted by plane and on December 19-21, 31 were seen from the sea (Prince Yamashina, *in litt.*).

The Japanese were by no means alone in the plume industry,

which was developed at the close of the 19th century, when tens
of thousands of bird skins reached the European market, especially
through Paris and London. The principal sources were Malaya
('Malacca'), Japan, Senegal and South America (Bogota, Trinidad,
Bahia). Plume dealers piled thousands of skins of all kinds in
boxes. Hummingbirds lay beside glossy starlings, emerald cuckoos,
birds of paradise and parakeets. There were also birds of such
humble plumage that it seems most unlikely they could have
interested a milliner.

This business does not seem to have had much effect on the avian
populations of South America but it was disastrous to oceanic
birds and egrets. The latter were hunted for their nuptial plumage,
which varies in form and texture according to species. Egrets were
massacred in their nesting colonies and the bodies abandoned after
the hunters had pulled out the long gossamer feathers. This sad
sight in the south-eastern United States led to a healthy reaction
and the establishment of the National Audubon Society, two of
whose guards were killed by plume hunters when the reserves were
established.

The plume trade declined gradually after the First World War
and disappeared in the Second. But a certain amount of trading in
plumes exists to-day, especially in birds of paradise, which are
secretly exported from the Moluccas to Indonesia, where they
bring very high black-market prices. Several species are currently
in danger (P. Pfeffer, *Bull. ICBP* 9: 90–5, 1963).

7 AUSTRALIA

Australia has a highly specialized and largely unique fauna. This is
particularly true of the mammals, which consist of marsupials aside
from a group of very peculiar rodents and the dingo. These primitive mammals were at one time widely spread across the world, but
they declined when placental mammals appeared which were
better equipped to compete in the struggle for survival. Several
marsupials have persisted in South America, where the invasion of
the placental species was relatively late, but most modern forms are
confined to Australia.

Geological history shows that pouched mammals are usually

incapable of competing with placental forms. Their method of reproduction is less efficient in protecting the young from flesh-eating predators. This explains the ravages of animals imported by Europeans. Feral foxes, dogs and cats turned partially wild, proved dangerous enemies, while rabbits laid waste original habitats and competed for food with herbivorous forms. Man added to the disaster by tilling wild habitats or transforming them into sheep pastures. Modification of natural habitats is probably the essential cause of the marsupials' decline. Accustomed to well-defined plant communities, they lacked the ability to change.

Most of the marsupials that were abundant in the 19th century have become rare; some are already extinct. According to a report by J. H. Calaby (CSIRO, *Wildlife* 1, 1: 15–18, 1963), 35 forms are threatened with extinction in Australia—some only on the continent, for Tasmania seems to have become a sanctuary. The status of many others is very uncertain.

The Tasmanian 'devil' (*Sarcophilus harrisi*), a large flesh-eater, has vanished from Australia and is now found only in Tasmania. A killer of poultry and sheep, it was the most harmful of native quadrupeds. The wolf or thylacine (*Thylacinus cynocephalus*), largest of the group, was the size of a big dog (*fig* 19). It has left fossil remains in Australia and appears to have been driven from there by the dingo dog. When the Europeans arrived, the thylacine was still common in Tasmania, where it attacked sheep. This led to a war that lasted during the final decades of the 19th century. There was a reward of a pound for every animal killed, and the thylacine was practically exterminated.

Herbivorous marsupials have suffered just as much. The smallest, like the bandicoots and the kangaroo-rats (*Bettongia*), were hunted for their fine fur. Their habit of nesting in burrows made them particularly vulnerable to trappers as well as to imported flesh-eaters. Poisoned bait spread to destroy rabbits is often consumed by vegetarian marsupials. It has also harmed the kangaroo, many species of which are gravely threatened by the destruction of their habitat, and by the predation of foxes and fur trappers. Most kangaroos have a thick, soft fur, which was so prized during the 19th century that many professional hunters earned their living by killing them.

The curious little koalas (*Phascolarctos cinereus*) were also hunted

Fig. 19
Thylacine or Tasmanian wolf, Thylacinus cynocephalus.

for their thick, woolly coats. These marsupials, resembling small bears, live in trees and feed on the leaves of several species of eucalyptus. When the Europeans arrived, there were millions of koalas but to-day only a few thousand remain. The specialized diet of the koala makes it sensitive to any change in its habitat, but hunting is responsible for most of the slaughter. In 1924 no less than two million koala skins were exported under the name of 'wombat' and in 1927 600,000 koalas were killed in Queensland alone.[1] Several hundred survivors were taken to Philip Island, where they thrived. During World War II the Department of Fisheries and Game was able to begin restocking the mainland. Over seven thousand koalas have been transported, and they are once again becoming plentiful in forest country.

Although Australian birds have suffered less than mammals, some have almost disappeared. The Australian scrub-bird or 'feathered mouse' (*Atrichornis clamosus*), a little songbird native to Australia, had been regarded as extinct since 1889 but was rediscovered on the slopes of Mount Gardner, near Albany, in 1961. Only some forty

[1] On 20th September, 1967, the Minister of Primary Industries wrote (*in litt.*): 'The 1927 figure for koalas may be fictitious, and refers to a sale which may have covered skins taken over a considerable period of time. Probably this figure covers skins of opossums and koalas, the former being the major portion.'

Female Transcaspian wild ass or kulan with her foal:
Barsa Kelmes Island, Aral Sea

Indian wild asses: Little Rann of Kutch, Gujarat

Above Hunting elephant in South Africa. From an engraving in
W. C. Harris's *The Wild Sport of South Africa*, London 1844: this
shows the abundance of the elephant in a part of southern Africa
from which it has now practically disappeared

Below Quagga zebra. From an engraving in W. C. Harris's
Portraits of the Game and Wild Animals of Southern Africa, London
1840. This species became extinct between 1870 and 1880

Hunting at the beginning of this century: a contemporary
photograph which was probably taken in East Africa or the Congo

Above *Encephalartos* station, an arborescent species of the family Cycadaceae of South Africa: Zuurberg Forest Reserve, near Port Elizabeth. *Below* Station of *Encephalartos horridus*, a stemless species of the family Cycadaceae of South Africa: near Amanzi. These plants, living fossils, are destroyed by brush fires to which their seeds are highly sensitive

Fig. 20
Australian terrestrial parrots. In the foreground: Australian night parrot,
Geopsittacus occidentalis, *found in deserts in the centre of western*
Australia; at the back: ground parrot, Pezoporus wallicus, *found in*
southern Australia. The two species have become quite rare since their
habitats were transformed and predatory mammals introduced.

pairs survive. The introduction of cats and rats, coupled with the
destruction of the habitat, practically wiped out the population
of this little bird. The same factors were responsible for the disappearance of two small parrots: *Pezoporus wallicus*, of southern
Australia and Tasmania, and *Geopsittacus occidentalis*, which inhabits the deserts of the south and west (*fig* 20). As these birds live
on the ground and nest in a hollow they are ready prey for introduced predators. Both are on the verge of extinction.

But the most spectacular loss among Australian birds is the black
emu (*Dromaeus ater*), of King Island, in Bass Strait (Jouanin, 1959).
This bird is known to us only from skins brought back by the
French expedition of Captain Baudin in 1804 and from subfossil
remains. It seems to have been exterminated early in the 19th
century by sealers who trained dogs to hunt it. The emus (*Dromaeus
novae-hollandiae*) are threatened with extinction on the Australian
continent where they are accused of damaging wheat fields. They
were machine-gunned until 1932, and even to-day there is a price
on their heads.

8 AFRICA

In Africa, as in North America, so-called civilized man has upset the balance of nature and particularly affected the large fauna. Destruction began in ancient times in North Africa and on the borders of the Sahara. The elephants hunted by Carthaginians in Libya vanished a long time ago.

The lion (*Panthera leo leo*) disappeared during the 19th century. Relatively abundant from north-western Tunisia to Morocco, it ranged as far as the Atlantic until the 16th century, then gradually withdrew from the coastal plains to the Atlas Mountains. But wilderness clearing, road building, and superior weapons proved too much. Between 1873 and 1883, 202 lions were 'officially' killed in Algeria, and the last one fell at Souk-Ahras in 1891. The lion survived until about 1922 in the forests of the central Atlas in Morocco. So the population dwindled as hostile tribes were pacified and civilization advanced.

The North African hartebeest (*Alcelaphus b. buselaphus*) met the same fate. This northern representative of a species still widespread in tropical Africa was abundant in the 18th century, when large herds roamed through southern Algeria and part of the Atlas Mountains. Gradually it abandoned the lower parts of its habitat for the mountains, which acted as refuges as the plains became settled. In 1925 the hartebeest was still found on the border of Morocco and Algeria, but it is now considered extinct.

North Africa has a mixed population of animals from both Africa and Europe. Among large mammals is the Barbary deer, closely allied to the European deer. Herds formerly inhabited wooded mountains from Morocco to Tunisia but the animal seems to have disappeared from the western portion of its habitat in Roman times. That it was a favourite target for sportsmen is evident from numerous hunting scenes on Roman mosaics in North Africa. Transformation of the forest was fatal to this animal, which now survives only in forests on the Algerian-Tunisian frontier. Some 300 deer were thought to live there in 1953. In 1964 the population on Tunisian territory was estimated at about one hundred and fifty, of which about one hundred are supposed to be intermittently on Tunisian and Algerian territory. No data are available about the Algerian side.

South of the Sahara, Africa has suffered an almost unparalleled destruction of wildlife at the hands of 'civilized' man. The black continent was far from being 'virgin' when the first Europeans arrived. It bore profound traces of man's activity and, except for damp rain-forests, it is probable that the habitats had already been modified by brush fires and shifting cultivation. There were already signs of soil deterioration. But the density of the African population, reduced by disease and slavery, was very low, in contrast for instance to South-east Asia.

Africa has a very special fauna, including a unique collection of mammals which represent the last survivors of a biological complex that has vanished elsewhere. Nowhere else in the world are ungulates, or hoofed mammals, so specialized and diversified. The present African mammalian fauna is the equivalent of the Tertiary (fossil) fauna of Europe.

Most of these animals are highly evolved and strictly dependent on their environment. Their diet and the large domain they require make them vulnerable. Many of them move long distances in accordance with the seasons and fluctuations in plant cover. No sooner did the Europeans come than they began to slaughter the animals and transform the habitats.

The first explorers were overwhelmed by the sight of enormous herds covering the plains. Like the bison of North America, thousands of elephants, antelopes of all kinds, zebras and giraffes gave the impression that nature was inexhaustible. Devastation began in the 18th century when the Dutch settled southern Africa and then moved north following the Anglo-Boer wars. This part of the country was inhabited by a fauna unequalled elsewhere. Immense herds inhabited the savannas and performed regular migrations; but to-day they have disappeared save in a few areas, and several species are extinct.

The bluebuck or blaauwbok (*Hippotragus leucophaeus*) has the sad privilege of being the first African ungulate exterminated by man (*fig* 21). It occupied a very small territory in South Africa, never going beyond the Swellendam district in Cape Province. Lichtenstein believes the last survivors were shot about 1800.

Several zebras met the same fate, notably the quagga (*Equus quagga*

Fig. 21
Bluebuck or blaauwbok, Hippotragus leucophaeus.

quagga), the southern form of an East African species characterized by a lack of stripes on the rear part of the body (*fig* 22). Although restricted to the Cape area and the Orange Free State and never going north of the Vaal River, they were numerous even at the beginning of the 19th century. The Boers massacred them in their deliberate policy of eliminating all large animals from the territories they proposed to develop. The last quagga south of the Orange River was killed in 1858. The animal survived for a longer period north of the river, where the Boers did not establish any colonies until about 1885. This marked the beginning of a wholesale slaughter to obtain leather for export and the production of grain bags. It is not known exactly when the quagga became extinct, but it was probably between 1870 and 1880. It thus vanished only a short time before the Burchell zebra (*Equus quagga burchelli*), another

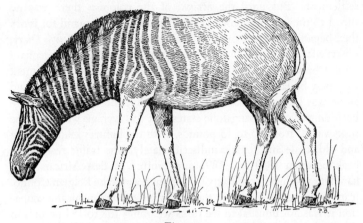

Fig. 22
Quagga, Equus quagga quagga.

representative of the same group native to Bechuanaland and the Orange Free State, which, although abundant, was soon driven from most parts of its habitat. The last one died in the London Zoological Garden early in the 20th century. A related form, *E.q. antiquorum*, is still represented by a few animals in the western part of S. W. Africa.

Most antelope populations have nearly vanished. The bontebok (*Damaliscus p. pygargus*), an inhabitant of south-western Cape Province, and the blesbok (*Damaliscus p. albifrons*) covered the karroo to the limits of the Transvaal and Bechuanaland and were the commonest antelopes in South Africa, but have now mostly disappeared. The white-tailed gnu (*Connochaetes gnou*), mountain zebra (*Equus zebra*) and the elephant (*Loxodonta africana*), which was still abundant in the Cape Peninsula in the 17th century, have been practically exterminated in southern Africa.

An incredibly rich fauna was thus systematically destroyed, and less than a century was required for the disappearance of this priceless natural treasure. The rest of the African continent followed the same course, large mammals vanishing as European penetration advanced. Elephants used to roam over all the habitable land south of the Sahara. They had for centuries been hunted for their ivory, the chief trade product—together with slaves—of the coastal settlements. But until the arrival of the colonists there was no threat to the very existence of the elephant. The demand for ivory then began to increase rapidly. Meinertzhagen, in his *Kenya Diary*, observed: 'It is a pity that an intelligent creature like the elephant should be shot in order that creatures not much more intelligent may play billiards with balls made from its teeth.' By 1860 England alone was importing 550,000 tons annually, and the animals were becoming scarce. Livingstone states that the average weight of the tusks varied from 13 to 15 pounds, with the hunters killing young and old, male and female indiscriminately. The traffic reached its peak between 1880 and 1890 and centred in East African ports handling products from Kenya, Tanganyika and the Belgian Congo. Jeannin wrote (1947) that at the beginning of the European occupation it was not unusual to see tusks weighing 132 to 154 pounds in the former Belgian Congo, with 33 as the average. This declined to 22 by 1890, to 17 by 1910 and by 1920 it was down to 13. A similar tendency is noted in Uganda, where the tusks weighed 55 pounds in 1926 and 40 in 1958 (Brooks and Buss, *Mammalia*, 26: 10–34, 1962). About 1880 between 60,000 and 70,000 elephants were killed annually to satisfy the demands of the European market. Actually the total was higher because tusks were carved in Africa if they were not considered good enough for export.

The rhinoceros was another victim. The horn, which had led to its destruction in Asia, also brought about a massacre in Africa. Populations dwindled rapidly first in South and then in East Africa. The white rhinoceros (*Ceratotherium simum*), once abundant in South Africa, suffered severely. So too did the race *cottoni* on the borders of the Sudan, the Congo and the Ubangi.

Other large herbivores decreased in proportion to the destructive scale of hunting. As white hunters were usually trying to outshoot their predecessors, the plains were covered with skeletons abandoned to hyenas and vultures. The rhinoceros had practically disappeared from territories under French rule by 1932. The hippopotamus was vanishing everywhere, and so was the giraffe, especially in West Africa where the population is now so small that it will be difficult to rebuild (*fig* 23). Better firearms dealt the deathblow to these large animals.

Professional hunters had other increasingly commercial outlets. They supplied fresh or dried meat (biltong) to men working in

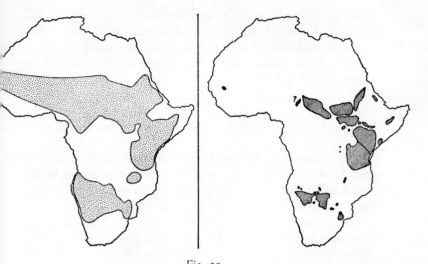

Fig. 23

Reduction of the territory of the giraffe, Giraffa camelopardalis, *in Africa. On the left: original distribution; on the right: distribution today Notice the splintering of the territory and the almost total disappearance of this ungulate from West Africa. From A. Innis Dagg* Mammalia 1962.

camps and fields. At the same time the hide business was established. It is very difficult to determine how many antelope were slaughtered for this purpose, but according to Marty (1955), 750,000 skins, chiefly duikers, were examined in 1953 on their way out of the territories which then constituted the French Union. These figures do not give a true picture because they deal only with skins that went through customs and not those worked by Africans. It is estimated that about two million duikers were killed annually for their hides. The figures are similar in East Africa, especially Somaliland. Funaioli and Simonetta (1961) state that this country exported annually about 350,000 dikdik skins (*Madoqua, Rhynchotragus*) and about 70,000 antelope skins, the majority of which (80%) were giraffe-gazelles or gerenuks (*Litocranius walleri*).

The large fauna was therefore threatened by the very rapid evolution of the African continent. Its destruction was accompanied by the less spectacular but equally serious ravages that followed

European colonization. Forest exploitation, often poorly planned, endangered some species, while contributing to the degradation of fragile habitats that were also menaced by clearing for farms. The pillage of Africa south of the Sahara thus had incalculable consequences.

9 MADAGASCAR AND THE MASCARENE ISLES

Owing to their isolation, these islands have served as sanctuaries for animals of a primitive type and for species representing highly specialized evolutionary lines. Human settlement, particularly the impact of modern man, has had disastrous results.

The Mascarenes had an impoverished but unique fauna. Although there were no native mammals, some birds had become flightless, and so were especially vulnerable. Discovered in 1505, these islands were uninhabited until the beginning of the 17th century, when destruction of the plant cover and massacre of the fauna began. Without counting those birds known only from bones, which are hard to identify, 24 of the 28 primitive terrestrial species have disappeared—one of the highest percentages in the world.

They vanished for the usual reasons: overhunting, the introduction of various foreign birds and mammals and domestic animals which reverted to the wild state (especially rats, mice and monkeys), degeneration of habitats, and deforestation of islands that early travellers described as a garden of Eden.

The most highly differentiated birds were gigantic terrestrial pigeons: the dodo of Mauritius (*Raphus cucullatus*) (*fig* 24), the dronte of Reunion (*R. solitarius*) and the solitaire of Rodriguez (*Pezophaps solitarius*). These three, each native to an island, were unable to fly because their wings were so diminutive. Furthermore, their weight, some fifty pounds, would have prevented them from flying. They belong at the end of an evolutionary line, and survived only because they had no natural enemies. The only remains that have been preserved are skeletons, and their description is based on drawings and paintings by Dutch artists of specimens brought to the Netherlands in the 16th and 17th centuries.

These defenceless birds provided fresh meat for ships, as three or four of them could feed an entire crew. Thirty or more were taken

Golden cat, widespread throughout Asia, but becoming very rare in many places

Asiatic lion (Gir Forest, Gujarat), now confined to an area of some 500 square miles in the Indian province of Kathiawar

Notornis or takahe, a native of New Zealand. For fifty years it was considered extinct: in 1948 it was rediscovered in the Murchison Mountains

Fig. 24
Dodo of Mauritius Island, Raphus cucullatus.

on board for the journey, and this pillage, coupled with the introduction of dogs, cats, pigs and macaques, which pursued the adults and devoured eggs and young, wiped out the birds. The dodo disappeared from Mauritius about 1680; the species indigenous to Reunion and Rodriguez vanished during the 18th century.

Other birds of the Mascarenes are better known because they survived until recent times. The last Mascarene parrot (*Mascarinus mascarinus*) of Reunion was still living in captivity in 1834, and the famous Bourbon starling (*Fregilupus varius*) was last collected about 1840 in Reunion (*fig* 25).

Overpopulation and its inevitable consequences are responsible for this destruction. Reunion, which was deserted in the 16th century, had 12 inhabitants in 1665 and 37,000 in 1772. In 1950 there were over 200,000. This led to massive deforestation and slaughter of even the smallest birds. Ph. Milon tells me he saw Zosterops skinned in 1950. There are said to be only 10 to 15 kestrels (*Falco punctatus*) left on Mauritius because their habitat has been destroyed. As birds vanished or dwindled in numbers, others were brought to replace them. Seventeen species, or 58% of the birds now on Réunion, were introduced, including the Indian mynah (*Acridotheres tristis*) which multiplies with alarming speed. These birds compete with the surviving native songbirds, that have found no refuge save in the remaining forest where few introduced birds ever go.

Other animals that have suffered from man are the giant terrestrial tortoises (*Testudo gigantea*) which are hunted for their oil and flesh, as they are on the Galapagos.

The Mascarenes thus show how a highly developed fauna, already degenerate because of the peculiar circumstances of its habitat, can vanish before 'civilization'.

In Madagascar the wild habitat was degraded by man long before the arrival of Europeans. Originally the east was covered with dense rain-forest and the drier centre and west with deciduous forest. But the island was soon defaced. The axe gradually felled the rain-forests and fire destroyed the dry ones. Such a transformation caused climatic changes; erosion and soil degeneration turned a good part of Madagascar into an almost unproductive desert, and to-day the island is one of the areas most tragically eroded by man.

The native plants and animals have inevitably suffered as well. Madagascar is the true home of lemurs, one of the most interesting groups of primates because they have retained their primitive characteristics. They are so closely linked to their forest habitat that its destruction entails their own disappearance. Madagascans have kept them and hunted them for food from earliest times. It is therefore not surprising that the lemur is one of the most seriously threatened of all mammals.

10 SUBANTARCTIC ISLANDS

These small islands scattered along the border of the Antarctic include South Georgia, Amsterdam, St Paul, Kerguelen, Crozet and Macquarie. The fauna is poor as ecological conditions are unfavourable and the islands remote. No mammal, save marine species, has found its way there, but there were rich colonies of sea birds: penguins, albatrosses and petrels.

Fig. 25
Bourbon starling, Fregilupus varius.

Man has upset the balance in these simple and hence extremely fragile areas. Seals were slaughtered for fur, and other animals for fun. Albatross bones, for example, were used to make sailors' pipe stems. But man's most serious crime was to introduce exotic mammals—rats, mice, rabbits, goats, pigs and cats. Rats were the worst, for they attacked birds nesting in burrows or on the ground, and devoured eggs, young and adults. Petrel colonies were ravaged everywhere except in spots that the predators were unable to reach. According to Jouanin and Paulian (*Proc. XII int. Orn. Congr. Helsinki* (1958): 368-72, 1960), only four species are thriving on Amsterdam Island, while countless bones give evidence of the petrels that have vanished (*Bulweria, Puffinus, Pachyptila, Pelagodroma, Pelecanoides*).

These threats to the flora and fauna go back to the 18th century, but they have become much more serious since permanent bases were set up on the islands. The presence of men causes profound changes in communities that have evolved in remote areas (Holdgate and Wace, 1961: Dorst and Milon, 1964).

11 SEAS

The seas have long been thought inexhaustible. Their exploitation —particularly by fishing—intensified as man perfected his techniques. As the dangers of overfishing did not become apparent until very recently, however, we shall not discuss the subject here.

For a long time, the number of sea mammals has been receding, particularly in the case of the whale. This animal seems to have been hunted first by Basques in the Gulf of Gascony, and whaling was already an important industry in the 12th century. As the right whale (*Eubalaena glacialis*) soon became rare, the Basques had to go farther and farther west, and they may have reached Newfoundland before Christopher Columbus 'officially' discovered America. By the beginning of the 19th century this whale had disappeared from European waters. Its populations then dwindled in the western Atlantic, while a related form, *Eubalaena sieboldi*, declined in the North Pacific. These two whales have become so rare that they comprise a very small part of the global catch; Townsend (*in* G. M. Allen, 1942) counted only 35, or 0·2% out of a total of 17,862 captured between 1910 and 1920. These whales have practically vanished because of exploitation. The grey whale (*Eschrichtius glaucus*) almost vanished during the first decades of this century. Now protected, its numbers have increased satisfactorily to almost 5,000.

As whales grew scarcer, the centres of exploitation moved. By the 17th century whalemen of all nationalities were in the Arctic seas, especially the waters between Spitzbergen and northern Canada. The principal prey was the bowhead (*Balaena mysticetus*). Later the hunt moved north-west along the coasts of Greenland and Baffinland, favourite grounds during the 18th century. Logbooks show that the takes were large. Between 1814 and 1817 586 vessels sent out by Great Britain captured 5,030 whales, most of them bowheads. During the 19th century the number decreased until the hunt was no longer profitable. After 1887 only a score of ships ploughed these waters; in 1911 8 vessels succeeded in taking 7 whales. Since that time the population seems to have increased, and, as its density is too low for industrial exploitation, the species does not at the moment seem threatened with extinction.

North American whalers hunted the sperm whale (*Physeter catodon*) in warm waters. By the second half of the 18th century business was flourishing near New England. Then the hunters spread out to all parts of the world, and American whaling reached its peak in the first half of the 19th century. Decrease in numbers and the use of kerosene lamps in place of whale oil effectively ended the industry. The sperm whale was never in danger of extinction, but now that it is becoming the chief prey of modern whaling the species is seriously threatened.

A final phase concerns the hunt for Antarctic whales. Several species of rorquals or finbacks form the principal quarry. Prized for their oil, they are captured in such large numbers as to endanger the species.

Most seals have suffered from intensive hunting. Populations in New Zealand and southern Australia (*Arctocephalus forsteri*, *A. doriferus*, *A. tasmanicus*) were reduced and some colonies destroyed in the 19th century. The Kerguelen seal (*A. gazella*) was almost exterminated about 1850 by an American sealer. The numbers recovered, but 3,000 animals were slaughtered in 1880 and the population has remained small since then. More than 70,000 skins of the Cape seal (*A. pusillus*) were shipped annually to London at the close of the 19th century. A massacre wiped out enormous colonies of the fur seal (*A. p. philippi*) on the Juan Fernandez Islands off Chile. These probably numbered between two and three million in the last years of the 17th century. It is estimated that, a hundred years later, three million skins were taken within seven years, most of which were sold in Canton. The species is now extinct, although a small population (200 to 500 animals) of a related subspecies (*A. p. townsendi*) survives on Guadelupe Island, Lower California. The same story might have been told of the fur seal of the Pribilof Islands, but we shall come back to this later.

Steller's sea cow (*Hydrodamalis stelleri*) was native to the North Pacific, especially to the seas surrounding the Commander Islands off Kamchatka (*fig* 26). About 26 feet long, this animal lived in shallow bays and fed chiefly on algae, particularly Laminaria. Bering found it there in 1741. In 1768, barely a quarter of a century after its discovery, the sea cow had been exterminated by sailors and Russian fur trappers. It is known only from skeletons, fragments of skin, drawings and stories told by travellers.

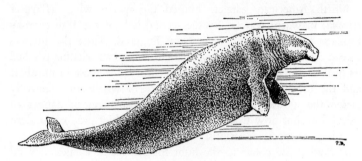

Fig. 26
Steller's sea cow, Hydrodamalis stelleri.

The sea otter (*Enhydra lutris*) was also exterminated in the North Pacific. This large animal, weighing up to 67 pounds, was well adapted to marine life, but its dense, resistant fur had made it a target for trappers by the middle of the 18th century. In 1742 Bering himself returned to Petropavlovsk with a cargo of 900 skins on board. The sea otter soon began to decline, as is evident from the decrease in the take at the Pribilof Islands. The price of skins rose from 20 to 465 dollars between 1850 and 1900, when the species was almost extinct. During that year measures were taken to enable the animal to recover and to-day the population in Alaska numbers 40,000 and the species is expanding towards the south. They were seen at Point Lobos, California, in July 1966.

We have made a very rapid analysis of the principal devastations for which man is to blame during past centuries, particularly during the 19th. Slow at first, except in a few places, this process was greatly accelerated as mechanical power and technical methods became available.

The chief causes of destruction have been hunting, the transformation of habitats particularly through massive deforestation, and the introduction of foreign plants and animals. From the last serious chain reactions ensue, especially on islands where the fauna is much more fragile than on large continental masses. It is also possible that diseases transmitted to native forms by introduced animals contributed to their destruction. Similar instances are known among human beings.

Highly specialized plants and animals have suffered most. The irruption of the white man was marked by catastrophe in insular regions and occasionally on entire continents, such as Africa where the large fauna proved extremely fragile. Man has acted like the Sorcerer's Apprentice, without knowledge of the laws governing the natural balance.

During the 19th century, the era of great industrial development, man literally assaulted the world in his need for raw materials of all kinds. Even to-day certain collectors seize all the specimens of a rare and often localized species. Entomologists are some of the worst offenders in this respect; some have captured in a single season twelve thousand very rare Lepidoptera of the Zygaenidae family, and localized carabus beetles are hunted so intensively that their numbers decline every season.

Rare plants are pillaged to satisfy the demands of horticulturists or collectors of herbaria. Societies that exchange specimens and insist on 'centuries', or one hundred specimens of a species, have caused widespread damage. The vandalism of unscrupulous 'naturalists' has been responsible for the disappearance of a number of smaller native forms, particularly in the Mediterranean region.

This abuse has led to certain legislative measures. Many Alpine plants are now protected in Switzerland, some insects, including the large Capricorn-beetle (*Cerambyx cerdo*), in Sweden, and in Germany, for example, the Apollo butterfly (*Parnassius apollo*) (*fig* 27).

Fig. 27
Apollo butterfly from Bavaria,
Parnassius apollo melliculus,
male. This well-differentiated
race has suffered from excessive
hunting by unscrupulous
collectors.

3 Man to the aid of Nature

At the end of the 19th century irrational exploitation, coupled with massive destruction, threatened the natural balance of the earth. It seemed that total eradication of the wild flora and fauna was imminent, with the exception of a few highly resistant species which had become accustomed to man and even dependent on him.

Then it was that a few clear-sighted men became aware of the gravity of the situation. The book of George P. Marsh, *Man and Nature; or Physical Geography as modified by Human Action*, which was published in London in 1864, is still a pioneering classic in its statements about the harmony which should exist between man and his natural habitat. A powerful reaction was organized by a handful of naturalists and financiers, and to them we owe the partial survival of nature in the world to-day.

A history of the protection of nature would undoubtedly reveal that the idea is very old. Authors of antiquity called attention to ravages in the Mediterranean region and reported that stony areas, barely capable of supporting a few scrawny goats, had once been covered with forests and springs. During the Middle Ages many laws were passed to protect the large European fauna and to save the forests. Although the majority of these measures were designed to secure a monopoly on game and to preserve hunting areas for the nobles, they protected the fauna by retarding the degradation of nature.

For example, the kings and princes of Poland took steps to preserve the aurochs, which had hitherto been abundant in eastern Europe. About the end of the 13th century Duke Boleslaus of Mazovia forbade hunting the animal in his domain, and a century later King Jagellon passed laws covering a larger area. In the 16th century King Sigismund III, aware that only a few of the animals survived, formed their territories into a reservation but did not succeed in saving them. Similar regulations were applied to the bison in both Poland and Russia.

Addax, North of Chad: this desert antelope of the Sahara is threatened by intensive hunting. A true creature of the desert, it lives wholly without drinking, deriving moisture from the plants on which it feeds

Above Emperor penguins in a blizzard: Adelie Land. These birds, which are well adapted to the polar climate, are relatively few in number: nesting in large colonies, they are sensitive to disturbances caused by human beings

Left Male, female and young fur-seals, Amsterdam Island. This species was pursued relentlessly and almost exterminated at the close of the last century: today there are less than 3000 individuals on this island in the South Indian Ocean

Above Sea otter on rocks which are uncovered at low tide: Amchitka Island, Alaska *Below* Sea otter floating on its back and breaking between its paws the molluscs that constitute its diet

Numerous examples could be listed in Asia, where philosophical and religious concepts encourage man to preserve nature. Some legislation advocating conservation is far older than any we have noted in Europe. About 242 BC the Indian Emperor Asoka granted his protection to fishes, terrestrial animals and forests. Areas called Abhayarana were real natural reserves. Appropriate laws were proclaimed by other Asiatic sovereigns, like the great Mongol Lord Kublai Khan, who, according to Marco Polo, prohibited hunting during the breeding season of birds and mammals.

Despite these forerunners, public opinion was not alive to the necessity of conserving parts of the globe until the second half of the 19th century. The first natural reserve seems to have been established during the Second Empire in France. In 1853 a group of painters belonging to the Barbizon School established a 1541-acre reserve in the forest of Fontainebleau, which was sanctioned by a decree of 13th August, 1861.

The concept of large reserves was born in the United States, where the catastrophic devastations of the 19th century provoked a healthy reaction. In 1864 Congress ceded the Valley of the Yosemite and Mariposa Grove to the State of California to establish a natural reserve and protect the sequoias. The idea of a national park came to several men who had spent six weeks exploring the Yellowstone region in 1870. Marvelling at the majestic scenery in this part of the Rocky Mountains, they organized a campaign which led to the promulgation of the law of 1st March, 1872, establishing the first National Park 'as a public park of pleasure ground for the benefit and the enjoyment of the people'.

Little by little the idea spread, and most countries passed legislation to establish reserves where the fauna and flora would be safe from man and could so build up their stocks. The aim was to protect certain areas there, so that by forbidding all human activity their original habitats and, in Alexander Humboldt's phrase, their 'natural monuments' could be preserved.

During this first phase people believed that if human influence were removed, a place would become 'an animal paradise' immediately. They soon realized this was a mistake, for nothing is stable in nature. In very large reservations natural forces are not affected by man's action in neighbouring areas, but in smaller places this does not hold true. So man often has to intervene to counterbalance influences which cannot be eliminated. This must be done intelligently. Some conservationists were prejudiced against predators which keep in check the numbers of their prey. They therefore destroyed the large carnivores and birds of prey to build up populations of vegetarians. In most instances this led to disaster, for overproduction caused degradation of the habitat. The value of a reservation does not depend on the number of animals it shelters but on the natural habitats and whether the animal and plant populations are in balance with their environment.

Man thus has to intervene in most reservations according to their size and the goals he wishes to obtain. This led to the establishment of a number of categories, of which the principal ones are as follows:

Natural Reserves are territories where man does not interfere at all. They are open only to scientists working under special conditions.

National Parks are usually large territories where protection of nature is combined with education and recreation. Their scientific or tourist appeal may be enhanced by special facilities. Visitors are admitted, provided they observe certain rules.

Partial Reserves are designed to protect a definite category of plants or animals, and, occasionally, minerals or soils as well. Other elements are considered only in their relationship to the protected ones, and they can be modified in accordance with established rules. Grazing or agriculture is possible so long as it does not interfere with the purpose of the reservation.

Special Reserves are designed to afford partial protection to certain elements of a biological complex. Hunting and fishing reservations are classic examples.

Protected zones are occasionally established around national parks or natural reserves to provide a belt area where a certain amount of human activity is authorized, but where hunting and transformation of habitats are restricted.

In every country an increasingly complex legislative apparatus has been designed to control exploitation of natural resources. Damage to forests, transformation of habitats and marsh-draining are now subject to precise laws. Governments alone can establish large reservations. They determine the categories of zones and provide for their maintenance. Many small and medium-size reservations, however, have been created by individuals and private societies.

The battle for the protection of nature has been a daily one, and there is no victory, for the same questions are constantly being raised anew. Doubtless the concept of 'protection' is now out of date, but we owe an eternal debt of gratitude to the men who worked courageously and unselfishly to preserve the landscapes and the flora and fauna of the world.

In 1962 the United Nations published *A List of National Parks and equivalent reserves* (second edition IUCN, 1967). Without listing them, we shall consider some of the outstanding achievements in this domain.

1 NORTH AMERICA

The USA has one of the best systems of national parks and reserves of any country, and one of the best methods of combining wildlife protection with well-organized tourism.

Some zones are directly governed by the federal government. These national parks are grouped under the authority of the National Park Service, Department of the Interior. In September 1967 this Service listed 259 areas under its administration. It provides for 33 national parks and 81 National Monuments, most of them in the West, which is wilder and particularly rich in beautiful landscapes (*fig* 28). 139 million visitors passed through one or another of these parks in 1967. 2,210,000 visited Yellowstone, the oldest and largest of the national parks, on the borders of Wyoming, Montana and Idaho. The volcanic nature of the soil is revealed in various ways, of which the 3,000 geysers are the best known. The fauna alone would justify the millions of visitors who have come to the Park since it was established in 1872. Large animals abound, including grizzlies, moose, wapitis and mountain sheep.

It would take too long to list the other parks scattered through the West. The most famous are the Grand Canyon in Arizona, the most spectacular geological phenomenon in the world, Yosemite N.P. in the Sierra Nevada and Sequoia N.P. to the south of it, both of which have forests of giant sequoias, while the latter includes Mount Whitney, the highest peak in the USA if Mt McKinley in

Alaska is excluded. In the east, the Everglades National Park, in the extreme south of Florida, is outstanding for its tropical aquatic habitats and very rich fauna, unique in the United States.

This system of national parks is completed by a series of National Wildlife Refuges administered by the US Fish and Wildlife Service. In 1966 there were 312 of these covering more than 28·5 million acres. Some are extremely important, such as the Aransas National Wildlife Refuge in Texas, the only known wintering ground of the whooping crane. There are also a number of very large areas administered by the Forest Service.

The most important private organization is the National Audubon Society, which has its own reserves and maintains centres where young and old can learn about the natural sciences. This Society also edits numerous publications and has done more to protect nature than any other private group in the world.

Other societies do fine work locally, like the National Wildlife Federation and the Hawk Mountain Association, which has set aside a reserve in the Pennsylvania hills to protect thousands of large birds of prey that come south in autumn. These unfortunate birds were ruthlessly hunted until part of their migratory route was specially protected.

In 1887 Canada created its first National Park (2,564 square miles) at Banff in the Rocky Mountains. Together with Jasper N.P. (4,200 square miles) to the north, it forms a great group of mountains sheltering a rich fauna, especially Rocky Mountain goats and mountain sheep. Other parks in the plains, like Prince Albert N.P., covering 957,427 acres in Saskatchewan, have a thriving aquatic fauna and mammals such as elk, caribou and beaver. Wood Buffalo National Park, with 17,300 square miles, shelters the only surviving herd of wood buffalo (*Bison bison athabascae*). The whooping crane nests there and is thus protected both at the beginning and the end of its long migratory flights.

Attempts have been made to ensure wildlife protection in Mexico, but the situation is far from satisfactory. The country was pillaged long ago. Furthermore, as in most Latin countries, the inhabitants have not felt any great responsibility toward nature. Several national parks are now being organized, however, and there is reason to believe that they will be properly administered in the near future.

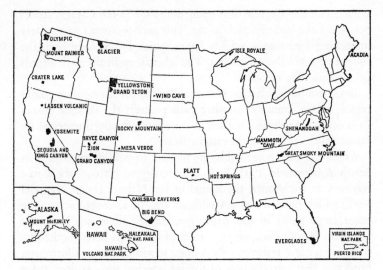

Fig. 28

*National Parks in the USA, administered by the National Park Service,
US Department of the Interior. In addition to these thirty-three parks,
with a total of over 13 million acres, the Service administers other areas,
including historic sites and national monuments.*

2 SOUTH AMERICA

As South America was despoiled by man later than other parts of
the world, there was not the same pressure to establish national
parks there. Protective laws for the flora and fauna were enacted by
the Spanish court in the sixteenth century. Admirable in intention
they were not well enforced. Some areas have been set aside as reserves. In Colombia measures have been taken to prevent deforestation, particularly in the river basins that supply water for large
cities. In 1935 Ecuador passed laws to protect the biological associations on the Galapagos Islands. Unfortunately these were not at first
enforced, but the recent creation of the Charles Darwin Research
Station directed by an international foundation working closely
with the Ecuadorian government, makes it likely that this inestim-
ably valuable scientific material may yet be saved.

Venezuela has established several national parks, the largest of which, Rancho Grande, was opened in 1937 in the Caracas Andes between Lake Valencia and the sea. This park protects a particularly interesting forest area, with a fauna which has already been the subject of a number of studies. The laboratory in the park affords fine facilities for research.

Brazil established Itatiaia National Park in the most mountainous region of the country; another park protects the famous Iguazu Falls on the Argentine border. Nature is especially threatened by industrial developments in eastern Brazil.

Argentina was indisputably the pioneer in wildlife protection in South America. In 1903, F. P. Moreno gave his country a vast territory in the Andes, the kernel of the Nahuel Huapi National Park, which opened in 1934 with an area of 1,939,813 acres. The other large parks in the Argentine, one of them adjoining the Brazilian Iguazu Park, cover a total of 6,532,135 acres. Some districts are natural reserves, others open to visitors. It is unfortunate, however, that introduction of foreign species, such as deer, trout and salmon, has modified the original balance. Chile has created several national parks to protect its Andean habitats and the rainforests with their native species.

There are two remarkable research centres among the sanctuaries in Central America and the Caribbean region: the New York Zoological Society's biological station in the northern chain of Trinidad (Simla), and Barro Colorado, in Panama, where the Smithsonian Institution created a station on an artificial island formed by the Panama Canal. Both preserve their original habitats and provide fine natural laboratories for the biologist in inaccessible areas.

3 EUROPE

The density of the population, a high degree of industrialization and a very ancient modification of the natural habitats are serious obstacles to the establishment of national parks in this part of the world. Nevertheless, most countries have set aside reserves, however small.

The most famous one in France is the Camargue Reserve, established in 1928 by the French National Society for the Protection of Nature. The Camargue is a large area of swamps and brackish lagoons between the two arms of the Rhône. It was set aside thanks to the collaboration of large industrial companies which own the land, despite protests from salt and rice interests that have been expanding there since the last world war. The Camargue is a paradise for the biologist, with its interesting fauna and one of the few European colonies of the rose flamingo (*Phoenicopterus antiquorum*). As the Camargue's natural habitats range from fresh to brackish water, there is nothing comparable in Europe, except for the recently established Marismas of the Guadalquivir, Spain.

France has several other preserves both in the mountains and on the coast, such as the Réserve des Sept Iles, off the Côtes-du-Nord (Brittany), which was founded in 1912 by the League for Bird Protection to preserve marine species, particularly gannets (*Sula bassana*) and fulmars (*Fulmarus glacialis*). In 1960 Parliament voted to establish national parks; one has already been created in Savoy (Vanoise National Park), another at Port Cros, off the Var coast, and a third in the Pyrenees. At the instigation of the *Conseil supérieur de la chasse*, an organization which has made laudable efforts to protect the fauna and ensure wise hunting practices, a number of small preserves have been set up along the migratory routes of waterfowl.

In Great Britain, where the public is enthusiastic about natural history, wildlife protection has been under the aegis of private organizations, although a number are more or less subject to state control. Founded in 1895, the National Trust administers a great many areas, but the most representative group, the only one officially responsible for the preservation of nature, is the Nature Conservancy established in 1949. This organization manages a large number of reserves very efficiently. However small some of these may be, they are adequate to ensure the preservation of an interesting habitat. Scientific studies, especially in the field of ecology, are conducted in these areas.

Belgium and the Netherlands have had considerable difficulty trying to save what remains of their wildlife. Their populations, of a density unequalled in any other European country, and their industrialization have made conservation problems more complicated than elsewhere. In the Netherlands protection of nature was the work of one man, P. G. van Tienhoven. Numerous preserves controlled by scientists and several national parks shelter the most threatened habitats. Many of them sustain a rich avifauna, particularly the Frisian Islands and Naadermeer, a marsh near Amsterdam famous for its rare plants and aquatic birds.

Although work began in Belgium thirty years ago, it is only since the last war that concerted efforts have been made to protect wildlife. A network of national parks and preserves, which are often small but well-placed, assures protection for rare plants and nesting sites for small populations of migrating birds.

Switzerland has favoured the protection of nature since the Middle Ages. On St Lawrence Day (August 10) 1548, the inhabitants of Glaris Canton named the Kärpf Mountain area, near Schwanden, a 'free district'; this has been a preserve for more than 400 years. Under the sponsorship of the Swiss League for the Protection of Nature, established in 1909, and other groups, a number of bird sanctuaries have been established. In 1914 a federal law created a national park in the Lower Engadine, at an altitude between 4,921 and 12,467 feet. Since then no human intervention has modified the region, which now covers 41,687 acres, and animal populations, particularly deer, have increased rapidly. The ibex, which was reintroduced in 1920, is now thriving; so are chamois and other mountain animals, including large birds of prey.

Italy may well be proud of the national park, Great Paradise, in the Piedmont Alps, which made it possible to save the ibex (Couturier, 1962). This territory, formerly a royal hunting domain, was turned into a national park in 1922, with 136,953 acres. The number of ibex increased to 3,865 in 1933. Political developments were responsible for another decline and in 1945 only 419 remained. By1961 the population had risen again to 3,479. They are probably too numerous at present; but this excess has made it possible to repopulate other Alpine areas, particularly in Switzerland, Austria and Germany. The creation of a park in Savoy, which will cover a considerable distance along the frontier, will doubtless permit some of the population to move there. Italy's other national parks and preserves do not seem to be very successful, except in the Abruzzi region.

All the other Mediterranean countries have made efforts to protect their wildlife. From the Iberian Peninsula to Greece preserves have been established with varying success. Spain has several national parks, particularly to protect the Spanish ibex.

Alpine ibex: Great Paradise, Italy. Preserved in this national park, its numbers increased enough to repopulate other Alpine areas

Small waders and terns on migration: Aiguillon Bay on the
Vendée coast

Jugoslavia still has many wild areas. It has also created national parks to protect some of its most famous natural monuments; the outstanding one, Plitvicka Jezera, established in 1949, has 35,858 acres, with a chain of lakes and waterfalls famous all over Europe. The rich fauna includes bear, chamois, wolf and numerous large birds of prey.

Greece is famous for its native flora. Many indigenous forms combined with various importations have made it one of the richest in Europe. Some of the animals are of great interest, particularly the wild goats whose different races inhabit some of the islands in the Aegean Sea. A national park has been established on Mount Olympus, and another one in Crete (Samaria). The Greeks have also assured the protection of the wild goats on the Mediterranean islands (see Schultze-Westrum, 1963, *Säugetierkundl. Mitt.* **11:** 145–82).

The reserves in central and northern Europe are often better kept than those in the south. In Austria the famous Neusiedl Lake, south of Vienna, shelters many aquatic birds, and plant life is well protected in certain zones of the Austrian Alps. The preserves of West Germany cover some 398,193 acres. East Germany has classified the habitats of rare animal and plant species; there are 210 such preserves in the German Democratic Republic, in addition to a number of classified natural monuments.

Despite their tragic recent history, the Poles have one of the best programmes for the protection of wildlife in Europe. One of their first achievements was to save the bison in the Bialowieza Forest. The skeleton herd remaining after the First World War rapidly recovered, and exchanges made it possible to avoid inbreeding. The Second World War nearly proved fatal because so many animals were slaughtered and scientific management was poor. To-day, however, Poland has the largest numbe of bison of any country. There is also a Society for the Protection of European Bison which co-ordinates the effotts of breeders. A fine biological station is attached to Bialowieza National Park. Scattered throughout the country 8 other parks, including Pieniny and Tatras, preserve high mountain districts near the Czech frontier. Some 450 preserves complete the park system and protect remarkable forests, peat bogs, swamps or special geological formations.

Czechoslovakia has established more than 300 reservations and national parks. Those in Sweden, particularly the ones at Sarek (469,509 acres) and Stora Sjöfallet (341,011 acres), safeguard a subarctic fauna, including many rare mammals.

The USSR organized a gigantic system, continuing efforts made before the Revolution, to protect the forests and regulate hunting. To-day there are 76 national parks or territories covering 15,735,514 acres. Most of them have research laboratories, since conservation of nature is inseparable from scientific research. When these reservations were established, legislative measures were taken to ensure the protection of every species threatened. But the administration of the national parks in the USSR follows a somewhat different pattern from that of the USA or western Europe. Economics is often considered more important than conservation. Since most of the parks are used as experimental stations, foreign animals and plants are often introduced. This is very bad practice in a protected zone.

4 AFRICA SOUTH OF THE SAHARA

A healthy reaction followed the catastrophic devastation of Africa, so the continent is now dotted with remarkable reservations. The oldest, created as the Sabi Game Reserve on 26th March, 1898, was rechristened Krüger Park in 1926. Located along the Mozambique frontier and covering 7,340 square miles, this area in the Transvaal has a very rich fauna, consisting chiefly of large mammals. It is one of the great tourist attractions of the South African Republic.

Numerous other regions have been classified as reservations in the southern part of the continent. The largest is the Kalahari Gemsbok National Park, but several others are no less important in preserving wildlife. Bontebok National Park, for example, in Cape Province, has the only surviving bonteboks. The last elephants of southern Africa are in Addo National Park and the Knysna Forest Reserve, near Port Elizabeth. To protect the elephants and keep them from invading cultivated fields, their forests are surrounded by solid barricades of railroad tracks. These living conditions are somewhat artificial—the elephants are fed oranges to supplement their diet—but they make it possible to preserve animals which would otherwise have vanished from South Africa long ago. It has also been possible to save several species of large mammals by keeping them in captivity, especially the mountain zebra (*Equus zebra*), of which only about eighty survive.

In other regions two ideas governed the creation and management of reservations. The first aimed to establish national parks with the status of natural reserves. In 1925 King Albert of Belgium signed a decree creating the famous park bearing his name. This was only the first step in a series that endowed the eastern Congo with the best parks on the continent (*fig* 29). Under the direction of Professor V. van Straelen, the Garamba, Albert, Upemba and Kagera National Parks, the latter in Rwanda, were created to provide protection for the most famous habitats in Africa. Albert Park is doubtless the best known (*fig* 30). Its 1,999,119 acres cover the western slope of the Ruwenzori, the rich savannas of the Semliki and Rutshuru to the north and south of Lake Edward, and the chain of volcanoes north of Lake Kivu. The diversity of biological habitats is enormous, extending from dry savannas to cactoid *Euphorbia* and from rain-forests to the lofty bamboo forests and Alpine prairies dotted with lobelias and giant groundsel. The steep graben slopes form the natural boundaries of this park, which is located on broad plains between two deep faults. Consequently there is a rich and well-diversified fauna. Among the best known animals are mountain gorillas, living on the volcanoes of the eastern Congo, innumerable elephants, buffaloes and antelopes, while the shores of the Rwindi and Rutshuru rivers shelter the largest concentration of hippopotamuses in the world.

Garamba National Park, on the border of the Sudan, was established to protect the giraffe and white rhinoceros, now found only in the Congo. The largest, Upemba N.P., with 2,898,600 acres, is located between the Katangan and the central African regions. Finally, Kagera N.P. preserves original habitats with the remains of a fauna that has disappeared elsewhere because of over-grazing. Its huge swamps contain a large number of animals.

The national parks of the Congo thus form a spectacular ensemble where nature has been completely protected. Although they are open to visitors, most of their area is reserved for scientific research. That the most important works on African flora and fauna have been written within their boundaries is evident from the series of reports published by the Institute of National Parks

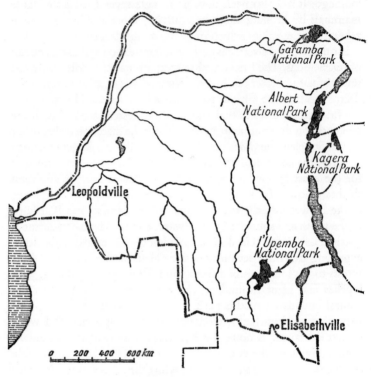

Fig. 29
National parks in the Congo and Rwanda.

of the Belgian Congo. The new Congolese government has made
every effort to preserve these sanctuaries, and some of the wardens
gave their lives to protect them.

The second reservation policy prevailed in territories under
British rule. Vast areas were set aside as reserves in which a certain
amount of human intervention is permitted, both on the part of
natives and of tourists. The park at Nairobi is the city's most
interesting attraction. Lions, giraffes and various antelopes wander
about on the outskirts of a modern metropolis. Tsavo, the largest
park in Kenya, with over 4,942 million acres, was established west
of Mombasa in 1948 to shelter a rich fauna that included elephants
and lesser kudus.

Since the last war Uganda has established two large parks. Murchison Falls National Park, with an area of 1,504 square miles, is centred around the famous falls where the Nile cuts into a very narrow gorge. Queen Elizabeth National Park adjoins the Congo National Park on the other side of Lake Edward, and its interesting landscapes and abundant fauna cover 764 square miles.

In 1951 Tanganyika (Tanzania) created several parks, including the Serengeti with 4,450 square miles. Unfortunately part of this territory has now been withdrawn because of pressure from the Masaï and their flocks. The famous Ngorongoro Crater, where there are numerous wildebeest, Thomson gazelles and zebras, is classed as a reservation, and there are also 10 'game reserves', rich in fauna.

Rhodesia has set up several national parks, including Wankie National Park, with 5,060 square miles, and Zambia has Kafue N.P., open to the public since 1955, with 8,650 square miles and a fine fauna. Other reservations have been established for the protection of such natural monuments as the famous Victoria Falls.

French-speaking countries have created many reservations. West Africa has undoubtedly witnessed a greater destruction of its fauna than Central or East Africa, but large numbers of the big animals have been preserved. Niokolo-Koba National Park was established in Senegal in 1954, with some 625,000 acres of Sudanese savannas interspersed with gallery-forests. It shelters numerous herbivores, including Buffon cobs and hartebeest.

The best-known reservation in Guinea is Mount Nimba. The savannas on the summit are populated by some astonishing native forms. This territory has often been despoiled on account of its mineral wealth. It has a laboratory attached to it.

Cameroon has many reserves designed to protect some of its landscape and fauna; Waza N.P. to the north, with 420,087 acres, shelters large mammals and aquatic birds. In 1958 Chad opened Zakouma Park, with 798,750 acres, as well as some fine game preserves where hunting is regulated. The protection of animals thus goes hand in hand with a tourist sport which has proved very profitable to the country.

Finally, Madagascar is sprinkled with a series of reserves that have saved beautiful fragments of primitive forest on the island, much of which has been converted into lateritic desert. There are 12

Fig. 30
Principal vegetation zones in Albert National Park, Congo.
1 equatorial and mountain rain-forests
2 bamboo forests

natural reserves, covering 1,235,550 acres, 13 special reserves, and a national park with 45,500 acres established on Amber Mountain in 1958. Laws for the protection of the lemur population are frequently disregarded.

Africa has therefore seen a large number of measures intended to safeguard its fauna, especially its large mammals. All its territories have enacted hunting legislation but though these measures have helped, in many areas they served only to slow down the phenomena of degradation.

5 ASIA

All Asiatic countries have made efforts to preserve their fauna and flora, and many have obtained very satisfactory results. In India there is a strong feeling that animals should be protected. Reservations have multiplied, but they are difficult to describe since the administrative system is so complex. The famous Kaziranga Reserve in Assam shelters in its 166 square miles more than half of the surviving Indian rhinoceroses, while the others are in various reserves in Nepal. Visitors can tour on elephant-back and observe rhinoceroses in their swampy habitats. The artificial Lake Periyar in the southern part of the peninsula attracts tourists who come to see elephants and gaurs in the surrounding forest. Ceylon has fine reserves and even some national parks, such as Wilpattu, Gal Oya and Ruhuna, which protect the remnants of the natural habitat, notably the 1000 to 1500 surviving elephants.

In 1938 Malaya established King George V National Park: 1760 square miles of mountainous country, inhabited by elephants, rhinoceroses, tapirs and other large flesh-eaters. In Indonesia the

3 grassland and wooded savannas
4 plant formations at high altitude (Hagenias, *tree heather, Alpine formations*)
This park has a good balance and includes all the natural habitats to be found in this part of Africa. From Robyns Les territoires biogéographiques du P. N. Albert *Brussels 1948, simplified.*

Dutch administration and some private groups created a series of reserves that numbered 100 in 1939. The new Indonesian directors indicated at once that they intended to preserve the 116 sanctuaries, covering 5,436,420 acres. The most precious is the Udjung Kulon-Panailan Reserve in western Java, dating from 1921; its 102,800 acres shelter the last Javan rhinoceroses, the world's most threatened animals. In 1966 there were said to be 25 in the reserve and some 40 altogether. This peninsula is not open to the public, for the rhinoceroses are also protected by tigers, animals which enjoy a bad reputation among poachers.

Other important reserves are those which, at Rintja and Komodo in the Little Sunda Islands, protect the Komodo varan or 'dragon-lizard of Komodo' (*Varanus komodoensis*), a gigantic, flesh-eating reptile, native to these islands.

Despite their chronic overpopulation, the Japanese, who are people of taste and tradition, have established and maintained 19 national parks, covering 4,364,516 acres. The most famous is Fuji-Hakone-Izu, with Fujiyama in its centre. Others preserve the Japanese Alpine landscapes and the beauties of Hokkaido Island where there is still a rich fauna.

Unfortunately, there are almost no large reserves in the other Far Eastern territories, particularly in the Indo-Chinese peninsula. Nevertheless, a start is now being made in this direction.

6 AUSTRALIA AND NEIGHBOURING TERRITORIES

New Guinea has remained unspoiled in a considerable part of its territory, unlike Australia where the government has had to create a large number of national parks and reserves, most of them in eastern Australia and Tasmania. They cover a vast area (the national parks alone occupy 3,157,176 square miles) if forest reserves are included. As of 30th June, 1967, there are 252 national parks and 173 scenic areas in Queensland alone and they cover 2,306,388 acres. In New South Wales, Kosciusko National Park, with an area of nearly 1,500,000 acres, preserves almost primitive habitats on Mount Kosciusko, the highest peak in Australia.

Unfortunately, fire continues to do severe damage to the forest

Young Japanese crested ibis ready to leave their nest: Sado Island, Niigata Prefecture. There are today only 12 Japanese crested ibis left in Japan, 8 wild birds on Sado Island, 1 on the Noto peninsular and 3 in confinement. These are the only survivors of a species which was common 80 years ago; it has been exterminated by hunting and destruction of its habitat (Dr Yamashina *in litt.*)

Komodo varan: a gigantic, flesh-eating reptile native to the Little
Sunda Islands

Duvaucel or Barasingha deer: Kanha National Park, Madhya
Pradesh, Central India

Indian buffalo: Kaziranga Reserve, Assam

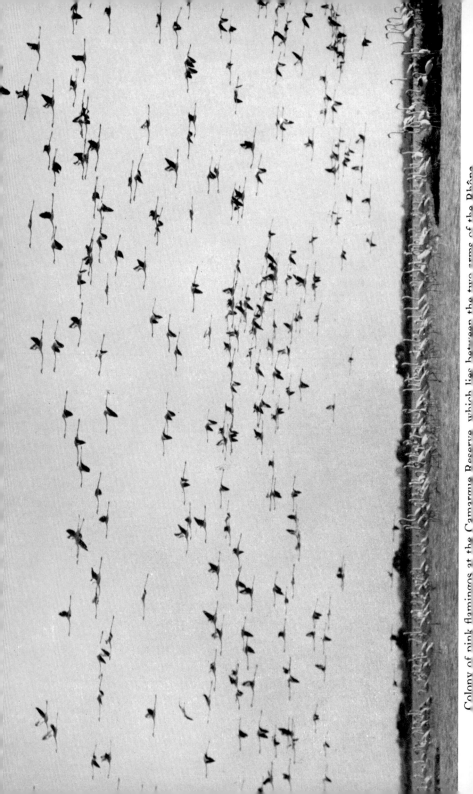

Colony of pink flamingos at the Camargue Reserve, which lies between the two arms of the Rhône

cover in much of the country, and national parks are not protected from ravages caused by introduced animals, particularly rabbits, cats and foxes, or by tourists. Some parks are really only vast camping sites. This only increases the value of smaller reserves on islands not yet reached by imported animals, such as the Flinders Chase Reserve on Kangaroo Island, off the southern coast of Australia. Hunting marsupials is now controlled by law, and many are rigidly protected.

New Zealand has also taken measures to protect its wildlife. Tongariro N.P. on North Island was established in 1894. At present nine national parks cover about 3,700,000 acres, of which Fiordland N.P. on South Island occupies 2,922,853. Some small islands surrounding New Zealand have been converted into bird sanctuaries and 20% of the whole country now enjoys 'protected' status.

7 INTERNATIONAL CO-OPERATION

It was soon obvious that attempts to protect nature would be fruitless unless they were put on an international basis. All countries face problems, such as the protection of migrating birds, which do not recognize frontiers.

In 1913 the Swiss Paul Sarasin called a meeting in Berne of an International Conference for the Protection of Nature. Seventeen countries sent delegates, who decided to create a permanent commission. Unfortunately, further activity was prevented by the war. In 1928 the Dutchman P. J. van Tienhoven set up the International Bureau for the Protection of Nature in Brussels and Amsterdam to disseminate ideas about protection and serve as a documentation centre. This organization lasted until the Second World War.

Meetings held in Paris in 1895 and 1902 established a convention for bird protection that was included in the legislation of a number of countries. Following this success, the International Council for Bird Preservation was created in London in 1922 to bring together national sections of each member country. Since the last war it has achieved a great deal.

Occasionally agreement has been arranged on a geographical

basis. African nations and colonial countries felt it necessary to work together to save their flora and fauna. At the suggestion of Great Britain, an International Conference held in London in 1933 assembled delegates from all interested countries under the presidency of the Duke of Brabant, later to reign as Leopold III. His speech on this occasion may be considered the charter for the protection of nature in Africa. The conference prepared a treaty, later ratified by most of the countries, which was designed to create reserves and national parks, to assure the survival of wild species, to preserve specimens of habitats in their original state, and to regulate hunting as a means of preventing useless slaughter of large fauna. To achieve this goal, the treaty specified measures dealing with hunting, the sale of hides, and special protection for threatened species. Two lists of endangered species were drawn up. Class A includes animals requiring total protection, such as the gorilla, the Madagascan lemur, okapi, mountain zebra, white rhinoceros, shoebill or Balaeniceps and, among plants, *Welwitschia*, which are really living fossils adapted to life in South African deserts. Class B lists animals that may be hunted under certain conditions, notably the chimpanzee, colobus, giant eland, giraffe, white-tailed gnu, black rhinoceros, ostrich and secretary-bird.

This conference made a notable contribution to the preservation of wildlife in Africa. Periodic meetings were planned, and the first was held in London in 1938. War prevented further conferences until 1953, when a meeting was held in Bukavu, Congo, under the auspices of the Commission for Technical Co-operation in Africa (CTCA). This conference made it possible for members to modify their plans in accordance with the current political and economic situation.

In February 1963 a *Charte africaine pour la protection et la conservation de la nature* was signed at Dar es Salaam. This led to a new convention binding the now independent African states, and is a logical sequel to the statement of Sir J. K. Nyerere, Prime Minister of Tanganyika (Tanzania), at the Arusha Conference in 1961. This 'Arusha Manifesto' reads:

'The survival of our wildlife is a matter of grave concern to all of us in Africa. These wild creatures amid the wild places they inhabit are not only important as a source of wonder and inspiration but are an integral part of our natural resources and of our future livelihood and well-being.

In accepting the trusteeship of our wildlife we solemnly declare that we will do everything in our power to make sure that our children's grandchildren will be able to enjoy this rich and precious inheritance.

The conservation of wildlife and wild places calls for specialized knowledge, trained manpower and money, and we look to other nations to co-operate in this important task—the success or failure of which not only affects the continent of Africa but the rest of the world as well.'

In 1965 a Convention on Protection and Utilization of African Wildlife was held in Kampala and in 1967 a Symposium on Wildlife Management and Land Use Practices in Nairobi.

For a long time, however, people had felt the need of a more general international organization. Although Paul Sarasin's efforts were unfortunately not crowned with success, his compatriots of the Swiss League for the Protection of Nature started a movement which led to a conference in Basel in 1946 and another in Brunnen in 1947. An International League was established and ratified the next year in Fontainebleau, the very place where the first European reserves were created. Several years later the organization took the name of the International Union for Conservation of Nature and Natural Resources (IUCN). It is responsible for collecting information about the protection of nature, for studying current technical problems and for discovering methods of repairing the injuries inflicted by man on nature.

There are at present international organizations well equipped to coordinate individual efforts. UNESCO, responsible for the creation of IUCN, has taken the initiative a number of times to ensure real protection for natural resources throughout the world. Its determination to help save them is shown in a *Recommandation concernant la sauvegarde de la beauté et du caractère des paysages et des sites* which was adopted by its Twelfth General Conference on 11th December, 1962. This text, a world charter for nature conservation, lists the points of chief importance to naturalists, namely the protection of habitats, the classification of sites and the establishment of reserves and national parks.

The World Wildlife Fund also deserves mention. This private

international foundation collects large sums to purchase territories for reserves or to safeguard threatened species. It has achieved notable results in all parts of the world.

An even closer collaboration is revealed by the establishment of international reserves, the best example of which is the Pieniny N.P. in Poland which merges into another park in Czechoslovakia. The idea of this collaboration originated in 1924, but it was 1957 before the Polish and Czech governments agreed to turn their frontier into a large park and thus preserve the magnificent Dunajec limestone gorges of the Pieniny. At present each country administers the portion on its national territory but under the same regulations. A similar project could link Great Paradise National Park in Italy and the National Park in Savoy to assure the protection of a vast Alpine area in Italy and France.

Thus, after the devastations of the 19th century, the first years of the 20th were favourable, on the whole, to nature. Simultaneously there was an awakening of public interest, thanks to an active propaganda campaign among school children, in the press, on the radio and on television. The problems of nature conservation are now familiar to everyone. The number of tourists visiting national parks and other reserves grows constantly, while documentary films and books disseminate basic knowledge about the natural sciences.

TO-DAY

Introduction

The relationship between modern man and the planet . . . has been that not of symbiotic partners, but of the tapeworm and the infested dog, of fungus and the blighted potato.

Aldous Huxley, *Ape and Essence*

By the end of the last century it was thought that reserves and national parks would be able to preserve the wild flora and fauna forever. All that was necessary was to set aside the largest territories possible and to regard them as 'sanctuaries'; then the rest of the planet could be freely exploited. There were two kinds of territories: those abandoned to human influences, and reserves.

Although this attitude was once helpful, the situation has changed since the wars. The fragile balance enjoyed by nature during the first decades of this century is increasingly threatened. Slaughter of animals has reached tremendous proportions. Population increase, industrialization, bad agricultural practices and an unreasonable exploitation of lands and seas are forcing men continually to turn toward virgin or barely modified territories.

It is obvious that setting aside a few parcels of land will not preserve nature. The national park and the 'sanctuary' are purely a local solution. As the world is a single unit, the whole planet must be administered for man's best interests. It is also increasingly apparent that human activities are harming our own species. Man poisons the air, the river water and the soil. Deplorable agricultural methods impoverish the earth, and over-exploitation of the seas diminishes their resources. Paradoxically one might almost say that the most pressing problem in conservation to-day is the protection of man against himself.

4 The 20th century population explosion

Problems of conservation and rational exploitation of natural resources must be envisaged in the light of an unprecedented increase in human populations. This population explosion, with its incalculable consequences, is the outstanding feature of our century, even surpassing nuclear fission.

Homo sapiens, as Linnaeus named him in 1758, appeared some 600,000 years ago. It has taken him all this time to attain a population of three billion but, at the current rate, the figure will have doubled in thirty-five years. This growth threatens our very means of livelihood and makes all other problems seem minor in comparison.

A United Nations report (Demographic Studies, No. 28, United Nations, New York, 1958) states that, if the present rate of increase continued for 500 years, the number of human beings on earth would be such that each one would have only one square yard at his disposal.

Since Confucius people have wondered whether excessive population growth would not cause wars by lowering the standard of living, but the population problem was not posed as such until the 18th century. In 1798 Thomas Robert Malthus published his famous *Essay on the Principle of Population*, in which he demonstrated that population increases more rapidly than the quantity of available food. According to him, the former follows a geometric progression; the subsistence curve is arithmetical.

During the 18th and 19th centuries economists expressed contradictory views. Some, like Adam Smith, Jeremy Bentham, James Mill and J. B. Say, shared Malthus's ideas and advocated a restriction in population increase. On the other hand, the pre-Marxists and Marxists affirmed that overpopulation would vanish with capitalist society. Although Malthus made some mistakes, chiefly because he did not anticipate the growth of our technological society, he was right in that the current expansion of human populations transcends all social and economic development. At stake is the very existence of our species.

To the naturalist this phenomenon resembles a swarming, such as one finds in the animal world, but the problem in man is much more complex, since irrational motive powers, moral and religious concepts, and ancient traditions exert great influence. The facts, however, are essentially the same. As for the future, the rhythm of growth, accelerated for barely a century, will continue unless there is a catastrophe, or unless man becomes aware of the peril. We must choose whether to be rational human beings, limiting our expansion in accordance with available resources, or swarming creatures, degrading our own habitat.

We shall show how the population increased, slowly at first, with fluctuations not unlike those of animal populations, and then how it exploded in the phenomenon we are currently witnessing. We shall discuss the effect of this massive growth on the means of subsistence and on the 'moral climate' in which we live. Overpopulation threatens not only the fate of the wild fauna and flora; it threatens the survival of mankind.

1 MAN BEFORE MODERN TIMES

Until modern times population density was tied to the capacity for production. Technical progress made it possible to clear the soil more rapidly, thus increasing pastoral and agricultural harvests and permitting population increase.

During the Palaeolithic period populations were very small and widely scattered. Comparable to these were the people living from gathering and hunting in modern times. Before the Europeans came there were, on average, 21 inhabitants per 100 square miles in Australia (in populated zones) and 42 in North America.

During the Neolithic period—that is, between 8000 and 7000 BC —development of grazing and cultivation provided new bases for human economy in the eastern Mediterranean basin. Agricultural progress and the construction of dikes and terraces attracted large numbers of people. In the Valley of the Nile and Mesopotamia, this happened about 4000 BC. These same techniques appeared in the Yellow River Valley in China and in South and Central America.

On the whole, however, populations remained small. The Roman Empire had about 54 million inhabitants at the death of Augustus in AD 14, with an average density of 42 per square mile; Egypt had 470 per square mile and Italy about 63. Under the Han dynasty at the beginning of the Christian era there were 60 to 70 million inhabitants in China. India had between 100 and 140 million inhabitants at the time of Asoka, in the second century BC.

By the middle of the 17th century the global population had risen to 500–550 million, which implies an average annual increase of between 0·5 and 1·0 per thousand. In Europe there is a definite correlation between the increase of the population north of the Alps and Carpathians and the progress of clearing land. The same ecological law applies to all animal populations, namely that population increases according to the amount of habitable land and the quantity of food available. This increase fluctuated enormously in accordance with epidemics, wars and their sequels.

In France the population, estimated at 6·7 million at the time of the Roman conquest, rose to 8·5 million under the Antonines but did not go beyond this figure until Charlemagne's era. It then increased at a steady tempo until it numbered some 20 million about the middle of the 13th century. During the Hundred Years War it decreased by a third or even half, then rose again until the 16th century when it diminished during the Wars of Religion. Later a slow but steady increase carried the population to about 18 million by 1712. Thereafter it continued to rise until the Revolution.

Similar fluctuations occurred in Great Britain. Under Roman domination there were 1 million inhabitants, 1·1 million in 1086 and 3·7 million about 1348. By 1377 the plague had carried off about 40% of the population. The story is the same in the German states. The population increased from 2 or 3 million in Caesar's time to 17 million at the beginning of the 17th century, as the amount of land under cultivation increased. In Italy the population rose from 7·1 million in the days of Augustus to 11 million in 1560, remaining at this level until the beginning of the 18th century.

Similar phenomena occurred in Asia but there were greater

fluctuations due to the vicissitudes of the civilizations which succeeded one another. Ceylon, for example, had a highly developed agricultural civilization, with a population of 20 million in the 12th century; it then declined, and by the beginning of the 19th century there were only 3 million inhabitants.

2 MAN SINCE THE BEGINNING OF MODERN TIMES

The colonization of the New World greatly enlarged the scope of western civilization. At the same time, the industrialization of western Europe, which began in the 18th century, enabled a larger population to prosper by providing supplementary resources and freeing it from a strictly biological dependence.

Various economic and political factors determined a strong current of immigration towards the virgin lands of the western hemisphere. Just as an animal population introduced into a new habitat spreads rapidly since limiting factors, especially the quantity of available food, are suppressed, so in North America the birth-rate was at once very high.

In the zone of European civilization—that is to say, Europe, Russian Asia, America and the Pacific islands—population rose because of an accelerated birth-rate from the 16th to the second half of the 19th century. Despite fluctuations caused by various economic and political factors, an increase in births over deaths became constant in 18th century Europe. In 1947, when the total zone of European civilization numbered 902 million inhabitants, 24·3 million births and 13 million deaths were recorded; this implies a natural increase of 12·5 per thousand. Several countries, however, have registered a decline. In Ireland the population fell from 8·2 million in 1841 to 4·4 million in 1861 and to less than 3 million in 1966. Famines, emigration and a low birth-rate are the responsible factors.

In other parts of the world where the white race has spread the population has grown much more rapidly. In North America the natural rate was higher than in Europe at the beginning of the 19th century. It then dropped until the First World War, but this was compensated by immigration. In 1966 the growth rate in the United States, 1·15%, reached the lowest level since 1936. In South America the increase has been much faster. In Brazil the rate was 131% from 1840 to 1890, and 190% from 1890 to 1940, making an annual increase of 16·9 per thousand. For Latin America as a whole, the average is increasing faster than in any other part of the world—nearly 3% a year. In Mexico it rose from 6 per thousand in 1922 to 17 per thousand in 1932, to 19 per thousand in 1937, and to 29 per thousand in 1947. This growth is explained in part by large-scale immigration, in Brazil for example, but the real causes lie in a high birth-rate and much lower mortality. If the present growth-rate continues, the population in Latin America will be 385 million in 1985.

Non-Europeans are showing the same tendency under the influence of western civilization, particularly in the fields of hygiene and warfare against native diseases. Asiatic populations have greatly increased since the beginning of the last century. In China the population tripled between 1650 and 1850, passing from 113 to 350 million. If the peripheral territories outside the eighteen provinces are included, the population was 450 million in 1933; about 1946 it dropped to 400 million due to famines and wars, but in 1953 it was 583 million and in 1968, 690 million.

Progressive acceleration has been far greater in India. It is estimated that the population rose from 100 million in 1600 to 255 million in 1877, with an annual increase of 3·5 per thousand. This tendency then accelerated, as a constant high birth-rate was accompanied by a decrease in mortality. In 1967 India's population passed the 500 million mark; it is now increasing by a million a month. The following table shows the increase in the rate of annual growth.

EVALUATION OF THE AVERAGE ANNUAL BIRTH-RATE AND
MORTALITY IN INDIA

Periods	Births per 1000 inhabitants	Deaths per 1000 inhabitants	Approximate difference
1901–1911	48	42.6	5
1911–1921	49	48.6	
1921–1931	46	36.3	10
1931–1941	45	31.2	14

A similar evolution is found in other parts of tropical Asia, particularly Ceylon, where the population is increasing very rapidly due to spectacular advances in public hygiene. The following table shows the increase in the annual growth-rate on this island.

Periods	Annual rate of natural increase per 1000 inhabitants
1871–1880	4·6
1881–1890	5·0
1891–1900	6·8
1901–1910	9·3
1911–1920	7·4
1921–1930	13·4
1931–1940	13·4
1941–1945	17·1
1946	18·1
1947	25·1
1948	27·4
1949	27·3

The Near East is undergoing a considerable increase as well. According to information from the United Nations, its population rose from 55 million in 1920 to 75 million in 1950, the average annual rate being in the neighbourhood of 20 per thousand between 1945 and 1950. The United Arab Republic had 26 million inhabitants in 1960. In Algeria the 2·5 million of 1856 had become 7·2 million in 1936, partly on account of European immigration, but chiefly because the Moslem population rose from 2·3 to 6·1 million. In 1965 the annual increase was 0.09%.

Africa is a special case because tribal wars, slave raids and numerous epidemics kept the population practically stationary between the 17th and the end of the 19th century. But it has doubled since 1850. Some regions are still underpopulated but there is very high density in others. Zambia and Rhodesia have created a record, for their population has doubled in a generation. In Tanzania the population, estimated at 4,145,000 in 1913, rose to 7,410,269 in 1948 and to 8,788,000 in 1964. In Uganda the population rose from 4,917,555 inhabitants in 1948 to 6,450,973 in 1959, an increase of 31%. In 1964 it was 6,547,000. Some demographers have stated that the percentage of growth in Rwanda and Burundi is 33 per thousand, although this figure may be exaggerated. These two countries are the most densely populated in tropical Africa, with 265 inhabitants per square mile in Rwanda and 214 in Burundi.

This compares with 14·5 in the Congo, 24 in Tanzania, and 61 in Uganda.[1]

These examples could be multiplied to show the numerical expansion of our species around the planet. It is clear that since the beginning of 'modern times', and particularly since 1850, the global population has been increasing at a faster tempo; the variation in the rate of average annual growth in the following table makes this clear (see also *figs* 31 and 32).

RATES OF ANNUAL AVERAGE GROWTH PER THOUSAND (World average)

| | According to information[2] from: | |
	Willcox and the UN	*Carr-Saunders and the UN*
1650–1950 (Average)	5	5
1650–1750	4	3
1750–1800	6	4
1800–1850	3	5
1850–1900	7	6
1900–1950	9	8
1900–1920	8	7
1920–1930	9	9
1930–1940	10	10
1940–1950	8	8

This acceleration is largely due to a reduction in mortality, caused by better hygiene and a rise in the standard of living. The spread of new European structures upset the old social and economic

[1] According to J. P. Harroy, *Bull. Séances Acad. Royale Sci. Outre-mer*, Brussels, N.S. 8: 524-30, 1962.

[2] As there is no exact world census, demographers have to estimate populations in former centuries. The two basic works are: W. F. Willcox, *Studies in American Demography*, Ithaca, 1940; and A.M. Carr-Saunders, *World Population: Past Growth and Present Trends*, Oxford 1936. As these experts vary slightly in their estimates, it is customary to give their figures in parallel columns.

systems which, though often out of date, were better suited to their biological environment.

In the past, enormous fluctuations took place in certain populations, but each time overpopulation occurred a kind of auto-regulation intervened.

WORLD POPULATION (in millions of inhabitants)

Year	World	Africa	North America	Latin America	Asia (except USSR)	Europe & USSR	The Pacific
Data from Willcox							
1650	470	100	1	7	257	103	2
1750	694	100	1	10	437	144	2
1800	919	100	6	23	595	193	2
1850	1091	100	26	33	656	274	2
1900	1571	141	81	63	857	423	6
Data from Carr-Saunders							
1650	545	100	1	12	357	103	2
1750	728	95	1	11	475	144	2
1800	906	90	6	19	597	192	2
1850	1171	95	26	33	741	274	2
1900	1608	120	81	63	915	423	6
Data from UN							
1920	1811	141	117	91	966	487	8·8
1930	2015	157	135	109	1072	532	10·4
1940	2249	176	146	131	1212	573	11·3
1950	2510	206	167	162	1386	576	13·0
1960	2995	254	199	206	1679	641	16·5

Rate of annual growth during the period 1950–1960(%)

	1·8	2·2	1·8	2·5	1·9	0·8	2·4
						(USSR 1·7)	

The figures in this table show that population increase follows, fairly exactly, a geometric progression, but that it also increases in absolute value, since humanity, with its higher birth-rate and decline in mortality, requires less and less time to double in numbers. These new phenomena constitute the population explosion.

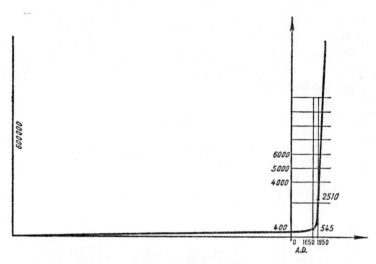

Fig. 31

Increase in population since man's appearance on earth some 600,000 years ago. In ordinates: numbers in millions. The form of the curve justifies Ritchie Calder's remark: 'The graph of population is like an aircraft taking off. For most of the quarter million years, it just skims along the time-axes. Then, about 1600, we raise the undercarriage and begin to soar. To-day, it is like a rocket rising from the launching pad.'

3 POPULATION INCREASE IN THE NEAR FUTURE

On the basis of the current rate of increase of the human population and the tendencies apparent since the beginning of the 20th century it is possible to estimate populations in the near future. The demographic service of the United Nations published estimates in 1951, 1954 and 1958, but each time it underestimated the speed of the changes. The low estimates are to-day close to the high estimates of 1954 and far above those of 1951. (The latter did not take into consideration recent censuses in China which were not published until later.) According to the latest calculations, it is thought that in 1980 there will be a world population of between 3,850 and 4,280 million. In the latter case it is reckoned that North

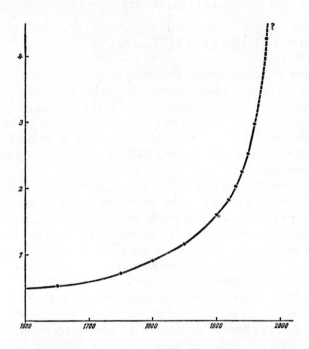

Fig. 32
Increase in world population from 1650 to 1960 and forecasts to 1980. From data by Carr-Saunders and the UN. The estimates for the 1960–80 period are in broken lines.

America, Europe (except eastern Europe) and the Pacific will have 652 million, Latin America, eastern Europe, the USSR and Japan 893 million, and the rest of Asia and Africa 2,735 million (*fig 33*). According to a report published in 1965, the UN experts expect the world population of 3·3 billion to be almost doubled by the end of the century. In 1967 it was increasing at the net rate of 180,000 every 24 hours. In a recent publication, 'The State of Food and Agriculture 1965', the FAO emphasises that output of food has been lagging precisely in those regions of the world that have the highest rates of population growth.

4 POPULATION AND LIVELIHOOD

In view of the contemporary situation, there is some apprehension about the disproportion between the number of consumers and the volume of food resources. Hunger is as old as humanity. In Europe the history of antiquity and the Middle Ages is marked by famines up to the last century. In the East they are tragically frequent, and China alone has had 1,828 since the beginning of the Christian era.

Occasionally these catastrophes seemed accidental, particularly in the West. As it was impossible to preserve perishable goods and transport was difficult, there was no method of balancing good and bad harvests; but men hoped to survive the lean years and famines were epidemic. In other parts of the globe hunger has been and still is chronic. Some populations have been resigned to malnutrition for centuries but continue to multiply.

At first it seems surprising that hunger was considered unavoidable for such a long time, but the science of dietetics is relatively new. An exact knowledge of man's needs for energy is only about sixty years old, and even more recently malnutrition has been blamed for a series of pathological, physiological, and even social disorders which had previously been attributed to more immediate or more mysterious causes.

Physiologists tell us that man and animals function like machines which require a certain amount of energy to enable them to carry out their tasks. The quantity of 'fuel' needed for the organic 'motor' is evaluated in calories provided by food. Daily caloric requirements for an adult man vary, but in general they come to between 2300 and 3800 calories, sometimes more.

The food requirement of an individual is not measured by calories alone, because the human machine also needs certain substances to form or maintain tissues that are constantly being repaired. As the organism does not combine them and as they cannot replace one another, each human being has to have a balanced ration containing minimal quantities of each. Some, like minerals, vitamins and some amino-acids, are needed in very small doses but their absence prevents normal physiological functioning and causes serious trouble.

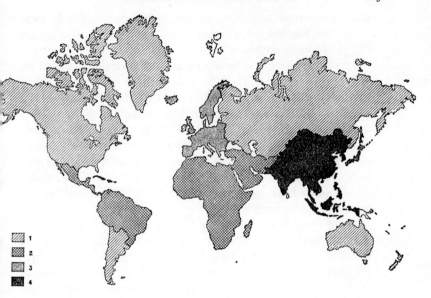

Fig. 33
World regions listed in accordance with population density and current
rate of growth.
   1 Group I: light density, moderate growth
   2 Group II: light density, rapid growth
   3 Group III: high density, moderate growth
   4 Group IV: high density, rapid growth
From UN Yearbook 1961.

Thus there are two kinds of hunger: the global one related to an insufficient number of calories, and the specific one, malnutrition. In practice, they occur together in acute or chronic famines, but produce different effects. Specific hungers are deadlier from certain points of view. Diseases caused by deficiencies are very numerous; *kwashiorkor*, resulting from insufficient animal proteins, is the most famous. Protein deficiencies occur chiefly in tropical regions and by lowering the resistance of the organism promote tuberculosis, typhus, conjunctivitis and parasitic diseases.

Malnutrition is thus accompanied by a lamentable series of physiological troubles. It also scars men's spirits, 'dehumanizing' them more than any other environmental factor. The laziness, apathy and fatalism found in some human groups are consequences of age-old malnutrition.

At present chronic malnutrition and nutritional deficiencies are acute problems. Multiple surveys have been made and contradictory results obtained. In 1950 the FAO declared that two-thirds of the world population suffered from hunger (J. B. Orr, 1950, *Scientific American*, 183, 11; see also FAO *Second World Food Survey*, 1952). Later it was discovered that these statements were completely inaccurate. According to more recent information, experts have reduced these figures to 10–15% (see Colin Clark, 1963). This estimate has been accepted by the FAO (*Third World Survey*), but seems too optimistic.

There are various reasons for these differences of opinion. The diets of Europeans and North Americans must not be used as a standard as they are too rich. Furthermore, it is very difficult to establish an exact nutritional balance sheet for all parts of the world. It is equally difficult to obtain significant figures and to analyze them statistically. Finally, some conclusions are unreliable because statisticians have modified them in accordance with their preconceived theories.

The fact remains that a notable section of humanity suffers from various types of chronic hunger. The situation is particularly grave in the Far East. In India it is tragic. Other countries with serious deficiencies include Egypt, certain tropical African states, and northeastern Brazil. Malnutrition causes a very high mortality rate, particularly among children. Life expectancy is 47 (till recently, 32) years in India, as against 69 in France and the United States. India, with its swarming, passive throngs of starving humanity, is the very image of chronic hunger. The situation is aggravated by destruction. To give just one example: the population in the Indus Valley goes up by ten every five minutes, but in the same time one acre is lost by waterclogging.

This deplorable situation is not so much the result of overpopulation as of a profound social, economic and political disproportion both on the international and the national level. The organization of international exchanges, the flow of raw materials and agricultural products, blatant inequalities between peoples and social classes, and the trade economy are responsible for the uneven distribution of foodstuffs and the chronic hunger of a large part of the world.

The solution, an economic one, consists of a global redistribution of the most essential commodities although food resources will never be able to keep pace with the massive, accelerated growth of human populations. Agricultural yields have risen considerably. The Paleolithic hunter required 3·86 square miles to provide food for himself; the Neolithic shepherd, 24·71 acres; the peasant of the Middle Ages, 1·6 acres of arable land. To-day the Japanese farmer can live on 0·15 of an acre. When Japan was opened to western civilization, it was 'underdeveloped' in the modern sense of the term. The population was increasing by 1% a year, although the country was already overcrowded. Japan has succeeded in increasing agricultural productivity by 3·5% per year and creating an industry to make up the deficit.

Technical advances will produce larger agricultural yields in the future, and new diets are being developed in the laboratories. Algae, plankton and synthetically grown plants are the best known of these substitutes for to-morrow's world.

A reasonable increase in human population is still possible if man can exploit this planet sensibly, without degrading the soil. But the difficulties involved in distributing foodstuffs and financial inequalities among populations will not disappear easily, if at all. As Dasmann observed (1959), while there is only one world to the biologist, there are several on the economic plane. For all these reasons it seems that the world's hunger is likely to increase despite men's best efforts. Unwise multiplication of the human race will upset the food balance and degrade humanity.

5 MEDICAL AND SOCIAL RESULTS OF HUMAN SWARMING

Some economists have stated that the earth is biologically capable of feeding a much larger population: Colin Clark (1963) suggested 45 billion. But then we shall have to agree with Paul Sears: even if every man is assured adequate rations, it is still more pleasant not to have to eat standing up!

A fundamental aspect of the influence of overpopulation is its effect on human behaviour. Animal numbers are restricted by psychological as well as ecological factors. Reproduction in a population of vertebrates is often limited by social interactions long before the effects of a food shortage are felt, and the human species is no exception to this rule.

Population increase, combined with industrialization, has led to highly pronounced urbanization. It is reckoned that in the near future the towns between Amsterdam and the Belgian frontier will form a single city. In the United States the great cities in the east will combine in one gigantic anthill. Whereas in 1800 there was only one city in the world (London) with a million inhabitants, in 1967 there were 92. In the United States the percentage of people living in communities with more than 100,000 persons has risen from 1·3 in 1830 to 28·4 in 1960. Population density is acute in some districts. In parts of Chicago, there are 99,970 inhabitants per square mile; in parts of London, 179,990; Tokyo, 240,000; Hong Kong 783,700. They are like human termite nests.

Cities, moreover, often extend into excellent agricultural lands. Towns constructed in fertile regions or along communication routes have a natural tendency to spread into plains, where problems of construction and planning are less difficult to solve.

As a result of urbanization, cities have lost their souls. Not one of these large, built-up areas can or will ever constitute a human *community*. As Le Corbusier wrote (*Maniere de penser l'urbanisme*, Geneva (Gonthier)): 'In three-quarters of a century a brutal rupture, unique in the annals of history, has detached the entire social life of the West from a relatively traditional framework remarkably in harmony with geography.' Both city and village are out of balance and have lost their character of coherent organisms.

The sheer size of cities has also determined the nature of the human habitat. Men have to choose between box-like apartments and small private houses set farther and farther away from their work. The latter involve a considerable amount of commuting and much physical and nervous fatigue. Furthermore, beyond a certain level, cost of the habitat in roads, water and gas mains, transport and urban administration, rises much more rapidly than the number of inhabitants.

In the cities atmospheric pollution, noise, the stresses of public life have produced unhealthy ecological conditions. Studies by doctors, psychologists and sociologists justify the complaints of city dwellers that 'life has become unbearable.' The benefits of our technical civilization, such as hygiene, are thus largely counter-balanced by the growing number of physiological and mental neuroses. Cardio-vascular diseases linked to the life of 20th century man—the chief causes of death, along with diseases of old age—are on the increase. Furthermore, investigations have revealed that 10·9 to 23·4% of the inhabitants of large cities suffer from more or less serious mental illness. The *Manhattan Midtown Survey*, though not scientifically thorough, reveals the influence of a modern urban environment on the body and mind of city dwellers. P. Zivy has said (*Remarques sur la physiopathologie des cités modernes*): 'A city like Paris has become a factory for the production of sick people.'

These troubles foreshadow what men will face in the future. City dwellers will need to find activities capable of making up for the deficiencies in their urban way of life. The portions of the globe preserved in their natural state will alone be capable of serving as 'recreation areas'. Escape will be as necessary as food.

Such are the principal characteristics and consequences of the contemporary population explosion. The increase will continue at the same rhythm for several decades, but it cannot last. 'Let Venus alone,' Bergson said, 'and she will bring Mars.' No one who has studied the dynamics of populations could doubt that remark, and that wars may well have biological causes. Thus, the increasing number of people invited to the 'banquet of life' must finally make us question all our social gains.

5 Man's destruction of land

Our land, compared with what it was, is like the skeleton of a body wasted by disease. The plump soft parts have vanished, and all that remains is the bare carcass.

Plato. *Critias* III.

1 NATURAL AND ACCELERATED EROSION

Our most valuable natural asset is the soil. The survival and prosperity of terrestrial biological communities, whether natural or artificial, depend on this thin layer. As in the earliest days, and in spite of the progress of synthetic industries based on mineral products, man draws almost all his substance, and most raw materials for his clothing and everyday needs, from this source.

Far from being stable and inert, the soil is perpetually changing. Formed at the meeting point of the air and the earth, it participates in both, since it is related to the mineral world as well as to living organisms. Like the latter, soils have a real metabolism. Decomposition of the mother-rock through the action of various physical agents such as heat, wind, and rain, and their transformation by living beings, are constructive processes which produce soils. On the other hand, they may be destroyed by the same dynamic agents, thus making for erosion or destruction of the uppermost layers of the earth.

Man can modify erosion to a considerable degree. A slow natural erosion cannot be prevented. Disappearance of some materials in the soil is compensated by decomposition of the mother-rock and deposits brought by water. Thus soils are normally balanced, at least under average conditions prevailing to-day.

But in addition to this normal geological phenomenon, there is an accelerated erosion, caused by man's poor management of

Above Rill erosion on slopes of a hillside ravaged by bad
agricultural methods. Sherman County, Oregon
Below Gully erosion: Jonesboro, Arkansas

Above Wind erosion near Kimberley, South Africa. The acacias covering the soil were cut to be used as wood for the mines; the wild grasses replacing them were in turn replaced by corn, a plant which does not hold the soil. The wind did the rest on land which was fragile and poorly protected against erosion. *Below* Rill erosion and gullying, following deforestation. Note the beginning of the process at the forest edge

the soil and not compensated by natural factors. This brutal degeneration of the soil is a result of the modification, or total destruction, of original habitats no longer protected by an adequate plant cover.

Natural erosion is the basis of fertile soil. Transformation of mother-rocks produces 'living' soils. Materials collected by winds and rains enrich areas where they accumulate in layers of fertile alluvium. A classic example is the mud brought by the flooding Nile from high Ethiopian plateaus to enrich the delta and a narrow strip along the river. This soil, the only part of the country which can be cultivated, has made Egypt prosperous. In the 6th century BC the Greek geographer Hecataeus of Miletus called Egypt a present from the Nile.

All natural habitats get their wealth from these erosive processes at the origin of life. But this is not true of accelerated erosion, which constitutes to-day the most serious impact of man on his environment. Bad agricultural practices have ruined much of the globe. Furthermore, man has encroached on marginal lands whose productivity and balance can only be guaranteed by maintaining them as natural biological associations, at least in the current state of our knowledge. Destruction of some original habitats has resulted in disasters as apparent to the 'protector of nature' as to the economist.

Land areas eroded as a result of man's activity cover tremendous surfaces. In 1939 Hugh Hammond Bennett, director of the Soil Conservation Service and a leader in the battle against erosion, estimated that during the past 150 years 282 million acres of tillable soil had been ruined or seriously impoverished in the USA; and in 775 million additional acres accelerated erosion had removed a good portion of the fertile top-soil. Degradation has spread daily over 1,482 acres, 296 of which were cultivated, or a total of 543,620 acres annually. Every year erosion lifts 2·7 billion tons of solid material from fields and pastures in the United States, of which the Mississippi alone is responsible for 730 million. Even if one deducts the amount that would have vanished from natural erosion, these impressive figures show the impoverishment of a country almost intact a century and a half ago. Damages wrought by this erosion amounted to 400 million dollars in 1939, without counting secondary damage.

The same situation occurs in all parts of the world, but particularly in the Mediterranean region. In Algeria the equivalent of 494 acres of arable land is lost to the sea every day during the rainy season. In France (*fig* 34) 12·3 million acres show signs of erosion, 6·9 million of which are south of a line linking Andorra to Modena. 1,235,000 acres are affected by wind erosion, the rest by rain. (Investigation by the Ministry of Agriculture; see Hénin and Gobillot, *C. R. Acad. Sci.*; Paris 1950).

Accelerated erosion is even more apparent in tropical regions where, contrary to general opinion, soils are much less fertile and infinitely more fragile than in temperate regions.

In Madagascar the practice of clearing forests and setting brush fires on the plateaus, which is between five and twenty centuries old, has seriously damaged the island's fertility, as well as its wild flora and fauna. Humbert (1949) estimated that out of a total surface of 143 million acres only 12 million retain their original plant cover, while 4/5 of the island has felt the effects of active erosion.

Thus the evil is general, and it has assumed catastrophic proportions since modern man employed technical methods. We cannot discuss this problem in detail, but we shall show how lands became degraded. (On the subject, see the classic works of Bennett, 1939, and Harroy, 1944.) Then we shall examine the symptoms of accelerated erosion, how man causes it and what can be done to remedy it.

2 FORMS OF ACCELERATED EROSION

Erosion is sometimes caused by winds which lift particles between 0·004 and 0·0195 inch in diameter and hold in suspension those whose diameter is less than 0·0039 inch. Particles carried away are always relatively fine, for the wind rapidly abandons larger ones. The finest dusts can be carried to high altitudes, occasionally over 10,000 feet, and transported considerable distances before falling back on the soil. But the most powerful agent of soil destruction is violent rain which breaks up hard masses and scatters the natural soil binder. Sheet erosion scrapes off, especially on gentle slopes, the upper layer of rich humus without at first transforming the general appearance of the area. This is particularly dangerous since for a time it can be detected only by slight changes in the colour

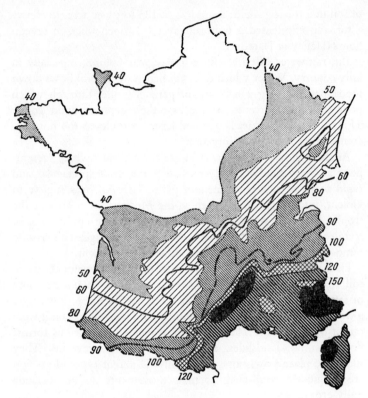

Fig. 34

Map showing the frequency of hydric erosion in France. The intensity of the phenomenon, illustrated by the density of the shaded areas, is proportionate to numerical variations as shown on the map. There is a close correlation between frequency of erosion and climatic characteristics (rainfall), if relief is taken into consideration.

From Hénin and Gobillot Chambres d'agriculture 24th year, suppl. to no. 26 1953.

of the soil and by the appearance of pebbles which remain when the materials that held them have vanished. With the removal of fine particles, the soil is deprived of nutritive elements and loses the power to hold water. This in turn causes a gradual disappearance of vegetation. In one week in Connecticut rain removed ·08 inch of soil in a tobacco field: a soil loss of 123 tons per acre. In Kenya a tornado eliminated a uniform layer 0·10 inch thick in several hours (Hailey *in* Harroy 1944).

But rainwater often acts in a less regular fashion, especially in hilly country. Water which does not penetrate the soil flows down the slopes, forming a network of parallel gullies through which pour miniature torrents. At the base their deposits build cones. This rill-erosion carries larger and larger particles as the flow becomes faster amd more impetuous.

As the hollows deepen, ravines are formed into which torrents pour at every rainfall. Gully-erosion is the most spectacular and rapid form of this phenomenon, particularly in areas subject to violent, intermittent rains, such as the Mediterranean area or the tropics. In several years a small hollow may become a gully 40 or 50 feet deep, in which waters from a vast basin converge. This erosion removes the soil and injures the mother-rock below it.

Finally, erosion may take the form of mass movements when soil is transported in lumps. These result from an undermining or saturation of the soil, either on the surface or deep down over a watertight shelf. In the latter instance a soil mass slides as if it were on an oiled surface. These mass movements take various forms: flowing mud, landslides, subterranean erosion, cave-ins. They may take place slowly or very rapidly. Different types of erosion are frequently combined, as mass movements do not exclude gully-erosion and so on.

There is one particularly effective way of killing soil. The liberation of large quantities of iron and oxide of aluminium, which accumulate in certain layers of the soil, then their oxidation and consolidation caused by deforestation and other bad agricultural practices, result in the formation of 'iron-stones' that are really inert rocks. Perfectly sterile, they can no longer evolve, and only geological time can bring new life to this soil. They, together with the deep gullies, constitute the most tragic aspect of the death of lands at the hand of man.

Fertility is seriously affected by transformation of the physical, chemical and biological structures of the soil. Although little is known about chemical changes in cultivated areas, the leaching of soils by rains and by agricultural practices which do not restore mineral elements, particularly nitrogens, is very serious. Studies conducted in Kansas have revealed a rapid loss in the amount of nutritive substances, especially proteins, in harvests. It has been calculated that the Mississippi carries away annually 62,188 tons of phosphorus, 1,626,312 tons of potassium, 22,446,379 tons of calcium and 5,179,788 tons of magnesium.

The effects are observed not only in the zones from which the materials are taken, but much farther downstream. Materials carried away by the waters accumulate in excessive quantities in low valleys or in mill-races with little or no current, such as lakes and reservoirs, and soon fill them with silt. In this way they upset the physical and biological balance of the areas. Finally, accelerated erosion affects waterflow by decreasing infiltration, lowering well surfaces, and establishing a torrential system of uncontrolled freshets which accentuates the processes of land degradation.

Natural habitats resist erosion much longer than habitats transformed by man, particularly if the latter have only a scattered or temporary plant cover. The forest with its undergrowth is the best defender of the soil because it has a complex plant cover, ranging from large trees with powerful root systems to plants whose roots form a fine network. It thus retains rain-water. Furon (1947) states that a square yard of moss, weighing 2·2 pounds normally, retains 11 pounds of water after a heavy rain. In a forest of 10,000 acres the moss alone retains 718,530 cubic feet of water.

The meadow is the next best protector of the soil. Plants have an excellent root system which often penetrates far into the ground, forming a pad that protects the soil from rain and sun. Cultivation, on the other hand, deprives the soil of its protecting plant cover for much of the year. Bare soil is beaten by rain, often violent in tropical countries, which hollows little craters. The energy produced by a drop of rain 0·234 inch in diameter is sufficient to raise a body weighing 0·65 ounces by 0·39 inch. The energy produced by a 0·8 inch rainfall lasting 80 minutes is sufficient to raise 45 ounces 0·39 inch (according to Mihara, *in* Fauck, *Rapport mission aux USA*, 1955).

Only part of the water penetrates the soil and the rest flows downhill, forming small torrents which bear away soil particles. It has been determined that there is a 27% runoff in a cornfield as against 11% in a nearby meadow. This causes ever deeper furrowing as more fertile land is carried away.

Physical evaporation is much greater on bare soil, three times higher in open country than in the forest. This drying effect causes a perceptible decline in dew, whose volume may in arid regions be equal to or larger than rainfall. The sun's rays, by warming the earth, cause destruction of the minute organisms which cannot withstand either rise in temperature or radiation. But these organisms are fundamental elements in the formation of humus and constitute an important part of the soil. Measurements made in England show that on 2,471 acres of land there were 140 tons of humus containing 2·2 tons of insects, worms, algae, fungi and bacteria, essential in the transformation of organic matter.

Finally, as a result of the clearing and tilling of forest habitats, local climates tend to become dry. All these factors, often combined, cause accelerated erosion and transform fertile soils into unproductive lands.

It is essential for soil conservation to maintain a natural or artificial plant cover. In Ohio it was reckoned that 174,000 years would be required to remove from 7 to 8 inches of top-soil by runoff in a forested area, 29,000 years in a meadow, 100 years if the soil is wisely planted with crop rotation and 15 years if corn alone is planted (Bennett, 1939). In the Congo it takes 40,000 years to remove 6 inches of soil under forest cover, 10,000 years with grassland and 28 to 10 years in a cotton field. Erosion may be much more rapid than this, for a tropical tornado can remove three-quarters of an inch of soil in a few hours. These figures are all the more striking when one recalls that it takes 300 to 1000 years to form 1·17 inch of soil, or between 2000 and 7000 years to produce the 7- to 8-inch layer necessary for cultivation.

Furon's figures (1947) give an idea of the importance of runoff and the rate of erosion, according to the nature of the plant cover and the slope of the terrain.

Slope	Runoff (inches)		Erosion (pounds per acre)	
	grassland	fields	grassland	fields
2	0·312	4·56	223	22,300
8	3·120	9·55	625	151,884
10	0·156	4·48	28·5	49,135
16	0·897	6·90	71·5	196,542
30	2·691	6·82	558	180,462

The causes of accelerated erosion are deforestation, fire, bad agricultural practices and overgrazing. The effects of these have been multiplied tenfold in modern times by new techniques and the population increase.

3 DEFORESTATION

In many parts of the world deforestation is still the first step in the destruction of natural habitats. It is particularly disastrous on slopes, where forest cover affords the only good protection.

Many reasons for felling trees have disappeared since wood is no longer used as fuel in metallurgy, but numerous new factors have been introduced. According to yearly reports published by the FAO, in 1953 44,137,500,000 cubic feet were felled—a figure that is probably too low. 38% of this was used for rough timber, 13% for paper pulp, 5% for various industrial uses, and 44% for cooking and food preparation. So the use of wood as fuel either directly or after the manufacture of charcoal, which is often produced by wasteful methods, still has first place. Two-thirds of mankind use it for cooking and 75% of Latin Americans have no other fuel. A growing need for pulp requires enormous exploitation of forests as tens of thousands of newspapers, magazines and books consume more and more paper. 168 million tons of wood were needed for this purpose in 1965. A large daily newspaper requires enough wood every year to cover 988 acres. A Sunday *New York Times* uses wood covering 190 acres of forest.

Population pressure and replacement of lands that have become sterile cause new zones to be cleared daily. Agriculture, at first confined to lowlands, tends to creep up along wooded slopes, depriving upper river basins of their protecting mantle. The lamentable experiences in the Mediterranean region and Central America are being repeated in other parts of the world. In addition, technical methods have been perfected and roads can penetrate areas once hard to reach. As machines do ten times the work of an axe, forest clearing becomes easy and rapid.

In Europe deforestation has been spread over centuries, and in wide areas forests have given way to highly productive lands that are relatively stable, since the climate is good and agricultural methods excellent. For the past century, furthermore, the number of trees planted in western Europe has been increasing. But this is not the case in Mediterranean countries, where most forest has given way to grassland. Spain, which was once forest-covered, has lost this protection in 7/8 of its territory. Greece has dropped from 65% to 15% forest, 4% only being productive forest; less than 2% of the cultivated land has retained its former structure, and the rest is deeply eroded.

In North Africa deforestation has been proceeding rapidly for generations, along with accelerated erosion and a profound change in the water system. It is estimated that in historical times the wooded area of the Berber country has decreased by more than 24,710 million acres and the percentage of timber has dropped from 30% to 14%. In Algeria the wooded or bushy area which disappeared between 1870 and 1940 is estimated at 2,471,000 million acres (according to P. Boudy, 1948, *Economie forestière nord-africaine*, Paris (Larose) Vol 1).

Deforestation has been much more devastating in North America, which was largely forested in the east. Even in Canada, where 43% of the country is still timbered, the southern agricultural area has lost two-thirds of its forest since colonization began. Of the original volume of 3,648 billion cubic feet of timber, 1,094 billion remained in 1912. Many agricultural projects have been abandoned because of the subsequent erosion.

In the United States 900 million acres were originally wooded with more than 1,100 species of trees, a hundred of which had great economic value. Only 647 remain and only 44 million acres have preserved their original forest. One can follow the progress of exploitation westward from New England to Pennsylvania, then about 1870 to Wisconsin and Minnesota, and southwards at the beginning of this century. Washington and Oregon have been the chief sufferers for many years. In addition to man's devastation, forest fires occasionally cause national catastrophes. In 1951 they wrought damage estimated at 46 million dollars. In 1952 780 million cubic feet of wood were destroyed by 188,000 fires which ravaged over 14 million acres. In 1965 this figure was reduced to 2½ million acres. Damage is also caused by fungus and harmful insects, some of which were introduced by man. 'Chestnut blight' was caused

Above Clouds of dust torn up by wind in the 'dust bowl'.
Springfield, Colorado, May 1937. *Below* Dust deposited by wind on
a Texas farm, which subsequently had to be abandoned

Above Effect of water erosion on a maize field
below Deeply eroded fields near Pretoria, South Africa

Above Slopes of eroded hills before their restoration by the
Tennessee Valley Authority
below Terrace cultivation following curves of the terrain

Tree, with roots laid bare by the wind, isolated in the midst of a desert: symbol of a poorly managed world

by a fungus brought from the Far East at the beginning of the
century and 'blister rust' originated in Germany. In 1952, over
2 billion board feet[1] of wood were destroyed by disease and 5
billion by insects. Only a small fraction of this could still be used
(figures quoted by Dasmann, 1959).

Deforestation is still worse in tropical regions, which were
severely affected before modern times by shifting cultivation. In
tropical Africa the large wooded areas which used to separate
warring tribes disappeared along with certain taboos that protected them. As population density increased, the rotation cycle
of cultivated sectors has accelerated to a point where the forest
cover can no longer regenerate. In Niger 3·2 million acres were
under cultivation in 1949, with an annual clearing of 370,000 to
617,000 acres for a period of cultivation lasting 3, 4 or 7 years at
the most. To enable the land to lie fallow from 4 to 20 years, a
permanent reserve of 4·4 to 7·4 million acres of fresh or renewed
land is needed. Since this does not exist owing to the population
density, rotation is speeded up and erosion accelerated (Guilloteau
1949, 1950).

Europeans have cleared huge areas in order to plant products
for export. This has led to much more serious deforestation than
any entailed by native agriculture. Such cultivation throughout
the tropics aims to get a maximum yield in a minimum amount of
time. It has thus led to rapid regression of the forest and to soil
impoverishment.

Deforestation has assumed dramatic proportions in parts of
Africa(fig 35). Shantz (1948) estimates that two-thirds of the tropical
trees on the continent have been felled. In Ghana cocoa plantations
increase by 185,000 acres every year, to the detriment of the forest
which now covers only 15% of the country. In Nigeria 617,000
acres are replaced annually by plantations that are soon eroded.
In ex-French Equatorial Africa the figure is 247,100 acres. In
Kenya and Tanzania only 2% of the forest remains; in Rwanda
and Burundi it retreats 5/8 of a mile in circumference every year.

Exploitation of forests, particularly for such woods as mahogany
and gaboon, has been assisted by the perfecting of mechanical

[1] The board foot represents in the United States a piece of wood a foot
long, a foot wide, and an inch thick.

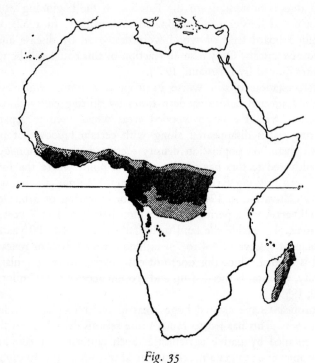

Fig. 35

Regression of rain-forest in Africa and Madagascar. In black: present area; in hatching: former area where the forest has vanished. From Aubréville, 1949.

methods to fell trees and transport rough timber. It is now possible to work increasingly remote areas (*fig 36*).

South America was, until recently, free from serious devastation except in certain areas such as eastern Brazil. This region has been ravaged since the colonial period, and the wooded façade of the Serra do Mar stretching along the Atlantic is only a screen hiding bare mountains and plateaus. The *Araucaria angustifolia* of the Southern States of Brazil is rapidly vanishing. In the State of Parana alone, it originally covered 18,829,020 acres; in 1953 this was reduced to 6,844,670. Nearly 12 million acres were thus felled in 20 years. These forests have no opportunity to grow again because the soil is cleared for grasslands which soon become unproductive.

In 30 to 40 years none of these trees will be left (Aubréville, *Etude écologique des principales formations végétales du Brésil*. Nogent sur Marne, 1961).

Erosion subsequent to deforestation is also affecting the Andes at tropical and subtropical levels. In Colombia, for example, it ravages some 494,000 acres every year, especially in the central Cordillera and the Santa Marta Mountains. New roads are being cut through Latin America, particularly through the Amazon basin which is no longer the enormous inviolate mass it once was. In Brazil part of Amazonia may lose its forest treasure during the next few years and the southern part has already been devastated.

In many sections of Asia erosion due to deforestation is centuries old. Only 18% of India is now wooded and only 9% of China.

The world's forest cover is thus decreasing rapidly, despite the efforts of foresters. Furthermore, modern forestry tends to think of 'fields' of trees like fields of wheat. Both are artificial in the eyes of the biologist, who is concerned with the disappearance of natural communities. Many imported species, especially eucalyptus and resinous forms, have been planted, but, while these may provide a good yield and restore eroded soil, such forests lack the numerous plants and animals found in a primitive forest.

Some writers believe all the tropical 'virgin forest' will disappear during the next generation. It is estimated that the demand for wood will increase 17% between 1950 and 1975. Consumption for industrial use will decline, but there will be an increase in the use of paper pulp (60%) and veneering (90%) for which certain tropical woods are used. A reduction in the use of wood for fuel seems unlikely.

For all these reasons natural forests are seriously menaced, yet they alone preserve the innumerable living creatures dependent on closed habitats. And only an adequate forest mantle can protect the earth from an erosion of which man would be the inevitable victim.

4 BRUSH FIRES

Since immemorial times most of Africa south of the Sahara, aside from the large tropical forests and some temperate regions, has

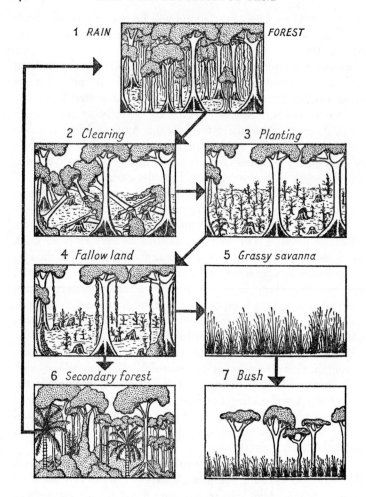

Fig. 36
Evolution of the primary rain-forest under the influence of man and
shifting cultivation.
1 primitive state before man's intervention
2 clearing for cultivation
3 planting (corn, cassava, etc.)
4 land fallow after cultivation is abandoned

been swept by man-made fires during the dry seasons. These brush fires are intended to improve pasturage or to encourage hunting. They are much more injurious in hilly country like Madagascar, than in a flat region such as Ubangi in Central Africa, according to Sillans (1958). But on the whole, they are powerful agents in the modification and destruction of habitats, and they often start serious erosion.

During the dry season shepherds set fire to dry savannas. When the rains arrive plants grow quickly in a soil free from dead grass, thus providing excellent pasturage for domestic animals. Though fire is said to reduce the number of parasites, especially ticks, there are now many means of destroying them. Burning the brush to kill ticks is, as H. Humbert said, like setting the house on fire to destroy fleas and bedbugs. The same kind of reasoning led people to set fires that spread over sixty-mile areas in Siberia to get rid of mosquitoes. It is easy to see why shepherds and foresters do not agree about brush fires, which have changed natural habitats in Africa very considerably. Fire is doubtless not to blame for the creation of great savannas at the expense of rain-forests, since it attacks only cleared areas. But it can spread under cover in dry forests and, in many cases, wooded savanna seems to represent a degraded dry forest.

Fire prevents forest recovery save in very unusual cases by destroying young shoots and saplings. Experiments have proved that the normal evolution of vegetable forms when protected from fire produces a reconstituted forest, which, however, differs from the original by the density and composition of its flora.

All travellers have been struck by the spectacular transformation of the plant landscape in zones subjected to brush fires (see Aubréville and Humbert). These areas are marked by widely scattered

------

5 *progressive transformation into grassland if cultivation is continued; under favourable conditions, imported species may turn it into wooded savanna* (7)

6 *If crops are abandoned after a short period of time, there is an evolution towards secondary forest which, in rare circumstances and if there is no further human intervention, may once again evolve towards 'primary' forest. From Sillans 1958.*

twisted trees, stunted bushes and coarse grass. Rise in temperature is the chief factor in this transformation. According to information quoted by Guilloteau (1958), ground temperatures have often been measured between 210°F and 482°F and they may reach 1292°F or even 1562°F. Temperature varies according to local conditions, such as wind fanning the fires.

Although fire acts differently on different species, it favours seeds with a very thick, woody integument. These burst under the heat, so accelerating germination. Perennial grasses with a highly developed root system that put forth new shoots quickly (like some *Andropogon* and *Cymbopogon*) are best adapted to high temperatures.

Plant associations are thus modified by brush fires. Closed habitats—such as wooded savannas—tend to become open habitats as trees disappear. An artificial balance is therefore maintained by annual fires.

These transformations also influence the animal population. Herbivores selecting herbaceous plants are favoured at the expense of those feeding on leaves and bushes. This explains certain shifts in balance among ungulates, such as the abundance of buffaloes in reserves that are periodically burned, like the Kruger Park in South Africa.

The influence of brush fires on the soil is just as important. Minimal at times, the temperature may be raised very high when the humus layer is dry. In Africa increased temperatures of 37°F to 129°F 0·78 inch below soil surface have been recorded, but they are often higher in country covered with underbrush where they may exceed 212°F. Humus fires have been recorded where the fire spreads below as well as above the surface. Roots of trees and seeds are burned, tiny animals and plants may be destroyed and the ground sterilized.

Fire paves the way for erosion, especially the formation of rivulets and leaching of minerals, which follow the disappearance of the protective mantle. The latter, however, grows again after the beginning of the rainy season.

From the ecological angle the brush fire is nonsensical and entirely artificial. Although fires have been ignited by lightning during storms preceding the rainy season or by fermentation of plant matter, these are most unusual. As Fraser Darling (1960) emphasized, the brush fire destroys a considerable amount of living organic matter, causing loss of energy for the whole habitat. Darling also noted that perennial plants on African savannas are not adapted to seasonal change. During the dry season they accumulate substances underground, but these are destroyed if fires are started too early. This loss of vegetable matter is particularly serious in regions where the climate varies from season to season. The botanist Gillet (1960) states that in the centre of Chad fire destroys the stubble, transformed by drought into straw or stalks, which constitutes the only food for cattle during the long dry season. He reports that a flight over an experimental ranch protected from fire reveals a striking contrast between the amount of straw within its boundaries and the sterile lands outside.

Some South African scientists (quoted by Guilloteau, 1958) hold a diametrically opposed view. They think that protection of the grasses results in an accumulation of old plant material and deterioration of the grass cover. These differences, doubtless based on dissimilar ecological conditions, show the danger of making premature generalizations.

On the whole, fire causes a profound transformation of habitats. If we follow Aubréville (1949), a specialist in African botany, we must admit that most of Africa to-day consists of secondary formations which have replaced true climatic communities. Withdrawal of the rain-forest is often rapid and marked by dense savannas covered with 'elephant grass' or *Pennisetum*. Pieces of ground are cleared, cultivated and then abandoned. Farther along these man-made formations give way to wooded savannas which resemble natural climatic formations but are only a stage in the decline of forest communities. Once the way is prepared for the invasion of grasses, fire assures their permanency by preventing regeneration of dense cover. The soil, exhausted and eroded by agriculture, fire and leaching is just capable of supporting savanna vegetation. Fire-resistant species colonize the habitat, which is now occupied by 'parasite' formations so old that they seem a natural part of the African landscape.

Unfortunately the evolution does not stop here, for loss of water entailed by the transformation from forest to savanna continues under the influence of poor cultural practices, overgrazing and destruction of vegetation. These factors produce accelerated erosion.

The climate too is affected, and man soon finds himself caught in a chain that turns whole regions into desert. Although fire is, of course, not the sole agent responsible for the evolution, it is the principal one, particularly in Africa, where some people consider it responsible for the transformation of the entire continent. Agents of natural deforestation include certain animals. The elephant, for example, tears down trees to get at the branches he feeds on (see Bourlière and Verschuren, 1960, who discuss habitat changes caused by elephants in Albert National Park, Congo).

Fire has thus changed and damaged natural habitats in Africa and Madagascar. It is the same story in other parts of the world where shepherds have used identical procedures—the Mediterranean region, North America, parts of South America (Venezuela, the high Andes) and South-east Asia.

The majority of conservationists are thus opposed to brush fires. Shepherds, however, draw some profit from them for they maintain and develop an important grass cover, destroying bushes which are unsuitable for domestic cattle. Studies show that 'bush encroachment' by undesirable shrubs and underbrush causes a loss of some sixty million dollars to cattle owners in Texas alone. It has also been observed that areas dotted with bushes are more eroded than grassland. In mixed habitats cattle tend to congregate in the best places and to cause local erosion.

In certain instances fire can lead to stable habitats highly profitable to man and his domestic animals. In some areas of the South African veld it produces a grassy association of *Themeda triandra*, an excellent pasture which protects the soil. The same situation prevails in East Africa, particularly in Kenya. On some of the Masaï plains the use of brush fires has led to stable areas covered with perennials that protect the soil and provide good fodder. As the nature of the soil and the flora vary, it is easy to understand why South African biologists do not share the opinions of those who have worked in West Africa. Damage wrought by fires also largely depends on the way they are used. It has been suggested that less harm would be done if preventive fires were set by the agricultural services instead of by shepherds. The action of the fire depends, to a certain degree, on the season. Some scientists believe early fires are less harmful, since at the beginning of the dry season fires cause less heat, cover smaller areas, and are easier to control.

Eroded lavaka field in Madagascar (near Anjozorobé) caused by
bad agricultural methods

Above Emaciated cattle feeding on tree branches cut by shepherds in Kenya. *Below* Masaï cattle moving across deeply eroded pastures

Other measures rely on an exact understanding of the use of the land. From the scientific point of view, brush fires are never justified, since they change the natural balance, transform closed habitats into open habitats and destroy climax formations. The forester condemns them, as they destroy the forest; the specialist in soil management condemns them as they degrade plant associations until they are unsuitable even for grazing. But in parts of eastern and southern Africa they have led to the establishment of excellent grazing areas, well protected against erosion.

As naturalists we deplore the reduction of forests, but we have to consider the economic necessities of human populations. The biologist must give way to these imperatives, provided the transformed lands are protected against degradation and accelerated erosion, and provided wise exploitation assures their permanent productivity. Brush fires are neither good nor bad in themselves; they are simply an instrument to modify habitats. When they are abused, they are always harmful, as is the case in Africa. In practice —and except for special instances—they are started without regard for the stability and permanent productivity of the land.

5 OVERGRAZING

Cattle-raising is a highly important source of food since it utilizes marginal zones unsuitable for agriculture, yet it also can lead to serious soil degradation. A given area is capable of nourishing only a specific number of animals, depending on the nature of the soil, the climate and the vegetation, as the speed of regeneration of the plant carpet must balance the grazing rate of the cattle.

Not more than 60 to 70% of the grassy plants in East Africa can be removed without endangering the plant cover. If the carrying-capacity of the land is exceeded, vegetation is impoverished and the soil degraded. Overgrazing is now practised everywhere, but chiefly in the Mediterranean region, North America and inter-tropical regions, especially Africa.

The burden that a pasturage can support is variable. There is a great difference between the dry areas of the western United States or tropical Africa, and prairies of the temperate zone, where there is always enough water to assure regeneration of the plant cover.

COMPARISON OF THE CARRYING-CAPACITY OF PASTURAGES IN DIFFERENT
PARTS OF THE WORLD (Bourlière, UNESCO, 1963, and a number of
authors)

Natural pasturages	Load in pounds per square mile
Argentine pampa	80,000
Texas prairie	62,800
South African high veld	48,500
Themeda savanna, Kenya	20,000–31,400
Savanna, Rhodesia	28,550

Artificial pasturages	Load in pounds per square mile
Kivu, Congo	371,150
Prairie, Belgium	274,080
Rubona, Rwanda	228,400
Nioka, Ituri, Congo	194,140
Kiyaka, Kwango, Congo	31,405
Range in good condition, Oklahoma	20,556

The carrying-capacity notion involves a general ecological law.
A certain area can 'support' a definite number of antelope or deer,
depending on the condition of the habitat and the food requirements
of the animals. If this load is surpassed, the populations of wild
animals regulate themselves by means of predation or diseases
caused by malnutrition. Except for certain instances where man is
involved, populations of wild herbivores are in balance with their
surroundings.

Domestic animals, on the other hand, have been largely withdrawn from the influence of natural laws. Economic factors,
particularly the high price of meat, leather and wool, encourage
an overload of cattle. Man has an unfortunate tendency to seek an
immediate profit rather than to administer wisely the natural
capital of grazing lands. Finally, we must not forget that cattle at
times have religious value—like the sacred cows of India—or
prestige value—as among the Masaï and Batutsi of East Africa.
In such cases there is no natural check on the number of head, as
they are not bred solely to satisfy food requirements.

Domestic animals have replaced wild animals in a good part of
the open habitats of the world, but their exploitation of the plant
cover is very different. Wild herbivores are scattered throughout
the whole habitat, those in savannas and steppes moving in accord-

ance with the season. The same area is inhabited by several species, each one exploiting its own ecological niche. The end result is a rational exploitation of the whole plant cover.

The extreme gregariousness of domestic cattle causes them to gather in large concentrations at certain points. The evolution of pastoralism—under the influence of a policy aiming to make nomad populations settle in the area—tends to place flocks within definite boundaries. Furthermore, the range of domesticated species, chiefly cattle, goats and sheep, is singularly small; like all vegetarians, cattle have a preference for certain plants which they eliminate. Other species of less nutritive value can then invade the pasturage. This is aggravated by the fact that domestic animals, particularly goats, often do more damage than wild herbivores.

Before the arrival of the Europeans, most agricultural tribes, particularly in Africa, applied the same laws to their cattle that prevail among wild animals. The number of head was determined by the carrying-capacity of pasturages, and nomadism checked over-exploitation. But there were already symptoms of erosion. European civilization has brought security to these people. Vaccines protect their herds from epidemics, but the cows remain skeleton-like because their number has exceeded the carrying-capacity of the pasturage. This problem of overgrazing, which is serious save in humid temperate zones, must also be placed in the context of a rapidly ascending population curve.

Erosion due to overpasturage is chiefly caused by grazing. Where there are too many animals, they remove more grass than can be replaced in a certain period of time. Instead of exploiting the plant growth, or its 'interest', the herbivore consumes the whole plant or basic 'capital'.

Trampling by herds also causes destruction. Cattle fenced within a limited area crush the plant cover and cut it off at soil level with their hoofs. Vegetation disappears gradually, especially on trails, at watering places and near kraals, where the cattle are penned at night. Erosive phenomena soon appear, particularly gullies which spread rapidly to adjacent areas. In Africa, as in America, some gorges thirty feet deep were at first only cattle paths. As cows always follow the same route, a little gully was formed through which water poured. The combined action of grazing and trampling causes a considerable decrease in the green cover. For Chad Gillet

(1960) gives a decline of from 40–50% to 20%. Plants become puny, often only half normal size.

The vegetal composition of the habitats is also transformed. Sampling by herbivores is always selective because of their food preferences, so plants once scorned, like those with poisonous elements or the hard or prickly ones, get the upper hand. The number of species is reduced and, in general, perennials are eliminated in favour of annuals. At Chad Gillet (1960) found only 5 species in a square yard 64 feet from a well, with a preponderance of 'cram-cram' (*Cenchrus biflorus*). This 'cram-cram' is a grasslike plant carried by herds and almost the only one found in zones where there is a great deal of grazing. 192 feet from this spot he found 13 species with more soil cover in a less grazed area. The impoverishment of grazed and trampled areas is more apparent when the comparison is made with zones sheltered from cattle.

As annuals have a less developed root system, they do not retain water so well. In Idaho it was found that pasturages eroded by overgrazing and with a predominance of annuals lost 61% of their water during violent rains from rivulets which carried away 16 tons of soil per $2\frac{1}{2}$ acres. In neighbouring grassland sheltered from overgrazing, and where there was a dominance of perennials, only 0·5% of the water ran off and 15·4 pounds of soil were lost per $2\frac{1}{2}$ acres.

Overgrazed lands are also subject to serious disproportions in their animal population. Swarming of pests is caused by modification of the plant cover and a change in the whole environment. This explains the multiplication of kangaroo-rats (*Dipodomys*), hares (*Lepus*) and ground squirrels (*Citellus*), a swarming further aggravated by destruction of their predators. Numerous observations show that rodents never swarm in zones covered with dense plant growth. They are the 'offspring' of overgrazing and not the cause of degradation and erosion. (See J. M. Linsdale, 1946, The California Ground Squirrel, *Univ. Calif. Press.*)

Insects also take advantage of degraded grassland, especially grasshoppers. In the USA, Soviet Asia, Australia and South Africa, swarming of crickets is partly due to overgrazing.

All these results vary in accordance with the physical and biological characteristics of the area. They also depend on the animals. Cattle, the most exacting, are responsible for the least damage.

But a book could be written on the misdeeds of goats, which have despoiled parts of the globe beginning with the Mediterranean basin. A classic example is the Island of Saint Helena, where the goat was introduced by the Portuguese in 1513; R. A. Wallace (*Island Life*, 1902) states that in 1588 thousands of them were attacking the rich plant cover of the soil. In 1709 the governor demanded that the animals be destroyed to protect the forests, but was told that the goat was more precious than ebony. By 1809 nothing remained of the forest, and the flora had been replaced by masses of exotic plants. The soil's advanced erosion was caused by violent rains and the hilliness of the island.

Some soil specialists praise goats for fighting against bush encroachment—wrongly. A goat can survive several days without water and live in zones with a fragile balance, where it uproots plants and therefore deprives grassland of any possibility of regenerating. It can even climb trees to devour branches when the grass cover has disappeared. That this behaviour was observed in antiquity is evident from numerous Sumerian representations of a goat up a tree.

Some economists think the goat is praiseworthy for being able to survive in areas where no other domestic animal can subsist. They regard it as a marvellous ally permitting man's survival in regions he would otherwise have to evacuate. This is blind-alley economy. In many parts of the world pastoral peoples have raised cattle; when the country was ravaged by bad exploitation, they replaced them with sheep, and when these could no longer survive, nothing was left except the goat. It is easy to sympathize with unfortunate cattlemen who have only 'a few poor goats.' In some areas this animal represents the only possible use of the plant cover, but everywhere else it deprives vegetation of any opportunity to regenerate. After the goat there is nothing; when it dies of hunger, man dies with it. Utilization of soil resources based on the goat is one of the best examples of destruction of habitats, especially when, as in most cases, the flock exceeds the carrying-capacity.

Overgrazing has not been restricted to any one part of the world. It was first known in the Mediterranean region, where its effects were added to those of deforestation and poor agricultural management. Tillable land soon became private property, while grasslands, like the woods, were subject to communal rights, which did not encourage shepherds to make wise use of them. Pasture lands were extended to the detriment of the forest, which still protected upper mountain slopes and where shepherds took their flocks to spend the summer. In Spain cattle raisers were grouped in a powerful corporation, the *Mesta*; as this was favoured for centuries by the government at the expense of farmers, shepherds led millions of sheep across the fields during the seasonal migrations. The nudity of the Iberian plateaus, particularly Castile, is the result of these depredations. The same thing occurred in the Apennines in Italy, in the Balkan Peninsula and in North Africa.

Overgrazing has become widespread in the USA. Colonization of the West opened the vast arid plains to grazing, and a 'rush' ensued comparable to the gold rush in California. The number of head of cattle rose rapidly, for breeders overestimated their prospects in regions subject to prolonged droughts. It is estimated that in 1850 there were some 500,000 sheep in the West; in 1890 there were 20 million. The State of Wyoming had 309,000 sheep in 1886 and over 2·6 million in 1900, with a corresponding decrease in cattle. In Montana sheep increased from 1 to 3·5 million in the same period.

When the first settlers established themselves in the West, the carrying-capacity was 112·5 million sheep units. (One unit is a sheep or goat; a head of cattle or a horse represents 5 units.) In 1930 it was down to 54 million units, but there were still at least 86·5 million domestic herbivores continuing the ravages caused in less than 60 years of occupation. Of 728,945 million acres of pasture land, about 593 million showed symptoms of erosion and only slightly over 93 million were in satisfactory condition. 55% of the pasturage had lost more than half its carrying-capacity.

In Iran, according to recent statistics, there are 27 million sheep, 12 million goats and 5·24 million cattle, or 66 million sheep units. The total grazing surface is 98 million acres, to which can be added 39 million acres of forest pasturage. As it takes 4·9 acres to feed a sheep during the year, the carrying-capacity is 26 million sheep or considerably less than half the livestock exploiting the territory. For administrative, social and economic reasons it is impossible to reduce the number of animals (Golesorkhi, Colloque, *Conservation et Restauration des sols*, Teheran 1960). The number of head of cattle in India increased from 84 million to 147 million between

1900 and 1940, while pasture lands decreased by 49 million acres (Abeywickrama, 1963). In 1950 there were 155 million cattle and in 1960 175 million. Meanwhile pasture land continued to decrease.

Africa, particularly East Africa, is another example of poor pastoral use of open habitats. Before colonization the natural habitat enjoyed a relative balance, as the number of grazing animals was limited by epidemics. Infections made grazing precarious in huge areas thus protected by the tsetses. Colonization has changed all this. Native population has increased, herds have grown and overgrazing of pasturage subject to severe drought has resulted. One problem is the artificial multiplication of watering holes. Until very recently the number available in the dry season determined the size of the herds. Colonists have dug new wells, but the amount of food resources still restricts the herbivore population. The same difficulty exists in reserves where dams have created reservoirs. A large number of big mammals can quench their thirst but cannot find food, so increased pressure is put on vegetation. The creation of water holes is justified only in regions where the supply of this precious liquid really determines the size of herds.

Examples of overgrazing could be selected from all parts of Africa. In Kenya it was estimated that the Suk region could support 20,000 head; but in 1935 there were 38,000 cattle, in addition to 150,000 sheep and goats. In the Machakos district, south-east of Nairobi, there were 1 cow and 2 goats to 2·4 acres, whereas 49 acres were needed to support them. Territories occupied by the Masaï show signs of erosion from overgrazing; in 1961 Kenya alone had 973,000 head of cattle, 660,000 goats and sheep and a great many asses. The extreme drought that year is said to have killed three-fifths of them, but in 1964 the cattle had increased to 7 million.

The situation is just as serious in certain parts of South Africa, where native reserves have been eroded by poor grazing practices, including an excess of goats and sheep. In some areas it is estimated that 75% of the soil surface is affected.

The first solution to the problem is to improve the quality of the cattle; grasslands must be enriched by introducing new species, by regulating brush fires and using better grazing methods. Above all, the number of animals should be reduced to a figure the area can support.

We have already observed that wild animals use the plant cover much more efficiently than domestic ones and that a larger number can graze an area without causing erosion. It has recently been suggested that big game be used to transform plant resources. A rational exploitation of wild fauna may provide a solution for marginal zones. It would preserve the fauna and the habitats, assure man a profitable return, and provide precious animal proteins lacking in numerous tropical areas.

6 BAD AGRICULTURAL PRACTICES

Agriculture, coming after clearing and deforestation, often completes the destruction of habitats. Bad agricultural practices accelerate the erosive processes and can cause the total ruin of a country.

From a strictly ecological angle, agriculture simplifies the environment, replacing the multiple species of primitive plant associations by a very small number of 'domesticated' forms. The solar energy falling on a particular area is captured and converted into a single product. Food chains are simplified, a process rendering the habitat increasingly sensitive as it removes most of its defences. Natural fertility need not be destroyed, and wise agricultural methods can often provide an acquired fertility, while also assuring stability. So the 'return' may be satisfactory, although the economy is orientated towards man.

In western and central Europe brown, leached soils are among the best for agriculture. Tilling creates a stable soil, which is constantly improved by spreading dung and fertilizers like lime and chalk. Complex agricultural procedures, rotation of crops, a mixed agriculture in which grazing has an important role, the maintenance of a mosaic of different habitats, have permitted man to increase soil fertility very considerably over the centuries.

The first European colonists used similar methods in the northeastern United States. The black soil zones, originally covered with a dense steppe-like vegetation, had a thick top layer rich in organic matter. They were fertile as long as conservation was practised, but steppes and savannas with a cover of low plant formation are much more fragile than forest soils and require greater attention.

Fertility has been maintained in countries with a long agricultural tradition. This is the case in western and central Europe and some low Asiatic regions, where, despite a large population, wise agricultural practices similar to those used in gardening have produced crops unequalled elsewhere. There is, furthermore, almost no erosion in rice fields, where only the finest particles are carried away by the waters.

China is one of the oldest agricultural countries. The Chinese classified soils 4000 years ago, or 1000 years before the siege of Troy (quoted by Bennett, 1939). But this has not prevented some areas from being among the most eroded parts of the world. Deforestation and bad agricultural practices in mountainous regions have removed soil from broad areas, produced serious floods and caused repeated famines. At the present time erosion is said to affect 395 million acres, or one-sixth of the country.

As long as the population in tropical regions remains below a certain density, shifting cultivation permits a satisfactory agricultural exploitation, provided crop rotation is rapid. When clearing and planting are followed by a short period of agricultural exploitation, the natural cover regenerates rapidly. In most instances, unfortunately, the peasant does not abandon the soil until it is ruined, and then a decade is required for it to recover. Tropical soils are usually very fragile despite the luxuriant vegetation covering them. The dispersal of hard materials and the loss of their constituents by erosion, especially by runoff following torrential rains, can ruin in a few months a structure which took centuries to form. Planting after clearing, and then a long rest as fallow land, may preserve the soil before crops have exhausted it; this cycle permits restoration of the plant cover and even the soil structure. But this practice was rapidly abandoned as population pressure increased, and the ruin of various hilly parts of the world was the sad consequence.

Profound changes occurred when a real agricultural revolution took place during the past century. Man discovered the wealth of the vast new grasslands at the same time as he developed agricultural machinery. Steppe soils have a natural structure resembling that of cultivated soils. So farmers abandoned old conservative methods and used the new machines which exploit vast surfaces with a reduced labour force. Draft animals were replaced by machinery as agriculture became industrialized. This led to the ecological monstrosity of monoculture, one of the curses of modern agriculture both economically and politically. From the strictly biological point of view, it is possible to assure the fixed return of a single plant, provided the soil is protected, the waste with its organic matter put back and the elements that are removed replaced by fertilizer. Since this is rarely possible, monoculture causes impoverishment of the cultivated soil. On the economic plane, it sensitizes the financial balance of a country whose fate is tied to the prices of a single product on the world market. Economic instability and ruin of the natural capital thus go hand in hand.

Polyculture, on the other hand, with its rotation of crops, including those which enrich, like peas and beans, makes it possible to exploit all the possibilities of the soil while giving it rest periods. Moreover, numerous crops, like cereals, leave the soil bare during a good part of the year, with no plant protection against wind and water erosion, and soil dries out more rapidly when exposed. Even during the period of growth, the single stratum formed by the cultivated plant does not provide as effective protection as a more complex system. No manure or fertilizer was used at first, and to-day chemical fertilizers are often the only ones employed. Natural fertilizers are not always available, as domestic animals have almost disappeared from regions where monoculture is practised. Chemical fertilizers may replace mineral elements needed by cultivated plants but they do not provide the organic substances required by the soil to preserve its structure

The classic example of soil degradation is that of the Great Plains of America (*fig* 37), which were first exploited in the second half of the 19th century when colonists arrived from the forested zone of the east. This was the period when the bison herds were systematically destroyed. The original grassy cover was replaced by fields of cereal and corn that afford much less protection to the soil. Cultivation, beginning about 1880, was favoured by abundant rains, but a decade later a period of prolonged drought caused many farmers to leave the region. At the beginning of the 20th century cultivation began again, and for a time there was abundant rainfall. Agricultural exploitation was extended, particularly during and after the First World War when there was a food shortage.

In the depression year, 1931, a drought began that was to last several years. The dry soil, completely degraded and lacking plant protection, was converted into a fine dust which the wind carried

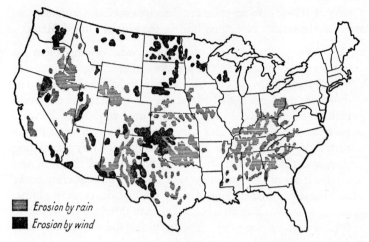

Erosion by rain

Erosion by wind

Fig. 37

Extent of erosion in the USA. The map shows only the most severely degraded zones; actually a much larger area reveals symptoms of degradation, except in the east. Notice the enormous 'dust bowl' on the borders of Kansas, Texas, and Oklahoma, where winds have stripped the soil. From Bennett, 1939, simplified.

off in tornadoes. The twelfth of May, 1934, will be recalled as a day of mourning in the annals of land use, for the Great Plains were victims of a catastrophe without precedent in American history. Winds blew the earth dust from a vast zone extending through Kansas, Texas, Oklahoma and eastern Colorado and carried it in black clouds over two-thirds of the continent. Part darkened the sky over Washington and New York; part was carried towards the Atlantic. The tornadoes laden with dust generally travelled about 650 miles on a front 300 miles in width, and transported dust particles at elevations up to 9,600 feet. Some of them, extending over 175,000 square miles, transported more than 200 million tons of soil. The wind removed it to a depth of 10 inches from the dust bowl. Dust falling on other areas caused more damage by covering tillable land, roads and houses. These events produced one of the greatest economic catastrophes caused by man's disregard of the most elementary natural laws. Millions of acres were ruined and farmers forced to seek new jobs. The first pages of John Steinbeck's *The*

Grapes of Wrath give an excellent description of the tempests that ravaged the poorly cultivated land in the central United States.

'A gentle wind followed the rain clouds, driving them on northward, a wind that softly clashed the drying corn. A day went by and the wind increased, steady, unbroken by gusts. The dust from the roads fluffed up and spread out and fell on the weeds beside the fields, and fell into the fields a little way. Now the wind grew strong and hard and it worked at the rain crust in the corn fields. Little by little the sky was darkened by the mixing dust, and the wind felt over the earth, loosened the dust, and carried it away. The wind grew stronger. The rain crust broke and the dust lifted up out of the fields and drove gray plumes into the air like sluggish smoke. The corn threshed the wind and made a dry, rushing sound. The finest dust did not settle back to earth now, but disappeared into the darkening sky.

The wind grew stronger, whisked under stones, carried up straws and old leaves, and even little clods, marking its course as it sailed across the fields. The air and the sky darkened and through them the sun shone redly, and there was a raw sting in the air. During a night the wind raced faster over the land, dug cunningly among the rootlets of the corn, and the corn fought the wind with its weakened leaves until the roots were freed by the prying wind and then each stalk settled wearily sideways toward the earth and pointed the direction of the wind.

The dawn came, but no day. In the gray sky a red sun appeared, a dim circle that gave a little light, like dusk; and as that day advanced, the dusk slipped back toward darkness, and the wind cried and whimpered over the fallen corn.'

In an endeavour to prevent further catastrophes, the American Government passed the Soil Conservation Act (1938) and the Taylor Grazing Control Act (1934). It also organized the Soil Conservation Service, which planted grass in ravaged districts and began a slow restoration of the soil. This was helped by the return of rains in 1940. During the Second World War increased demand for agricultural products, with a corresponding rise in prices, led farmers to cultivate these fragile lands again. The year 1950 brought another drought and again disaster struck, but without the same economic consequences. The damage, minor at first, was aggravated by torrential rains that started in 1957 immediately after the drought. They carried away torrents of mud, leaving bare rock over large areas, and destroying all hope of restoring the soil. It is hoped that farmers have learned their lesson now and will no longer practise monoculture. In 1965 the Dust Bowl was again bone dry after a two-year drought. Although much had been learned since the thirties, not all farmers took the necessary precautions, and it was estimated that 275,000 acres of wheat were damaged in Texas alone.

Modern man has committed equally serious mistakes in the tropics. His installation of a 'predatory economy'—the German *Raubwirtschaft*—has had deplorable effects. After destroying the forests and massacring the animals, civilized man set out to violate the earth by cultivating export products with no thought for the country's biological balance. Vast enterprises were established in Africa, Latin America and South-east Asia. Monoculture was responsible for much of the disaster, especially in the savannas.

Coffee is responsible for the destruction of the area in Brazil between Rio de Janeiro and Sao Paulo. After the forest was felled, coffee trees failed to protect the soil. Erosion spread rapidly and caused the abandonment of cultivation. The coffee 'front' moved westwards, leaving in its wake a country where only a subsistence economy could be maintained. As of February, 1967, Brazil's massive coffee-eradication programme was well under way with 20% of its 2·6 billion coffee trees eliminated. This frees over a million acres for other uses. Para-rubber plants, cotton and tea were also cultivated on a growing scale. Elsewhere tobacco and *Pyrethrum* were planted. The latter is to blame for the degradation of vast areas in East Africa and the Congo, since it exhausts the soil and leaves it unprotected, like all crops which have to be hoed.

The 'groundnut (peanut) scheme' was one of the most glaring failures of the post-war period. The project was abandoned after 36 million pounds sterling had been squandered in three districts of Tanzania between 1947 and 1952. Failure was due to poor soil management and exaggerated mechanization.

In West Africa gradual degradation of the soil follows the movement of peanut plantations: in Senegal to the south and east, in Niger to the north and north-east. As Guilloteau stated (1950): 'We have here an example of industrial cultivation exceeding the needs of the natives, pursued without precaution or restraint, for economic reasons.'

Much could be said about bad agricultural methods, such as the systematic removal of all 'parasite' plants in order to eliminate competition between the cultivated plant and 'weeds'. This leaves the soil bare under the cultivated plants—often trees or bushes—so it dries out more rapidly and is open to erosion. In native fields the ground is covered with all kinds of plants. No doubt this owes something to laziness, but the farmer also has an instinctive knowledge of an elementary ecological law. European settlers now see their mistake and soil specialists have drawn up a long list of cover plants which, together with those that are cultivated, form the semblance of a natural system.

We cannot discuss all the agricultural methods used after colonization in tropical countries. The subject is incredibly complex, as problems vary according to the nature of the area. Some settlements were a complete success, like the large farms in the highlands of East Africa. British colonists established prosperous farms in the 'White Highlands' of Kenya, where the climate is excellent. Crops provide a good proportion of the revenue of the country, 85% of which derives from agricultural exports, particularly coffee, tea and sisal. Although the natural habitat was Europeanized, the colonists produced stable and highly productive lands, and no 'protector of nature' can object to such changes. The same is true of other parts of the tropical zone.

Elsewhere the influence of western civilization has been extremely harmful. In some regions planters pushed the natives back into certain areas, and made them agricultural workers. (See Harroy, 1944, and René Dumont, L'Afrique noire est mal partie, Paris 1962.) The 'native reserves' drive the natives into special zones but refuse them the right to own property in districts reserved for colonists. Such ideas have not been applied in countries with a dense population and a strong political structure (for example, Asia and certain parts of Africa). In other places, planters transformed virgin or slightly modified lands to make a quick profit. This industrial exploitation is still continuing, with sordid interests often concealed beneath generous promises to the natives.

Differences in the rate of erosion between fields cultivated according to traditional African practices and those treated by modern industrial methods appear in an article by Fournier (*Contribution à l'étude de la conservation du sol en AOF;* unpublished) about peanut cultivation in Central Casamance (at Séfa, near Sedhiou). Two identical experimental fields were laid out, one according to native methods, the other by mechanized procedures including mechanical forest clearing, systematic removal of large stumps, rootcuttage (running a straight blade through the area at a depth of some 7 to 8 inches), and raking. After rotation of crops for four years, erosion was as follows:

		1954 Peanuts	1955 Fallow and rice	1956 Peanuts	1957 Rice
Runoff (%)	a	33·3	19·9	33·1	22·4
	b	47·0	49·3	39·5	25·3
Erosion (in tons	a	3587	1597	1646	1984
per square mile)	b	4934	7743	3069	2784

(a=fallow in the native field; b=rice in the mechanized field)

The runoff is larger and the soil loss much greater in the field cultivated by mechanical means. Annual erosion had removed 2200 tons per square mile in the field cultivated by native methods as against 4630 tons in the other. This is because clearing causes degradation of soil structure and machines lower its resistance. The mechanized method produces a larger crop (1644 pounds per acre of peanuts versus 866 pounds), but it is questionable whether this increase is justified in the long run.

When modern man first arrived in tropical countries—some of which, like a good part of Africa and most of Latin America, were almost unoccupied—he believed that agricultural methods used in temperate zones could be applied to the new regions. Since then governments have established institutes for agricultural research, and new technical documentation has made it possible to correct certain mistakes. However, much remains to be done. The political situation may change, but economic problems stay the same or worsen. The new African nations are desperately seeking funds. Let us hope they will not sacrifice their future to the present by using agricultural methods detrimental to the fertility of to-morrow. This is the real African drama, the one being played in 'under-developed' areas in other parts of the world.

Much research has been done to restore degraded soils and increase their yield, and many discoveries have been made in the domain of soil chemistry. Land management has become a science, like all the biological sciences, but 20th century technicians have not ceased to use many methods centuries old.

Some measures use engineering techniques. Terrace cultivation divides a long slope into a series of successive shelves bounded by ditches to intercept water. Terraces prevent erosion by cutting a mountain into a series of steps. Similar systems have been employed for centuries in Asia, the Mediterranean basin and the Andes.

Contour ploughing prevents furrows from following the steepest slope down to a small gully when rivulets turn into torrents. The struggle against furrowing requires the construction of supporting walls, often of considerable size, before any planting is done.

Other measures of a chemical nature aim to re-establish a balanced soil by restoring mineral and organic elements removed by crops. This is especially important in the case of nitrogen, essential for high protein products, and certain mineral salts like potassium and calcium.

Finally, some measures to re-establish a natural balance are biological and, at the moment, these are considered the best. Strict monoculture is being replaced by a mixed agricultural economy. Rotation is again being practised, particularly in the USA, where strip cropping takes place on a large scale, with regular rotation of cereals and plants that protect the soil. Wind erosion is checked by keeping the soil covered with a mulch of grasses that live through the dry season and by planting windbreaks such as cypress hedges in the Mediterranean region, poplars in temperate climates, and rows of acacias or similar plants in tropical areas. Forested zones, whether natural or artificial, protect upper water basins. They provide a kind of natural balance by dividing the territory into lots, each of which has a special purpose. Man thus realizes that the best way to assure good productivity is to manage nature instead of violating her laws.

Special precautions are required in tropical areas where soil is fragile. Monoculture and industrial culture would ruin these lands, which can be protected only by complex plant associations and particular agricultural methods. Although native practices have despoiled some areas, elsewhere, as on the Kilimanjaro and Meru slopes, which the Warush and Chagga tribes have cultivated intensively, conservational techniques aim to preserve a protective plant cover. Large trees form a shady stratum beneath which banana trees, coffee trees and harvest crops are grown. This association forms several strata above the soil and mingles root systems at different levels in the ground. Man has thus reconstituted a complex system to maintain soil fertility and provide balanced resources. Similar examples are found in Central Africa, where the Bantus protect the soil by planting associations in continuous sequences.

Man is beginning to learn at last that the real vocation of a region must be considered, and that many areas are not suitable for cultivation. Modern agriculture thought itself an industry and forgot that it was governed by strict laws that cannot be ignored. Even its basic material, the soil, is living and subject to modifications. The great catastrophes that have ravaged the world result from this denial.

7 EROSION AND WATER CONTROL

The problem of accelerated erosion is closely linked to that of water control. Within certain limits the fertility of a region is determined by the regularity of the water supply rather than its abundance. Civilizations are born and prosper in accordance with sound administration of this supply. The great civilizations of the Near East arose on the edge of deserts irrigated with water from neighbouring mountains, and their ruin was determined to a large extent by erosion of these mountains, which ceased to accumulate water. Vestiges of great cities in western Asia and North Africa bear this out. Other ruins in East Asia and Central and South America tell the same story.

These dramas are being re-enacted under our eyes as a result of accelerated erosion caused by man. His influence is apparent in the progressive drying out of the soil, in floods, and in the accumulation of debris in upper basins of water systems.

Water has a general tendency to flee from eroded regions. Soil, deprived of plant cover, changes its structure and loses the physico-chemical properties that retain water. Moreover, deep gullies lower the water table. In eroded zones, a large proportion of rain-water fails to penetrate the soil and what remains tends to descend to a considerable depth. Thus the upper layers progressively dry out and vegetation decreases. Meanwhile, man requires more and more water for industrial and domestic use. As most large cities use much more water than they obtain by normal rainfall, they are exhausting underground resources.

Transformation of habitats and resulting erosion have also affected the climate, though lack of objective information makes this a highly controversial problem. If we limit our consideration to the large equatorial rain-forest (see Aubréville, 1949), there is no doubt that it regulates mean and extreme temperatures by protecting soil from direct heat and humidifying the atmosphere. It also seems that forests increase the volume of rainfall by cooling upper air layers and causing vapour condensation. Further complications arise from the movements of air currents and from evaporation. This influence of the forest, which prolongs the rainy season, would also affect rainfall in zones adjacent to wooded mountains. Aubréville states there would be less rainfall in regions near the desert and the Sudan zone if the rain-forests in Guinea were felled. He writes: 'Dense rain-forests must be considered as a means of extending the influence of the seas to the centre of the continent.'

Action of the forests is also felt in temperate regions, and other habitats clearly exert considerable influence over rainfall and climate. Although no definite conclusions can be obtained from fragmentary observations, there are numerous historical accounts, particularly in the Mediterranean basin, which favour such an interpretation of climatic variations. In any case, it is certain that the loss of an adequate plant cover—whether forest or grass—considerably decreases condensations in the form of dew. This is a serious matter in dry regions.

Accelerated erosion thus causes a perceptible decrease in atmospheric precipitation, hastening the formation of deserts. By destroying natural habitats and denuding the soil, man unleashes an infernal mechanism whose repercussions even spread to the layers of atmosphere vital to his prosperity.

When water can no longer be absorbed by a saturated soil, it flows downward and causes rivers to rise. Freshets are especially common and exert the greatest influence in regions with a scanty plant cover. We have seen that man's poor agricultural methods have greatly decreased the soil's capacity to retain rainfall, laying eroded regions open to periodical flooding. It is said that in this respect a forest is equivalent to a dam.

The history of the Yellow River in China is a long struggle between the waters and the populations on its banks. But accelerated erosion has given catastrophic proportions to what was originally a natural phenomenon. The Chinese have succeeded in demolishing the forest throughout the greater part of their country.

Rivers in the United States also provoke terrible floods. Those in the west are particularly susceptible because of the aridity of the terrain, but the same is true of the Mississippi, where the damage is chiefly due to human intervention. Bennett (1939) estimated that between 1903 and 1938 floods caused losses of $1,697,507,124, excluding injury to the land. The great Mississippi flood of 1927 spread over 28,950 square miles, an area larger than Belgium and the Netherlands, and cost about 300 million dollars.

Materials detached by the water are carried from upper basins to lower levels, where some are deposited and others borne along to the sea. In normal circumstances this natural sedimentation acts as an element of agricultural wealth. The rich silt of the lower Nile valley is the best example of the fertilizing power of such deposits.

But this normal process is quite different from the accumulation of materials torn by waters from areas of accelerated erosion. The solid bodies include masses of gravel and rocks. They fill dams and reservoirs, choke river mouths and seal harbours. The destruction wrought upstream by erosion is thus doubled by the accumulation of rubbish.

The quantity of fine solid matter transported by the water may amount to 12·6 to 50·3 pounds per 100 cubic feet of water. So in one year the Mississippi carries a volume of 10,593,200,000 cubic feet of sediment. The Yellow River carries an annual average of 1,890 million tons of solid matter. The maximum measured in one year was 2,643 million tons, but in a single August day of 1933 it carried more than 500 million tons of mud near Chancheou. For the whole basin, a region the size of France, the corresponding degradation would be 7·3 to 7·7 tons per 1,000 acres (J. Messines, C. R. Colloque, *Conservation et Restauration des sols*, Teheran 1960).

China holds the record for volume, but the amount is relatively as great in other parts of the world. In the USA average degradation is 2·4 to 58·2 tons per 1,000 acres a year in the Los Angeles region. Elsewhere it amounts to 14·6 tons per 1,000 acres a year in the valley of a tributary of the Ganges in India; from 18·2 to 60·7 tons per 1,000 acres a year in the Oued el Oujda basin of Algeria; 182 tons per 1,000 acres a year in the upper basins of the Drac and Durance in France; and 667 to 728 tons per 1,000 acres a year in the Vorarlberg in Austria, though fortunately this occurs in small areas, measuring 24 to 988 acres.

When these materials are deposited in fertile soil, they may change it completely. The Nile silt, carried in thin layers, has high agricultural value, but many deposits contain gravel or boulders which remove the finer materials that enrich the fields.

The most dramatic consequence, however, is the speed at which sediments fill basins constructed for purposes of irrigation, the hydro-electric industry, or the control of water volume passing through a river. Algerian dams silt up at a rate of 10,594,200 cubic feet per year, while their feed basins deteriorate rapidly owing to deforestation and overgrazing. The Oued Fodda Dam, with an initial capacity of 7·945 million cubic feet, took in 21·188 million cubic feet of solids a year between 1932 and 1937, 44·15 million cubic feet between 1937 and 1941, and 132·45 million between 1941 and 1947. This corresponds to a scraping of the soil of 0·27 inches per year (Furon, 1953). If this process continues, the dam will last 80 years at most.

In Greece the dam erected on the Strymon (Kerkini) has lost a third of its capacity in 19 years, an annual decrease of 194 million cubic feet. If this erosion cannot be checked, all irrigation on the Serres plains will cease after 40 years.

Reservoirs are filling very rapidly in the USA. Some have filled 80% in 30 years, and it is estimated that 39% of them will be useless in less than half a century. In certain cases dams have become filled in 10 to 15 years. In Texas a dam on the Colorado River lost 47% of its original capacity in 6 years and 9 months; a new dam built to replace it lost 83% of its capacity in 9 years and 95% in 13 years (Bennett 1939).

An exceptional case is the famous Kwanting Dam built in 1951-54 on the Yungting Ho, near Peking, with an original capacity of 80,176 million cubic feet. Chinese engineers have calculated that the sedimentation is 3,178 million cubic feet, which means that the whole construction will be useless after 75 years. They are attempting to preserve this dam by reforesting its drained basin.

Clogging of reservoirs may have even more serious consequences by exerting too much pressure on construction works and causing them to burst. This occurred in Algeria at the Oued Fergoug Dam. In France the famous Serre-Ponçon Dam is threatened in the same way. Annual deposits are estimated at 102,400 million cubic feet. Lack of funds has prevented reforestation, so the possibility of a catastrophe must exist.

Research projects in the south-western United States revealed that fish populations have suffered severely from modifications in flowing water, and that these effects were increased by industrial pollution and other changes caused by man (Miller, 1961, 1963). Destruction of the plant cover, hydro-electric construction, introduction of exotic species, emptying of waste products and the use of selected poisons to eliminate so-called 'undesirable' fishes have entirely transformed the original balance of aquatic biological associations. In spawning areas such as Lake Erie in the USA ecological conditions are so changed that the animals are deserting them.

Many fishes are in serious danger, even extinct, because of man. Excessive accumulation of sediments may also cause serious damage in the sea. The choking of estuaries in Chesapeake Bay on the east coast of the USA is apparently caused by material torn by rivers from damaged lands (Tricart 1962). Erosion is thus responsible for disturbances that even affect the tides. The coast of Languedoc in southern France is threatened with sand-blocking which seems to come from hydro-electric installations. As the flow of the Petit Rhône has decreased considerably, a mass of silt is no longer borne along by the river. The coast is receding and currents carry away sand which they deposit to the west.

8 DESTRUCTION OF AQUATIC HABITATS

Aquatic habitats, particularly in temperate zones, are among the most threatened areas in the world. Highly important for the preservation of a large number of animal and plant species, they range from salt lagoons to freshwater swamps and lake areas. The contact of land and aquatic areas produces a considerable volume of plant and animal forms, especially along the coast where the sea, fresh water and land combine to produce a biological 'crop' unequalled elsewhere.

As far back as antiquity man endeavoured to drain marshes. In countries with an old civilization this practice has considerably reduced aquatic regions. Few of them are classed as reserves—about 10% in the USA and less than 2% in France, of which the Camargue alone accounts for about two-thirds. All are severely threatened.

In most cases aesthetic and moral reasons would alone justify the preservation of some aquatic habitats in their natural state. Most of them are very picturesque, and their preservation can maintain a large number of animals and plants which require very definite ecological conditions. There are also various economic reasons in favour of their conservation, for swampy zones play an important part in the regional balance by regularizing the flow of rivers and restoring large volumes of water during dry periods. They also help fertilize districts with organic matter. Finally, it has been proved that profit from swamps by way of hunting, fishing and grazing is often larger before they are transformed than after large sums have been invested in them.

It is obvious that drainage of some swampy areas is justified for economic reasons. Cultivation of flooded zones may yield good crops, and requirements of public health, especially in the battle against malaria, occasionally necessitate drainage of districts where mosquitoes breed. But it would be equally false to consider that all marshes should be scientifically drained.

In many instances solid scientific or economic arguments plead for the preservation of a series of aquatic habitats. Animal and plant communities established in humid zones must be preserved intact if the species are to be preserved. Long lists of small plants and animals would disappear if their habitats were destroyed. This is even true of numerous vertebrates, each of which has a special ecological niche.

Conservation of aquatic habitats is highly important for migratory waterfowl. On the whole, populations of water birds are much smaller than is generally thought. The International Wildfowl

Research Bureau states that the number of white-fronted geese wintering in western Europe does not exceed 70,000; the world population of the pink-footed goose is 40,000; that of the barnacle goose 30,000; and the European population of the brent goose not over 20,000.

Most of these ducks and geese nest in tundras of the Far North, where they are relatively protected because of their wide dispersion and the few changes man has made in their habitat. But they are all migrants and come south to winter. Their populations are thus concentrated in very restricted areas, which are used as migratory stations or winter quarters. Ducks and geese nesting from Iceland and northern Europe to western Siberia winter in a certain number of spots scattered through western Europe and tropical Africa. In the Netherlands it is not exceptional to find between 500,000 and 600,000 migrants on the muddy flats of Waddensee on Vlieland Island. There are very large concentrations in Aiguillon Bay on the Vendée coast, and in swampy zones of tropical Africa. The low Senegal valley shelters an enormous population of teal, as does the flood zone of the Niger.

These bird populations, remarkable in so many ways, cannot be protected unless enough reserves are placed along their migratory routes to provide winter quarters. Geese need damp open meadows, while little waders (Charadriidae) like mudflats and areas uncovered at low tide. Aiguillon Bay has large areas of this kind. A project is under consideration to build a dike separating the bay from the sea and to replace the mudflats by a freshwater lake. This would destroy a habitat essential for the survival of wildfowl in western Europe.

Large aquatic habitats must be preserved to safeguard wildfowl. This will require a vast effort of international co-operation, for the disappearance of several links in the chain would endanger the survival of already dwindling populations of migrants. These measures should be accompanied by sensible hunting regulations and by the elimination of spring hunting in countries where it is still permitted. Biologists have found that a large number of species of wildfowl breeding in Scandinavia do not have a population density corresponding to the habitats. (See Proc. 1st European meeting on Wildfowl Conservation, 1963, Nature Conservancy London 1964, especially Curry-Lindahl pp. 3–13.)

Public opinion tends to think of swampy regions as unproductive and useful only as depositories for refuse. Many people want to see them all drained. As Gabrielson said (1959), 'it seems that swamps were created to give engineers an opportunity to show their skill'. In temperate zones these habitats are always considered unhealthy, as breeding grounds for harmful 'miasmas'. In tropical zones swamps constitute real dangers for public health, as malaria is widespread.

Swamps have an important rôle to play, nevertheless. They regulate the flow of water, soaking it up like a sponge and then restoring it gradually. Marsh drainage contributes a great deal to the disorganization of river systems and catastrophic floods. Furthermore, swamps are far from unproductive. They supply good pasturage during droughts and considerable quantities of wood and aquatic plants. Swamps flooded at high tide provide fertilizer a long way from shore—an important factor in coastal fishing and oyster culture.

Studies in Georgia, USA, show that swamps in estuaries produce an average of 10 tons of dry organic matter per acre a year, whereas a wheat field in the same region yields about 3·4 tons, including straw and roots, and the most productive areas of western Europe do not produce more than 14 tons. Of course, these quantities do not compare in absolute value, for a much greater percentage of the wheat yield can be used for human consumption. The usefulness of the swamp product could, however, be considerably increased by fish culture. High yields have been obtained by this method in China and central Europe, and the profit is much greater than if these habitats had been transformed, at huge cost, into fields or meadows. Simple ecological considerations explain why a pond for plant-eating fishes yields a higher return in proteins than one drained for cattle-grazing. Warm-blooded animals, as Vibert and Lagler showed, need part of their energy to maintain a constant internal temperature, so they transfer less energy than cold-blooded animals. The yield may be twenty times greater in poor lands of the subtropical zone.

Many fishes, especially in tropical waters, perform local migrations which take them to zones that are flooded during the rainy season. The natives then do a great deal of fishing, for example in the tributaries of Lake Victoria, Kenya (Wasawo, 1963). Draining the swamps would destroy the breeding areas and upset the local economy.

Salt marshes bordering estuaries have particular economic importance because they are breeding grounds for marine fishes, and young eels spend the first months of their life there. Various species of fishes and crustaceans live in marshes, so fishing, both for profit and sport, provides an excellent return without any investment.

Waterfowl are also found in swamps, and the location of blinds and hunting grounds often provides a better return than the same land would if it were cultivated. In the USA, where hunting ducks and geese is a real business, almost two million hunting permits for waterfowl are issued annually, and it is estimated that hunters spend about $89,000,000. The association 'Ducks Unlimited' was founded in 1937 to counteract their marked decrease in North America. Funds are collected by subscription, especially in the USA, which provides 90% of the resources. They are used to administer nesting territories in Canada, principally in the provinces of Manitoba, Saskatchewan and Alberta where 75% of the ducks killed in the USA nest. This organization has an annual budget of over $500,000 and has spent $8,500,000 since it was established. The figures reveal the economic importance of these operations which keep the habitats in their original state, preserve the breeding stocks of ducks and yet assure an excellent profit.

Swampy zones also shelter fur-bearing mammals. Although the demand has dropped in recent years, partly because of breeding in captivity, the value of the mink, muskrat, and otter pelts collected in the USA is $10,500,000 a year. Reptiles, particularly alligators, also yield profits which would vanish if the habitats were transformed.

Finally, lake areas can be used for many sports from yachting to fishing. The latest statistics estimate that 21 million freshwater fishermen dedicate 385 million days a year to this sport in the USA. In France 2,717,000 permits were granted to anglers in 1963.

In many instances, marsh drainage has led to the creation of useless lands. The Netherlands has stopped costly transformation of swamps into fields. There is overproduction of a considerable number of agricultural products—especially butter and cheese—

whereas the rental of flooded areas for hunting, fishing or water sports is constantly rising.

The outstanding example of unsuccessful drainage is Lake Hornborgasjörn in Sweden. In its natural state the lake covered about 10 square miles and sheltered a luxuriant vegetation. Attempts to drain it were made in 1803, 1850 and 1870, and each time heavy losses were incurred. A fourth project in 1903 was equally unsuccessful, but a fifth was initiated in 1930. By 1958 4 million Swedish kroner had been spent, but Lake Hornborgasjörn is still a swampy area.

It is the same story in the case of certain vast programmes for the transformation of river basins. Fifty per cent of the waters of the Volga are now controlled by dams intended to produce electricity and irrigate arid districts. This has caused considerable evaporation in the irrigated zones, which did not receive as much water as was anticipated. Furthermore, it led to a drop in the level of the Caspian Sea (six feet between 1929 and 1946, and much more since then) and a progressive drying out of the Volga delta. These changes have had profound repercussions on the habitats; they have also caused a decline in the yield of fisheries and the production of Russian caviar, three-quarters of which comes from the Volga. In 1957 the take in the Caspian Sea was 65% lower than in 1917. Sturgeon has declined 50% since 1913. An incredibly rich complex is thus disappearing because of a series of mistakes on the part of man (Curry-Lindahl, *Europe—A Natural History*, New York (Random Press) 1965). In Egypt audacious projects are under way to domesticate the Nile, but no one can foresee the result.

In certain cases people have not hesitated to restore the original conditions. About half of Lake Mattamuskeet, covering 49,422 acres in North Carolina, was drained between 1915 and 1932. After a careful study, the lake was restored to increase the breeding of waterfowl.

Dam-building also threatens conservation of aquatic habitats. Hydro-electric installations change the flow of rivers, and artificial lakes often submerge areas where rare plants and animals are sheltered. Dams also prevent migration of fishes, particularly salmon, despite 'fish ladders'. After the construction of the Bonneville Dam on the Columbia River, the salmon catch dropped 80%, from 49·5 million pounds in 1911 to about 10 million in 1965.

Finally, some dams have completely disfigured beautiful mountain scenery. Lakes subject to rapid changes in elevation are surrounded by a lifeless girdle of dry mud. Construction of a dam should be regarded as part of the management of a region, in which conservation of natural habitats plays a part. Other sources of energy will soon be available but some landscapes should be preserved, even if a financial loss is entailed.[1]

The progressive reduction of humid zones is a source of anxiety to conservationists. In November 1962, the IUCN held an important conference in France at Saintes-Maries de la Mer, near the Camargue Reserve, in connection with the MAR project, a programme designed to preserve and administer wetlands in temperate zones. A detailed list of methods of conservation and restoration of wetlands was drawn up, together with an inventory of the most important areas to be preserved in Europe and North Africa. It is hoped that through international co-operation a conservation programme may be formulated.

9 WILL EROSION DEFEAT MAN?

The amount of soil that can be cultivated dwindles year by year because of man's poor management. We know, of course, that primitive man began to transform habitats by using fire, but in recent times erosion has been accelerated to a tremendous degree through an increasing need for wood, the establishment of industrial plantations, abandonment of conservative agricultural practices, and colonization of the world by western-style civilization. The economic and political evolution of certain continents, particularly Africa, spurs new nations to develop their resources to the detriment of the soil. At the same time human population is passing through an unparalleled crisis.

The 'protector of nature' can regret the transformation of wild habitats which caused the disappearance of animal and plant species. But the economist, the farmer and the businessman have seen how,

[1] *See Hydro-Electricity and Nature Protection*, IUCN 3rd Technical Meeting, Caracas (1952); same title *Pro Natura*, vol 2, 1955; and *The effects of dams on habitat and landscape*, IUCN 7th Technical Meeting, Athens (1958), Vol 2.

in a few years, lands have grown sterile and bare rock has appeared on hills scarred with gullies.

Once erosion has begun, there is a sort of natural self-destruction in which atmosphere, water and land work together to sterilize areas where man has upset the natural balance. Although there are still some very productive zones, the cancer of erosion has affected a large part of the earth. New zones are constantly being cleared and the cultivation 'front' advances like a wave unfurling amid zones which have hitherto been almost untouched. In its wake are impoverished lands and a ruined economy, while tornadoes carry away the soil in clouds of dust. The Mediterranean basin has long since lost a good part of its agricultural potential. The Great Plains in the USA have lost an alarming amount of their 'useful' surface. Erosive phenomena in Latin America are now posing serious social and economic problems, yet men continue to 'cultivate' untouched areas.

A large part of tropical Africa is eroded because of rapid deforestation, poor soil management and cultivation of products intended for export, which do not benefit the local biological economy. Asia is gradually being eroded, although the process, now thousands of years old, is slower than elsewhere.

The problem is an enormous one, involving the very existence of man. Pedology, or the science of soil, which was developed in Russia at the close of the 19th century, has become very important. Each country now has services studying the nature, evolution and conservation of soils. International organizations assure necessary co-ordination and prepare research programmes which have already borne fruit.

Moreover, farmers are now becoming aware of something biologists have known since the days of Aristotle: that there is an extraordinary diversity of natural habitats, as each one has a plant cover and an animal population directly related to its soil and climate. Farmers also realize that certain areas cannot be modified without running the risk of destroying them. These marginal zones must be preserved as they are, and all that man can do is to exploit their natural products, such as wood and game.

American specialists have divided soils into eight categories, according to the nature of the land (its physical and chemical composition), its slope, degree of erosion, climate and type of exploitation. The first three include lands which may properly be cultivated with or without special methods; the fourth includes land where temporary cultivation is possible; the next three include land unfit for agriculture, but where the plant cover may be exploited with or without special precautions, such as grasslands, forests, and moors; the last contains agriculturally unproductive land. This classification has been adopted, with certain modifications, by specialists all over the world.

CLASSIFICATION OF SOILS IN RELATION TO THEIR USE
(based on the land-classification system of the US Soil Conservation Service, which has been modified by several authors; Roman numerals refer to Land Class).

Characteristics	Principal use
1 Land suitable for cultivation	
i Flat land which can be cultivated without special precaution	Agriculture
ii Land which can be cultivated with elementary precautions (strip farming, grass cover)	Agriculture Grassland
iii Land which can be cultivated with intensive protection (long rotation, contouring, strip cropping)	Agriculture Grassland Maintenance of original vegetation
2 Land permitting temporary and limited cultivation	
iv Land which is very fragile because of its slope, soil structure or water system	Grassland Maintenance of original vegetation
3 Land unsuitable for agriculture	
v Land which is stable if it has a permanent plant cover and good management	Forest, extensive grassland Maintenance of original vegetation
vi Land requiring care to prevent accelerated erosion	Forest, extensive grassland Maintenance of original vegetation Urbanization
vii Very fragile land requiring great precautions	Forest, maintenance of original vegetation Urbanization Recreation

Characteristics	*Principal use*
4 Land unsuitable for exploitation	
viii Very fragile land, without pedologic structure, on a steep slope with a serious water problem	Maintenance of original vegetation Urbanization Recreation

NB Such a classification is based on the nature of the soil, slope, degree of erosion, climate and nature of exploitation. In reality, lands form a continuous series, and this justifies the sub-categories suggested by some authors.

Formations in categories v to viii are particularly well adapted for reserves to preserve the wild fauna and flora.

A certain balance must be maintained between forest, grassland and field. This balance made western and central Europe, part of Asia and the north-eastern United States rich. When they disregarded this principle, farmers ruined the great central plains of North America and the savannas of Africa and tropical America. Monoculture is a calamity for which we may have to pay a very high price.

This concept of balance has made it possible to restore certain areas. Under the direction of David E. Lilienthal, the Tennessee Valley Authority performed a gigantic task of restoration in 1935. Thanks to money advanced by the Federal Government, this organization built no less than 40 dams to produce electricity and regulate rivers. This checked erosion and made a great agricultural advance possible.

Programmes for agricultural renewal must be based on a preliminary ecological investigation by experts in a number of different disciplines. Let us hope that the population curve does not outstrip agricultural production resulting from wise land use. The terrible example of mountains reduced to bare rock should put us on our guard.

6 Pests and pesticides

Clearing land for agriculture has destroyed many animal and plant species, but it has also encouraged others to become predators or parasites. Introduction of alien forms upsets the natural balance, and the most harmful parasites are often animals or plants of foreign origin. When removed from surroundings where their populations are restricted by competitors and predators, they can increase very rapidly (see page 218).

'Pests,' particularly insects, must be regarded as an inevitable consequence of man's transformation of natural habitats (Kuenen, 1960). Multiplication of cultivated plants provides an enormous quantity of food for certain animals, whose numbers increase accordingly. This applies especially to cereals grown in newly cleared lands. Insects that had hitherto been restricted to wild grasses suddenly find tremendous food supplies. So wild grasslike associations are vast reservoirs of ravagers that switch to cultivated plants as soon as lands are tilled. In the semi-arid regions of the south-eastern USSR, 312 species of insects have been observed in uncultivated areas. Although only 135 of them appeared on newly-sown fields in the vicinity, the average density of insect population was nearly doubled. Among the score of very abundant insects in tilled areas the flea beetle is 20 times and the wheat thrips 360 times more numerous than in the wild grasses. An analogous transfer of the insect from the native plant host to the cultivated plant has been noted elsewhere, particularly in the case of the African sorghum (Uvarov, 1963).

Chemical weapons have been used to control these pests. The battle is directed chiefly at insects, animals most harmful to man because of their extraordinary abundance and destructive power. In the USA insects belonging to some 6500 species and about 2500 species of mites do more damage to forests than fire and disease combined. In India the loss of foodstuffs amounts to 360 million pounds sterling, sufficient to feed 40 million people. Some insects, moreover, are carriers of serious diseases affecting man, domestic animals, and occasionally cultivated plants.

Man has discovered that he can control harmful plants with herbicides, and the fungi destructive to crops with fungicides. Until quite recently almost all these substances belonged to the domain of mineral chemistry. A classic example is the famous 'Bordeaux mixture,' with a copper sulphate base, that is used as a spray to protect vineyards from parasitic diseases. Products with an arsenic base have also been used for a long time.

But now, thanks to the sensational progress of organic chemistry, man has at his disposal a large number of synthetic products. Dichlorodiphenyltrichloroethane, launched in 1942 as DDT, is a kind of pioneer in a realm where frequent new discoveries are still being made. It is the first of a long series of substances whose number has been multiplying since the end of the Second World War. In the United States alone 58,831 different brands of pesticides were officially registered under commercial names in 1966-7. In 1966 they represented an expenditure of 587 million dollars. Three hundred and fifty million pounds of pesticides are spread annually on about 85 to 100 million acres of cultivated land. These figures, although large, represent only 15% of the cultivated areas, 0·28% of the forests and 0·25% of the prairies, or a total of 4·62% of the surface of the USA (1962). Other countries, especially in western Europe, are close behind North America in the chemical warfare campaign. Many of these chemical substances have been known for a long time. DDT was synthesized in 1874 by Zeidler in Germany and HCH in 1825 by Faraday, or 68 and 118 years before they were known to be effective as insecticides.

Humanity owes a great deal to pesticides, which have made it possible to control dangerous plant parasites and reduce their destruction in every latitude. This is of paramount importance in view of the current food shortage. They have also enabled doctors to eliminate or check several diseases, notably malaria. The *Anopheles* was eradicated from the New World at the time of the great Brazil epidemic (see page 236). Until very recent times there were 400 million cases of malaria with 5 million deaths every year. Thanks to the campaign waged against insects in India, the number has dropped from 75 to 5 million, while average life expectancy has risen from 32 to 47 years. In Bengal the rice production of marshy

Right
Bald eagle (immature plumage): this large bird of prey, the American national emblem, is menaced by the indiscriminate use of pesticides

Below right
Common scoters killed by marine pollution caused by oil products: Sylt Island, Germany

Below left
Fish killed by pollution of the Broye waters, Switzerland

Above Pollution of cities by smoke and fog: industrial Sheffield
Below Pollution of rivers by detergents forming accumulations of toxic froth: River Trent, just below Nottingham

country has increased 15% as a result of improved sanitary conditions. In the Philippines absenteeism from schools due to malaria dropped from 40–50% in 1946 to 3% in 1949.

Synthetic pesticides represent a step forward in the defence of humanity, but they are violent poisons capable of eliminating all life. Some pesticides, related to substances affecting the human nervous system, were considered as weapons for chemical warfare, and the original discoveries, in Germany as well as elsewhere, were linked to research on the destruction of man rather than insects. Insecticides to-day kill useful as well as harmful insects. The majority are also toxic to other animals, especially cold-blooded vertebrates.

Of 95,000 fatal accidents in the USA in 1956, 152 were caused by these substances, and 94 of these were produced by pesticides with an arsenic base (*World Review of Pest Control* 1: 6–18, 1962). It is impossible to determine the long-range toxicity of synthetic insecticides, however, owing to the lack of objective information.

Some of these chemical substances can be transformed, under the influence of heat, humidity and sun radiations, into much more toxic bodies. Aldrin, for example, becomes the far more poisonous dieldrin (Rudd, 1960). Furthermore pesticides can be carried along the food-chain to areas where their harmful action is not counterbalanced by any usefulness. DDT was found in the liver of seals and penguins captured on the Antarctic continent, where no insecticide was sprayed. The abuse of pesticides thus leads to poisoning whose consequences are incalculable.

Numerous discussions have been devoted to this thorny problem. Rachel Carson's famous book, *Silent Spring*, first startled the world by drawing attention to it. Press articles bearing banner headlines aired the question in a spectacular fashion, while the reader would have benefited from a more considered treatment. It is difficult to be objective when conflicting interests such as chemical industry or agriculture obscure a problem about which we have extremely fragmentary data.

There is no doubt that the abuse of pesticides has caused disasters in the biological and even the economic realm. Pesticides are like drugs. Most of them are dangerous poisons, fatal if you take an overdose. No one would dream of taking ten to a hundred times the amount of medicine prescribed by a doctor, yet pesticides are sprayed regardless of the consequences.

1 PRINCIPAL INSECTICIDES IN USE

Numerous chemical substances are being used in the war against insects.[1] An inventory by J. Lhoste (*Les insecticides de synthèse*, Marseilles, 1962) gives more than 150, and this number keeps growing. The list does not include mineral and plant products still in use.

On the basis of their chemical composition and origin, insecticides can be divided into three major categories.

a *Mineral insecticides*. Most of these products have a base of arsenic (especially salts of arsenic acid or aceto-arsenites, such as 'Paris green,' an aceto-arsenite of copper) or fluorine (fluorides and fluorosilicates).

b *Insecticides of plant origin*. The most important are nicotine (extracted from tobacco), pyrethrum and rotenone.

c *Synthetic organic insecticides*. These are the leading products at present because they are manufactured on a large scale at relatively low cost.

Insecticides may be divided according to the chemical families to which they belong; Lhoste (*op. cit.*) groups them in 14 classes on this basis. Without going into detail the most important chlorine products are: HCH (hexachlorocyclohexane) and one of its compounds, lindane, chlordane, dieldrin, endrin, aldrin and toxaphene. DDT is still widely used along with some of its derivatives. Carbamates, such as dimetan, sevin and isolan, have recently become important. Others are the organophosphate compounds, such as JETP, TEPP, malathion, mevinphos and parathion; most of the new products belong to this chemical family.

It is also possible to classify insecticides according to their action. *Contact insecticides* penetrate the epidermis of the insect; DDT acts as if this cuticle did not exist. *Ingestion insecticides* penetrate through the digestive tract; and *inhalation insecticides* penetrate through the

---

[1] See especially 'Effects of pesticides on fish and wildlife: a review of investigations during 1960,' *Fish and Wildlife Service*, circ. no 143, Washington 1962; and Pesticide-Wildlife Studies. 'A review of Fish and Wildlife Service Investigations during 1961 and 1962.' *Fish and Wildlife Service*, circ. no 167, Washington, 1963.

respiratory tract. However, insecticides usually penetrate in various ways: HCM and aldrin through contact, ingestion and inhalation, dieldrin and toxaphene through the cutaneous covering and digestion.

Insecticides penetrate all the more rapidly if they are soluble in liquids; hence the solvent with which they are mixed is important. The most effective form is one which can mix with both fatty substances and water. These products are usually less toxic to vertebrates, as they are unable to penetrate their skin.

Insecticides affect both the metabolism, by paralysing respiratory mechanisms, and the nervous system, although at different speeds depending on the type of insect. They also poison higher animals. DDT is very toxic to cold-blooded vertebrates, less so to warm-blooded forms. Some phosphorus derivatives are violent poisons, although they rapidly decompose into much less harmful substances. Endrin and dieldrin are highly toxic; some are also more or less poisonous to plants, but the toxicity of these chemical substances varies largely with environmental conditions and the way in which they are used.

2 ABUSE OF INSECTICIDES

Although synthetic products have performed notable service in the fields of medicine and agriculture, their generalized use in increasing quantities has become a menace.

a: TOXICITY TO ANIMALS

All insects are sensitive in varying degree to substances which destroy entomological fauna. When a large area in France was sprayed with HCH to destroy maybugs, it was found that 48% of the species of Diptera, 21% of the Hymenoptera, 14% of the Coleoptera, 15% of the Hemiptera and 2% of the butterflies were destroyed simultaneously (Grison and Lhoste, 1960.) Changes in balance among different species are often produced, with consequences contrary to those desired. Insectivorous forms, including numerous useful species that attack crop ravagers, are frequently more sensitive than plant-eating insects the farmers wish to destroy.

Bees pay a heavy toll to insecticides, especially in Europe, when colza is treated. In 1954 20,000 hives were destroyed in the vicinity of Paris. Fortunately, legislation now requires French farmers to treat plants that produce honey with products non-poisonous to bees, such as toxaphene and diethion, and if possible, at a time when they are not in full bloom.

Most insecticides are also dangerous to other animals, including some economically important ones. Cold-blooded animals are poisoned together with aquatic larvae of mosquitoes or midges. Fishes poisoned by certain insecticides, particularly DDT, may die at once because of damage to their nervous system and their respiratory apparatus. In weaker doses these substances cause serious physiological disorders.

Treatment of swampy zones and mountain forests scored by torrents is often disastrous to fishes. Aerial spraying of DDT in the western USA and Canada caused the death of hundreds of thousands of trout and salmon. In Canada a count made over several years in the Miramichi Basin, New Brunswick, showed that DDT sprayed in adjacent forests poisoned or starved two-thirds of the salmon; there were no young fishes in 1954 or 1956, while insects preying on the forests thrived after each treatment. In British Columbia almost 100% of the salmon perished.

Grave repercussions may also be expected in tropical Africa following the treatment of certain expanses of water with insecticides. According to medical authorities, bilharziasis, a serious disease of parasitic origin, can only be suppressed by eradicating the mollusks which serve as intermediary hosts. So an entire freshwater fauna may disappear from the vicinity of inhabited areas. Even if mollusks are the only animals affected, their disappearance will have a profound effect on biological associations.

A similar instance is recorded by Blanc (1958) in the High Volta region. Large surfaces have been treated with lindane to conquer onchocerciasis, which causes blindness by forming cysts and ocular lesions. This ailment is transmitted by midges, whose aquatic larvae live on plants immersed in rapid streams. As no preventive remedy is known, the only means of combating the disease consists of eradicating the midges, and large-scale campaigns have been waged at regular intervals since 1955. This has caused the death of large numbers of fishes and also diminished food resources of the populations doctors were trying to protect. Measures have been taken to substitute DDT for lindane, so as to destroy the insects while causing less damage to the fish. Otherwise the inhabitants would have faced the unhappy alternative of either starvation or disease.

Pesticides affect coastal fisheries. Poured in increasing amounts on coastal marshes and estuaries they are then carried out to sea. All those whose toxicity has been examined in laboratories have been found harmful to crustaceans, mollusks, and marine fishes. The growth of young oysters has been prevented by doses of 3 in 100 million parts of chlordane, heptachlor and rotenone.

Insecticides are also poisonous to birds and mammals, including man. Lethal doses are relatively small for some of them. For example dieldrin is lethal to a rat at 0·13–0·20 grams per pound and endrin at 0·05 grams per pound. Birds feeding on prey containing insecticides can absorb a sufficient dose to kill themselves and their broods. Chemical warfare against rodents may lead to high mortality among other mammals. Poisoned bait for flesh-eaters causes serious losses among all vertebrates attracted by the food. For example, carcasses poisoned in certain European countries, notably Jugoslavia, to kill wolves, caused serious losses among vultures.

These effects, which are very apparent in the case of certain synthetic insecticides, are equally apparent when arsenicals and fluorine compounds are used. Fortunately, these are being used less and less. Campaigns against the fire ant in the USA caused such serious losses among warm-blooded vertebrates (up to 97% of the birds) that dieldrin had to be replaced by less toxic insecticides. In Indiana a single spraying of parathion caused the death of at least 65,000 robins and other songbirds. Losses reaching 80% of total populations have been recorded. Similar disasters have occurred in Europe. In Lincolnshire in 1960 no less than 10,000 deaths were caused by insecticides. Severe destruction has been caused by coating seeds with pesticides. Aldrin, dieldrin and heptachlor were used to combat certain insects, together with mercuric compounds acting like fungicides. Furthermore, insecticides often settle in the sexual glands of birds and cause partial or total sterility of the reproductive organs. This has been noted in numerous songbirds, especially the robin in the USA, and in ducks, geese and birds of prey like the sparrow hawk and bald eagle (*Haliaetus leucocephalus*).

which absorbs large amounts of insecticides from crabs and fish. When the tissues of 26 specimens of the bald eagle were analyzed by the Fish and Wildlife Service, 25 were found to contain DDT, occasionally in lethal quantity, for the species seems very sensitive to it. The rapid decline of the bird, the American national emblem, has in fact been ascribed to insecticides, for it has dwindled in coastal areas of the east which are often sprayed against mosquitoes. Only a small percentage of birds breed. In 1963 not a single nest was found in New England south of Maine and the average brood was much smaller in the Atlantic States than elsewhere.

In the Highlands of Scotland a widescale census of the golden eagle (*Aquila chrysaëtos*) revealed that the number of breeding pairs declined from 72% to 29% between 1937–60 and 1961-63. Observations show that decrease in reproduction and decline in populations are due to synthetic insecticides. Various pesticides have been found in the eggs of birds of prey (Lockie and Ratcliffe, 1964, see also Cramp, 1963).

Similar facts have been noted among birds of prey in other countries, particularly in Sweden (white-tailed eagle, eagle owl) and among pheasants and partridges, such as smaller clutches, sterile eggs and high mortality among the young.

In certain cases mortality due to insecticides is very high among warm-blooded vertebrates, but elsewhere deprivation, hunting, and disease are more effective killers. This was recently shown in England by experiments conducted by the Ministry of Agriculture.

Despite statements to the contrary there is no evidence of any relationship between the use of pesticides and diseases affecting human beings, such as cancer, leukemia and hepatitis.

b: TOXICITY IN RELATION TO PLANTS

Insecticides may cause direct harm to cultivated or wild plants. A large dose of HCH may retard plant growth and even affect the hereditary mechanism.

c: EFFECT ON THE SOIL

Large quantities of insecticides can cause partial sterilization of the soil, especially with regard to nitrogen-fixation processes. As sprayed products accumulate and often last a long time, the consequences are far-reaching.

d: DELAYED EFFECTS

Delayed effects may appear in different forms, particularly when chlorine derivatives are used. Insecticides do not cause animals to die immediately. They may accumulate until they are released with stored fat, especially during the winter, as Rudd (1960) observed in the muskrat. The effects being cumulative, the liberated doses prove lethal. Most insecticides accumulate in reserve fat, especially DDT, concentrating it at a rate of possibly 100 to 150 times the original proportion. Insecticides are also found in birds' eggs and milk of mammals, where they poison the young. Cows' milk is contaminated when the animals are given fodder treated with DDT.

But the greatest danger consists in a concentration of toxic substances along food chains. The pesticide is absorbed by a living being, where it becomes concentrated. It then passes into the body of a predator, which it may poison. The most famous case is that of the American robin (*Turdus migratorius*) (Barker 1958). Large quantities of DDT are sprayed to protect American elms from a disease transmitted by insects. The fraction falling on the ground is consumed by earthworms, which are not sensitive to DDT but concentrate it in their tissues. Robins eat great numbers of worms, absorb large amounts of toxic substances and die from locomotor paralysis and convulsions (*fig* 38). Three weeks after a spraying 86% of the nearby robins may be killed. Some ornithologists predict that the robin may have a fate comparable to that of the passenger pigeon. At least 140 species of birds in the USA are known to be victims of pesticides, chiefly because of concentration along food chains.

A similar concentration of toxic substances is found in aquatic biological associations along food chains passing from plankton to fishes, and then to water-fowl. Hunt and Bischoff (1960) found that when Clear Lake (California) was treated in 1949 with DDD, a substance related to DDT, to destroy mosquito larvae (*fig* 39), the product, applied at the rate of 1 dose in 70 millions, became concentrated in going from liquid form to the plankton (5: 1 million), then to plankton-eating and flesh-eating fishes, and finally

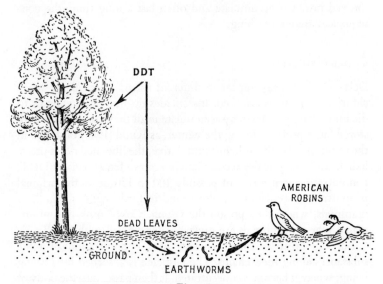

Fig. 38
Concentration along food chains of insecticide (DDT) *sprayed on trees.*

to grebes, where the doses varied from 40 to 2500 parts per million and caused a high mortality. Only 30 out of 1000 nesting pairs survived the treatment and these appeared sterile.

Such phenomena are observed in the case of most food chains. In addition to the transformation of pesticides into more toxic derivatives, this concentration shows the impossibility of determining the results of spraying in advance.

e: DISTURBANCES IN BIOLOGICAL BALANCES

The simplest change in the biological balance is a marked scarcity in the quantity of animal food available. In many cases insect populations decrease, with grave consequences to all insect-eating animals, especially birds. Rearing of their young depends on the supply of food, and, when insects disappear, this may be reduced to zero.

Even more significant are changes affecting the balance of differ-

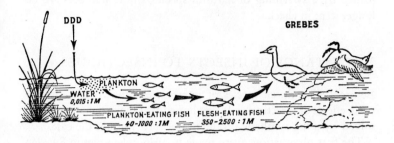

Fig. 39
Concentration along food chains of insecticide (DDD) *sprayed on Clear Lake, California. See explanation in text.*

ent species of insects, often to the detriment of man. A large population of parasitic insects on cultivated plants is accompanied by a population of predators which contribute to limiting the number of parasites. Synthetic products kill these human allies as well as the harmful insects. When the effects of the spraying vanish, populations of vegetarian insects have an excellent chance of reviving before the flesh-eating insects that prey on them. As the latter have second place in the food chains, increase in their numbers is slower. The destruction of an entire biological community is especially serious in areas near a balanced habitat, such as a tropical plantation. A sudden swarming of parasitic insects has often been observed after a pesticide treatment.

According to Basilewsky (*in* Kuenen, 1960), a flea (*Habrochila ghesquieri*) which parasitizes the coffee tree in the Congo and Uganda begins to swarm after DDT treatments on plantations. But another flea (*Apollodotus chinai*), a predator of the former, is destroyed by the same insecticides. Man has thus eliminated this ally and assisted the enemy of his trees.

In California applications of DDT to combat the lemon thrips (*Scirothrips citri*) and the cochineal insect attacking lemon trees (*Coccus pseudomagnoliarum*) have resulted in a multiplication of the number of insects which begin to swarm as soon as their predators vanish (Clausen, 1956). Massive infestations of this type have been observed in the case of numerous plant parasites.

In Europe destruction of flesh-eating insects is always accompanied by a swarming of harmful species whose numbers are no longer kept in check.

3 RESISTANCE OF INSECTS TO INSECTICIDES

Before 1945 a dozen species of insects were known to resist the toxic effects of insecticides. It was hoped that the problem could be solved by using synthetic products, but such was not the case.

The first observations were made in 1946, when flies in Sweden seemed to become immune to DDT. Similar resistance was then observed in Italy, Denmark, Egypt and the USA. In 1947 it was noted among mosquitoes (*Culex*) in Italy and among the *Anopheles*, resistant populations of which were observed in Greece in 1949, only three years after DDT was first used in the battle against malaria. A gradually increasing number of insects became immune, and some dangerous plant parasites and vectors of serious diseases like malaria and yellow fever appeared again. Almost every new chemical weapon devised was parried by the insect, though in certain conditions the resistance of an insect population is by no means irreversible.

At present more than 120 species are resistant to insecticides; half of these are plant parasites and the others disease carriers. These include 54 Diptera, 23 Hemiptera and 14 Lepidoptera (Brown, 1960). They are immune to DDT, to dieldrin and its derivatives, and to organophosphate products.

This resistance seems to be acquired by a Darwinian selection of stocks immunized naturally against toxic products which replace pre-existing populations. The resistance mechanism seems linked to the existence of detoxification enzymes which transform toxic products into harmless compounds. The process, common in the case of DDT and HCH, has not been so successful with organophosphate products. The phenomenon is closely related to the extraordinary fertility of insects and the rapidity with which one generation succeeds another.

Their physiological resistance is further complicated by a change in behaviour. Insects belonging to newly selected stocks have a behaviour pattern affording better protection from pesticides. The World Health Organization organized several meetings to discuss harmful insects, and its 8th General Assembly advocated an intensification of the struggle to eradicate disease carriers before they become resistant.

Insect resistance has also led to an increase of the chemical doses sprayed on habitats and the substitution of more toxic insecticides. As long as DDT was used in moderate doses, the mortality rate among birds and mammals was small. But its replacement by such products as dieldrin, heptachlor and organophosphate derivatives like parathion and malathion, has destroyed many animals, even though some of these products are less stable than DDT. The toxic nature of insecticides does not always follow an ascending curve. Arsenic and mercuric compounds, such as nicotine (fatal in a dose of 0·015 gram per 2·2 lbs.), were fully as dangerous as synthetic products, if not more so.

Resistance, one can predict, will develop as new products appear. If the exposure of insect populations to insecticides determines the selection of resistant strains, the same might apply to vertebrates that are accidentally slaughtered. This has been noted in the case of the trout (*Salmo trutta*) and the gambusia (*Gambusia affiinis*). But the phenomenon appears far more slowly owing to the much greater interval between generations.

4 CHEMICAL WARFARE AGAINST UNDESIRABLE PLANTS

Animals are not the only victims of an overdose of synthetic products. The use of herbicides to suppress a large number of weeds is also to blame for destruction of plant communities and for thinning out some species.

The farmer has many complaints against weeds. They deprive cultivated plants of water, air, light and mineral elements. Some have poisonous leaves, like the European tansy ragwort and water crowfoot which harm cattle, or poisonous seeds, such as the wheat smut (*Lychnis githago*). Weeds are also hosts to diseases or shelter harmful, plant-eating insects. Losses to agriculture from these plants are at times as great as those caused by insects.

The substances developed to eliminate these undesirable weeds are much more effective than the old methods. It is claimed that one gallon of herbicide has the same effect as seven men working with seven hoes for seven years. Some[1] destroy all plants, as, for example, chlorate of sodium and potassium, and urea substitutes, such as Monuron or CMU. Others are selective herbicides which may act by contact, such as the xanthates and calcic cyanimide that also functions as a fertilizer. These are the translocation or internal action herbicides, known as growth substances. Often derivatives of phenoxyacetic acid (2.4D was developed in the USA in 1942; MCPA in England that same year) act like plant hormones, although chemically different from them. Herbicides are composed of very divergent chemicals. Along with mineral products (sulphuric acid, cynanimide sulphates, borax, chlorates), numerous organic products are used (acetamides, derivatives of halogenous organic acids, derivatives of aryloxyacetic acids, derivatives of carbamic acid, carbolic acid and cresols). Minute doses produce abnormal growth and rapid wilting. Most of these herbicides destroy dicotyledons but are harmless to monocotyledons. Some of the latter however, like *Stratiotes* and sedges, are very sensitive to these substances. As their toxic effect on animals is very weak these herbicides cause minimal harm to biological associations, except in the case of a few, like 2.4D, which acts like a cumulative poison on birds, especially ducks.

Herbicides exert a great influence on plant associations, but are not injurious to fields or other artificial habitats, where they destroy many 'weeds'. Nevertheless the elimination of dicotyledons may cause certain species to become rare and may even harm pasture and fodder. To a naturalist the damage is even worse when herbicides are sprayed on slopes, dikes, railroad embankments and roadsides, as some plants seek refuge here after disappearing everywhere else.

The situation is even worse in aquatic areas. In trying to eradicate harmful plants, man runs the risk of destroying whole communities

[1] See Selective weed killers and growth regulators, *Journées françaises d'information de la Féd. nat. de protection des cultures*. Paris, Nov. 28-9, 1956

Lhoste, J., 1958. *Les désherbants chimiques*. Paris (Orstom)

Klingman, G. C. and Noordhoff, L. J., 1961. *Weed Control as a Science*, New York (J.Wiley)

Audus, L. J. (edit.) 1964. *The Physiology and Biochemistry of Herbicides*, London (Academic Press).

of aquatic forms, especially as herbicides are carried long distances. According to Westhoff and Zonderwijk (1960), 17% of the flora of the Netherlands could be destroyed by excessive use of herbicides in Dutch waters. The effects are aggravated by the fact that, as plant communities change, the balance of the aquatic fauna is upset, and some herbicides have toxic effects on fishes and spawn.

Finally, herbicides make it possible for man to change whole plant associations. This was attempted in the 'sagebrush' area in the western USA, a poor region economically but one of very great biological interest. Its animal communities included the pronghorn and the sage grouse. Cattle breeders developed a plan to replace sagebrush by cereals. Millions of acres were sprayed with herbicides, but the rain pattern and soil conditions do not seem favourable to any vegetation other than the one which developed naturally. So man may destroy an entire habitat without profit.

5 RATIONAL USE OF CHEMICAL WEAPONS

Since ancient times man has waged a battle against parasites and insect carriers of disease. With the development of synthetic chemical products about twenty years ago, he found that, for the first time, he could control most harmful insects. By immediately abusing these chemical weapons, man to-day may have literally poisoned the whole world.

Severe measures—short of a complete ban—should be taken against the abuse of toxic products. In ploughing fields, man has created an artificial habitat, the only one capable of providing his food. He has multiplied predatory animals, which can only be controlled by artificial means. Insecticides have thus become part of the agricultural pattern since natural methods will not control the swarming of pests in an artificial environment.

We can seek new methods of warfare, and one of the best is biological warfare, which destroys insects or other harmful living creatures by a rational use of their natural enemies. In its natural habitat every insect is accompanied by a certain number of predators that limit its populations. (There are 14 orders and 224 families of these insects). An insecticide treatment kills them all indiscriminately and often leads to a swarming of parasites. All birds, but especially songbirds, are enormous consumers of insects, particularly during the nesting season. In 1921 Forbush estimated that in the USA birds destroyed enough insects to save the national economy 444 million dollars. As in the case of insecticides, however, birds eliminate both good and harmful forms.

In a transformed area no natural brake can restrain the swarming of ravagers. To combat introduced insects which have become pests, man can use predatory forms to re-establish the original prey-predator balance of the native habitat. In 1881 the parasitic hymenopteran *Apanteles glomeratus* was acclimatized in the USA to combat an alien cabbage parasite. In June 1967, four gallons of ladybugs were brought from California to New York, where they were released in Riverside Park to devour aphids and other insect pests. At present no less than 95 species of parasites or predators of the insect pests have been acclimatized in the USA; 390 other species were introduced unsuccessfully Clausen, 1956). Similar experiments have been made in other parts of the world.

Good results can also be obtained by introducing insect diseases. Various micro-organisms, including viruses, bacteria and fungi, can cause these. Viruses are often very effective. For example they destroy the processionary caterpillars (*Thaumetopoea pityocampa*) which ravage French pine forests. Bacteria have an advantage in that they can be grown cheaply and sprayed like an insecticide. Also they only affect insects. 'Milky diseases' killed the larvae of the rutelid beetle (*Popillia japonica*) and the maybug (*Melolontha melolontha*). The bacillus *Bacillus thuringiensis* has been used on caterpillars of several moths. As it kills the insects by secreting certain poisons which have no effect on man and other animals, it acts like a biological insecticide (Grison and Lhoste, 1960).

New methods make it seem possible that man will be able to control some ravagers by a kind of auto-extinction of their numbers. This involves introducing sterilized males, to compete with normal males. The method, developed by E.F. Knipling,[1] has been tried on a large scale in Florida and the Dutch West Indies, in Curaçao, in the fight against a fly causing serious damage to cattle. *Callitroga hominivorax* lays its eggs in cattle sores, and the swarming larvae

[1] See The Eradication of the Screw-worm fly, *Scient. Amer.* 203 (4): 54-61, 1960.

produce infections and high mortality. In the USA these flies spend the winter in restricted areas—southern Florida, Texas, New Mexico, Arizona and California—from which they invade huge territories in the spring. As the population is small for several months, it has been calculated that if a number of sterilized males equal to twice the normal male population can be introduced, the reduction of the birth-rate will cause the population to become extinct in four generations. When males were sterilized by irradiation, their reproductive behaviour was not changed and the flies practically disappeared. A Florida insectarium provided 50 million flies a week. They were dispersed by light planes in bags, each of which contained several hundred sterilized males. When the operation was complete, some 3·5 million sterilized flies had been released.

Although this method presents numerous difficulties, due to the monogamous habits of some insects, it may play an important role in the restriction of insect pests. It could be greatly improved by sterilizing males without having to capture them. Unfortunately, the only sterilizing chemicals known to-day have cancerous properties.

While these methods are much less dangerous to the balance of nature than pesticides, the latter are still generally more effective. It is essential to study new synthetic products. Organic chemistry is rich in possibilities, and often a minute change in formula may modify the action of complex substances on living beings. It may even make them completely inactive. As every species of insect has a slightly different biology and a special chemical cellular 'mechanism,' we may hope that pesticides will be discovered which are harmful only to insects, and only to those we are trying to destroy.

The method of application also influences the toxicity of these products. For example, it can be arranged so that pesticides which are swallowed are consumed by plant-eating insects, the only plant parasites, and not by the flesh-eating insects most useful to man.

Systemic insecticides are interesting from this point of view. These are substances given to plants to make their sap poisonous to predatory insects. Similar insecticides have also been developed to combat animal parasites. Most of them belong to the series of organophosphate compounds. One of the first was schradan, discovered by G. Schrader in 1937 in Germany, but no longer used because it is highly toxic, even to plants. Other bodies like demethon and endothion have been used to combat flies and aphids. When put in contact with seeds or roots, these substances spread throughout the plant.

Excellent results have been obtained by using systemic insecticides on tropical plants and in temperate climates. They often produce better and more lasting results than powdered insecticides but, unfortunately, most of them are highly toxic to warm-blooded animals, and no one yet knows what effect they have on man and domestic animals on swallowing agricultural products treated with them. They should therefore be used with care. It is surprising to see how many substances are applied in massive doses before their impact on nature has been determined.

The method of application must also be considered. Any substance can be used safely in or near a dwelling provided it is not toxic to man. In fields and habitats transformed by man pesticides are not dangerous if used in normal amounts. Since these habitats are completely artificial, only chemical insecticides can control plant parasites, and repercussions on other animals are minimal. This does not mean that man should 'poison' these areas, as that would have serious consequences, particularly on the soil. It must be remembered that pesticides attack the evil, but not its causes; brutal limitation of an animal population does not prevent it from swarming immediately afterwards. Its recuperative power depends entirely on environmental conditions, rather than on how large a fraction of the population is eliminated. In so far as possible, chemical controls should be accompanied by agricultural practices favourable to a good biological balance.

The situation is altogether different in natural habitats, where the species are better balanced. There insecticides should be used merely as an aid to natural defences. This is particularly true of orchards, which, from the ecological point of view, are more or less equivalent to light woodland. An excellent example of such antiparasitic treatment was reported in Canadian apple orchards, one of the chief resources of Nova Scotia (Patterson, 1956; Pickett, 1960). When insect populations became resistant between 1930 and 1949, farmers replaced the poison they were using by DDT and other synthetic insecticides. These caused a decrease in the number of ravagers but, since they also exterminated the predators, each

Flowering water hyacinths

Water hyacinths invading an arm of the Congo at Stanley Pool: an example of an 'escaped' plant becoming a pest

Achatina shells strewn over a plantation; this shows the population density of these molluscs in tropical areas where they have been introduced. After three years, the potential progeny of a single mollusc is 8 billion individuals

treatment was immediately followed by a swarming of parasites.

The method of treatment was then changed, the doses reduced and spaced at greater intervals so as to preserve and assist the fauna limiting the predatory insects. Attacks became proportionately less numerous, and from 80 to 94% of the fruit was unharmed, the same result as from the massive treatments. Man was aiding the ecological defences instead of destroying the natural balance.

Similar experiments have been undertaken in other regions with varying results. Since there is no universal solution, each treatment must be adapted to the particular environmental conditions.

At times it is advantageous to keep cultivated terrains in a state comparable to that of a natural habitat. Grison and Lhoste (1960) cite an example illustrating how agricultural practices influence the abundance of predatory insects. In southern Italy, as in other Mediterranean regions, the current tendency is to remove all underbrush in olive groves. It was found that this caused a swarming of the olive fly (*Dacus oleae*) despite the use of insecticides. The weeds acted as shelters where insects parasitizing the fly took refuge when the olive trees were being sprayed. 'Clean culture' methods may thus be as injurious to cultivated plants as to the soil balance. In certain instances these adventitious plants may shelter the parasites which return to the plants as soon as the treatment is over. Fallow or abandoned lands may also serve as sources of infestation. The preservation of hedges, brambles and other plants, which at first seem useless, is very helpful in maintaining a balance between populations of insects and control of harmful species. Monoculture and the regrouping of plots of land thus destroy valuable aids to man.

Pesticides are even more dangerous in natural habitats, like forests and aquatic areas, where they can start chain reactions leading to serious disturbances of the natural balance. Accidents due to pesticides and the destruction of harmless animals are common in the USA where enormous quantities of these substances are used. Tropical countries are also beginning to abuse them. In some European countries, a better agricultural balance has preserved crops from any swarming of dangerous parasites. In France no pesticide can be sold without endorsement from the Ministries of Agriculture, Industry and Public Health. There are strict laws governing both the approval and the use of the new product.

Manufacture and sale of these substances are in the hands of the great chemical industry, which investigates their toxic effects. There is also international technical collaboration on several levels, for example FAO, WHO, and the International Commission on Methods of Analysing Pesticides, or ICMAP.

On the whole, man must consider pesticides as just one of the elements in the struggle against the enemies of his crops. Ecological studies, which should precede cultivation of any region, ought to include an analysis of the native insects, particularly those which might transfer to cultivated plants. This would make it possible to choose those least likely to be exposed to a swarming of parasites. Furthermore, agricultural methods unfavourable to ravagers ought to be used. Only then should man have recourse to the chemical weapons at his disposal. The International Union for Conservation of Nature and the International Council for Bird Preservation have pointed this out on numerous occasions.

In certain instances large-scale use of pesticides should be restricted to government services. They alone are capable of making the necessary preliminary tests and of determining the quantity and methods of application. The prescription of drugs is limited to the medical profession. Pesticides are also violent poisons, yet anyone can buy them and intoxicate nature as well as his compatriots. Man must learn that the chemical warfare in which he is engaged will result in a Pyrrhic victory unless he stops abusing powerful destructive weapons which can act either as beneficial drugs or as Borgian poisons.

7 Pollution by waste products

Man will be killed by the excess of so-called civilization.
J. H. Fabre, *Souvenirs entomologiques*, vi

Until quite recent times, or at least until the Industrial Revolution, waste products were chiefly organic and could easily be transformed by bacteria and fungi. Industry has produced more resistant substances with a greater 'duration of life'. Certain oil products, for example, are attacked only very slowly by certain very specialized bacteria. Beaches marked with long black lines bear witness to this. Special mention should be made of radioactive bodies—some of which are completely artificial—whose effects may last millions of years. The situation has worsened because industrial development, linked to the population explosion, has greatly increased the volume of waste.

Man's attitude towards these products has not changed. He continues to pour them into the air and the waters regardless of the consequences. So long as the speed of transformation matched the quantity of waste, there was a kind of balance. To-day, however, nature can no longer absorb either qualitatively or quantitatively the enormous mass which man goes on discarding. These products contain a thousand chemical compounds and are literally poisoning the earth.

The elimination of certain substances is not easy. Furthermore, purification of water and transformation of waste are so expensive that people prefer to close their eyes to the facts. However, some progress has been achieved now that every country has protective laws and international conventions govern the high seas. Technical procedures have been developed to filter various kinds of waste products. No area is safe when harmful bodies can be carried great distances by rivers, ocean currents and winds. The worst menace of all, the nuclear menace, is capable of poisoning the entire world.

1 POLLUTION OF FRESH WATERS

That pollution of fresh water is by no means new is evident from the fact that both the Zend Avesta and the Scriptures have precepts about waste and how to dispose of it so as to protect man and his water supply. The transformation of river water into 'blood', one of the ten Egyptian plagues described in Exodus, is probably due to a biological pollution and related to the 'red tides' of coastal waters. But the question did not give cause for alarm until recently. At the beginning of the 19th century M.P.s were still fishing for salmon at Westminster Bridge, and drinking water for the city of Paris was taken straight from the Seine until the end of the 18th century. Salmon has, unfortunately, vanished from the Thames, and below Clichy the Seine water in summer is half sewage.

The first cause for the pollution of fresh waters is, of course, the increase of human population and the growth of towns. Large cities discard an enormous volume of partially purified water that contaminates the reaches of rivers downstream. The second factor is linked to the development of industry, which deposits chemical waste products in the rivers.

The problem is extremely serious in Europe and North America, especially in the eastern United States. The Ruhr, Luxemburg, Belgium, northern France and England are sad examples of what has happened. In the USSR no less than 225,000 miles of rivers are seriously polluted.

The situation is deteriorating every year, especially as the modern tendency apparent in western Europe is to decentralize factories, putting them in areas which were hitherto agricultural and thus multiplying centres of contamination.

To make matters even worse, water requirements continue to rise. In the USA the annual consumption per person is 330,000 gallons, and it is estimated that this figure will double in the next forty years, excluding requirements for hydraulic energy and navigation. The quantity of surface and underground water is limited, and only a fraction of the latter can be utilized. Already a water shortage is apparent, even in areas with plenty of rainfall. At certain seasons the industrial zones of eastern and northern

France rely on weekends and vacations to permit the underground water table to return to normal.

The first cause of pollution is the waste carried off by sewers (Ellis, 1937; Klein, 1962; Erichsen, 1964). The continual growth of cities, various technical difficulties, and the high cost of equipment are responsible for inadequate or nonexistent garbage disposal. The Rhône below Geneva is periodically polluted by drainage from the Verbois dam, which receives sewer water from the city, and its effects are felt as far as Culoz, 37 miles downstream. The lower valley of the Seine used to be famous for its abundant fish, and 58 species could be caught at Quilleboeuf. They have all disappeared. The lakes of the Swiss and French Alps are polluted. The lower strata of Lakes Annecy, Nantua and Zurich lack oxygen from August to December because of sewer water and the resulting overturning of the chemical balance. The lake bottoms fill up, aquatic vegetation is replaced by fungus and bacteria, and even the fishes suffer, particularly the famous Grayling Chevalier. Elsewhere birds are the victims; in one day more than 7,000 dead or dying ducks were found along pools where the sewers of a California city are emptied.

The second and much more serious type of pollution results from industrial expansion. It can be divided into various categories, depending on the chemical nature of the products involved. Oil products spread in ugly streaks and form a surface film that prevents oxygen from diffusing in the water. Synthetic detergents, which are increasingly popular, are even more harmful because they change the surface tension. Their effects are far-reaching, since they diminish the water's capacity to retain oxygen, inhibit bacteria attacking organic substances, and produce froth that accumulates on the surface. In certain doses they are toxic to fishes and even aquatic plants. Anionic detergents, the most widely used, are toxic in doses of 0·038 to 0·095 grams per gallon. The water crowfoot (*Ranunculus aquatilis*) cannot grow when the water contains 0·004 grams per gallon of detergent, and the *Potamogeton's* growth is checked if 0·009 grams are present. When ducks frequent waters loaded with detergents, the fatty substances impregnating their wings are dissolved and the plumage absorbs water. Some birds in the USA are said to have drowned because of this (quoted by Klein, 1962).

Other substances, such as waste from coke plants and gas factories (phenols, tars, cyanide derivatives), numerous copper, zinc, lead and nickel salts, and fluorides act like real poisons. Trout are killed at a concentration of 0·002 grams per 1·7 pints of copper sulphate and perch at 0·101 grams per 1·7 pints. In the USA a mill-race over 9 miles long was completely sterilized by a deposit of copper salts producing a concentration of 0·015 to 0·030 grams per 1·7 pints. Other products have corrosive properties, particularly acids and bases which change the water's pH and thus modify the balance of the micro-organisms. Sprayed insecticides and herbicides also cause serious changes in fresh water.

These substances introduce bodies and violent poisons into waters which either did not have them at all or had them in infinitesimal quantities. Some can modify the colour, transparency, surface tension, even the resistance and temperature of the waters. Finally, they change the taste and smell, and they may render water unfit for human consumption or damaging to aquatic fauna.

These substances act in various ways in a highly complex natural milieu. Fresh waters form biological associations containing very different elements, with multiple food chains that start from a large number of micro-organisms, bacteria, algae and fungi. These transform organic matter so that it can be absorbed by higher creatures. The balance of mineral salts and organic substances is usually extremely unstable, and often a very slight change in the ionic equilibrium or the percentage of mineral or organic elements is sufficient to inhibit or accelerate certain transformations. Poisonous organic substances poured into this fragile habitat act differently from mineral pollutions.

Organic substances deposited in rivers are attacked by micro-organisms, chiefly bacteria that grow in oxygen. If the concentration does not exceed a certain point, the waters can regenerate themselves thanks to the bacteria in suspension. Nitrates, sulphates and phosphates are formed, while compounds rich in carbon become carbonates. These transformations require large amounts of oxygen, however, so the process involves a small concentration of the substance and a high percentage of dissolved air. The degree of pollution can be estimated by determining the biochemical demand for oxygen (BDO), which represents the quantity of oxygen the water absorbs in five days at a temperature of 64°F.

As soon as the concentration of polluting substances becomes too high, their degradation exhausts all the oxygen dissolved in the water. Fishes are literally asphyxiated. Furthermore, the action of aërobic bacteria is supplanted by that of anaërobic forms, which degrade oxygen combined in chemical bodies (nitrates, sulphates, organic compounds). The toxic substances thus formed cause putrefaction of the water by forming derivatives of methane, amines, sulphur or phosphorus. The deposit of too many organic products thus causes both lack of oxygen and serious poisoning produced by decomposition products. This is why apparently inoffensive organic substances, such as wood shavings, may have extremely grave effects on the chemical and biological balance of waters by diminishing their autopurifying power.

PRINCIPAL INDUSTRIAL POLLUTIONS (excluding radioactive pollutions; after Klein, 1962, simplified)

A: Mineral or chiefly mineral pollutions
    Chemical industries
    Mines (panning ore, waste)
    Electro-chemical industries
    Refrigeration waters (boilers, electric power stations

B: Organic pollutions
    a Oil products
        Oil refineries
        Plastic and rubber industries
        Miscellaneous industries (lubricants)
    b Phenol derivatives
        Gas works
        Coke plants
        Distillation of woods, tars, creosotes, etc.
        Dye-works
   c Pollutions caused by biological waste
        Tanneries
        Distilleries
        Breweries
        Sawmills
        Canning industries
        Sugar refineries
        Slaughterhouses
        Textile mills
        Paper mills

Fishes are extremely sensitive to certain chemical products and to the percentage of air in the waters. A large number of mineral salts, chiefly lead, zinc, copper, mercury, silver, nickel and cadmium, precipitate and solidify the mucus covering of the gills. Experiments have shown that fishes placed in waters with a certain percentage of heavy metal or acid salts display a notable acceleration of the movements of the gills. These motions then become irregular, slow down, and the fishes die of asphyxia.

Other substances commonly responsible for polluting fresh waters act like internal poisons, paralysing biochemical reactions and upsetting cellular oxidations. Cyanide compounds and soluble sulphurs massively reduce respiratory exchanges. Ammonia and its derivatives pass through the gills, spread in the blood and block respiration by transforming the pigment in the red corpuscles. They apparently attack the globules themselves.

Fishes are very sensitive to lack of oxygen. Although eels and most Cyprinidae can get along fairly well without it, numerous others, like the Salmonidae, are asphyxiated as soon as the amount of dissolved oxygen drops below a certain level.

Furthermore, as fishes are cold-blooded organisms, their metabolic rate depends strictly on temperature; a thermal rise of 18°F multiplies by 2·7 the oxygen consumption of a rainbow trout. The effects of pollution are much more telling in warm waters than in cold because physiological requirements there are greater.

As pollution of organic matter greatly reduces the percentage of dissolved oxygen, the sensitivity of fishes to pollution by mineral substances is increased. Experiments have shown that fishes in a well-aërated area can resist concentrations of toxic products which would be fatal in waters less rich in oxygen. And pollutions usually consist of mixtures of both organic and mineral substances.

Finally, the pollution of fresh water is highly detrimental to man. Most large cities depend on rivers for their water, and the treatment of highly polluted water is becoming more and more difficult. Traces of certain elements which no processing can remove may be injurious to public health.

Pollutions are also harmful to industry, for high concentrations of chemical products are incompatible with refrigerating machinery and, more directly, with the chemical industry, paper mills and food industries. Many factories are forced to treat water to rid it of products received upstream. They then deposit it again in the river, charged with new impurities. The industrialist is one of the first victims of his own pollution.

Most countries realize the gravity of these problems. Legal measures exist which forbid deposits and regulate the pouring out of waste water, and technical methods of purification are improving. Each case should be studied in relation to the nature of the pollutions, their volume and the possibilities of autopurification of water-courses. Then measures can be integrated in a plan covering the entire river basin.

Some countries have adopted a classification of rivers. They forbid the deposit of any waste in some, but allow others to become natural sewers. This is the case in the USA and Belgium. Others are trying to contain pollution by adequate technical measures. In Great Britain no waste water may be emptied until it is treated and deposited in communal sewers. Similar laws exist in Germany.

The technical measures, which we shall not discuss here, are extremely varied. The ideal solution in a factory is, of course, a 'recycling' of waters in a closed circuit with residues emptied somewhere else than in the river. On 30th June 1967, every State in the USA was required to submit its plans for combating pollution of interstate waters. In 1966, 791 plants were constructed to treat water waste as against 691 the previous year.

2 POLLUTION OF THE SEAS

For a long time waste products have been deposited in the seas.[1] Despite the large volume of water, these substances can have a great impact. Currents, instead of carrying deposits out to sea, may bring them back to shore far from the spot where they were emptied. Both in North America and in Europe famous beaches have been polluted by sewers and marred by surprising waste products.

Contamination of the seas can also modify the balance of marine organisms, particularly plankton, causing swarming of numerous algae which make the water putrid when they die. There is a

[1] See E. A. Pearson (editor), *Waste Disposal in the Marine Environment*, Oxford (Pergamon Press) 1960.

definite relationship between the composition of animal associations and the degree of pollution, as certain more resistant species can swarm where the marine fauna and flora are completely sterilized.

In Portugal and the Scandinavian fiords pollution has affected fisheries, while 'poisoned barriers' at river mouths prevent certain fishes, like salmon, from going upstream.

Constantly moving sea water can quickly make industrial and domestic waste harmless, but this does not apply to oil products which have been dumped into the sea in increasing quantities as industry and transport have developed (see Hawkes 1961, Tendron 1962, Zobell 1962). As these substances do not mix with water, they float on the surface, forming a film of varying thickness. Marine currents carry them great distances, especially towards beaches. This form of pollution is all the more serious since most oil products are remarkably stable and are attacked by only a small number of slow-working microbial organisms.

Thirty years ago British shipbuilders agreed that they would not dump any petrol product less than 50 miles from the coasts. Other countries in Europe followed suit, and in 1936 the USA applied the same prohibition to a 100-mile zone. These measures proved ineffectual because marine currents carry back to the coasts products deposited far out at sea, and also because the oil business has continued to expand. After the Second World War pollution of the seas reached a point which aroused international concern (see UN report, 1956). Most of these products come from oil-tankers transporting crude oil. After the contents are discharged the tankers are loaded with water to serve as ballast, but they still contain oil products which mix with the water and are eventually cast into the sea when the tanks are emptied of water. Even after this, a sticky mass remains in the cargo tanks; it solidifies and cannot be emptied when the cargo is discharged. This 'sludge', which fills tanks and obstructs pipes, has to be treated with steam and hot water under pressure to liquify it. It is then poured into the sea. A further source of pollution is water from various leaks which becomes charged with grease, oils and fuel before being dumped into the sea.

At first it is difficult to imagine the volume of waste deposited. During 1966 approximately 1,160 million tons of oil products were carried at sea. Assuming that only one-thousandth of these products becomes waste, that still leaves a million tons spread over ocean surfaces, principally along the American and European coasts. These figures are perfectly logical when one recalls that a large modern tanker empties between 3,000 and 5,000 tons of water containing 100 to 200 tons of oil products every time it clears its cargo tanks. Tendron (1958) estimates the proportion of waste as 1%, which means that in 1955, for example, when 295 million tons of oil products were carried, 2·95 million or 250·73 cubic feet a day were deposited in the world oceans.

Among the most seriously polluted areas are the Mediterranean, which is used by all the oil-tankers from the Near East, the eastern Atlantic, with the Brittany coasts exposed to N. W. winds, the English Channel, and the North Sea. Cold seas seem to be more polluted than warm ones, and shallow seas more polluted than deep ones.

The first to suffer are the birds. When they alight on the surface, their feathers become soaked with ineradicable oil products. Their plumage thus loses its insulation and waterproofing properties and the bird soon dies from congestion and poor thermo-regulation, as it is no longer isolated from the liquid environment by the air mattress enclosed within its feathers. It is difficult to estimate the numerical loss since most birds die on the high seas. The only guide is the number of bodies found on beaches. On the Avalon Peninsula of Newfoundland, 464 bodies of thick-billed murres (*Uria lomvia*) were counted on each mile of the west coast in March, 1956, in addition to birds of 11 other species. This situation is especially serious, since numerous marine birds winter in this part of the Atlantic, and oil traffic has intensified since the opening of the St. Lawrence seaway. It also explains how a colony of auks, consisting of at least 250,000 birds, could be destroyed in two years in these waters. It has been estimated that between 20,000 and 50,000 birds —belonging to some fifty species, including 14 species of ducks— are victims of oil pollution along the Dutch coasts in a single year. There are probably 250,000 annual victims in Great Britain —especially auks, scoters, gulls and divers. It is the same story in other coastal areas of Europe, especially the North Sea which acts as the winter quarters of numerous ducks from the Arctic, notably the long-tailed duck or 'old squaw' (*Clangula hyemalis*).

On 16th April, 1967, dead and dying birds were washed ashore along a 40-mile stretch of Cape Cod. About 40 birds per mile were collected on the beaches, their feathers covered with a layer of thick, gummy oil. Only one bird survived out of 200 taken to the Audubon Society.

On 11th April at least 1,500 wild ducks died when thick black oil drenched them on their feeding grounds off the South Jersey coast. The coast guard said the oil had probably been dumped far out at sea by a tanker.

Of 6,000 birds brought ashore after the *Torrey Canyon* disaster in March 1967, less than 500 were saved. Some 25,000 sea birds perished at one of the largest bird sanctuaries in western Europe, Ile Rouzic in Brittany.

Birds are not the only animals to suffer from oil products. They change the surface tension so important to planktonic animals while some of their chemical components poison marine invertebrates, crustaceans, and even certain fishes. Serious losses have been reported on famous fishing grounds. Distilled oil and tar products act on the nervous system by causing abnormal excitement and hypersensitivity. Difficulties in balance, locomotion, and breathing follow and the mortality rate is high. This is especially true of fishes like mullet, which feed on small prey and organic debris charged with oil. The spawn, particularly in the form of eggs floating on the surface, is also affected. In April 1967, French fishermen moved millions of young oysters from beds in northern Brittany, away from the oil of the tanker *Torrey Canyon*.

Man is seriously threatened by cancerous compounds of oil products, such as benzopyrene, found in shellfish, oysters, mussels and razor-fish (*Solen*). Although nothing is known about how these bodies are metabolized, it is possible that, as in insecticides, there is a kind of concentration along food chains with man as the final victim. Mud contains sizable proportions of certain bodies derived from oil products (Vasserot, 1962; Mallet, 1961; Tendron, 1962) and these substances may then pass into the bodies of mollusks used for human consumption.

Furthermore, oil wastes, driven by winds and currents, collect on beaches in long streaks and solid masses. These accumulations are a menace to coastal organisms and a serious inconvenience to bathers. And the situation is going to worsen. European consumption of oil products, which came to 134 million tons in 1957, will

total at least 340 million in 1975, thus doubling the danger of polluting the seas. In 1926 the USA called a conference in Washington
(Preliminary Conference on the Pollution of Navigable Waters by
Oil), and in 1935 there was another at the League of Nations. In
1953 a conference was held in London under the sponsorship of the
Intergovernmental Maritime Consultative Organization (IMCO),
the 12th UN institution charged with problems of international
commercial navigation. In 1954 the delegates signed a Convention
defining a certain number of zones within which it was forbidden
to clean or drain ballast tanks; waste was to be discharged outside
definite boundaries or eliminated by means of separators in harbours.

Thirty nations ratified this Convention, but several countries
with large fleets of oil tankers did not. Since currents carry wastes
back to the coasts, the results were still unsatisfactory, and pollution
continued.

In March-April 1962, another conference met in London with
55 nations participating. This conference adopted certain amendments to complete the 1954 text and constitute what was in effect a
new international Convention for the Prevention of Pollution of
the Sea by Hydrocarbons. It applies to all vessels over 150 tons
except warships. Contracting nations admit in principle that no
oil products should be discharged in the sea, while recognizing
that this cannot be applied at present, except in the case of tankers
with a raw load of over 20,000 tons. The most important practical
measure is the extension of the perimeters to include Canadian
waters, the north-western Atlantic, seas bordering Iceland, Norway,
the whole North Sea and the Baltic (*fig* 40). Prohibited zones were
created in the Mediterranean, Red Sea and Persian Gulf, as well as
around India and Madagascar, in preparation for new maritime
routes when the tonnage of oil tankers exceeds the capacity of the
Suez Canal. By the end of 1965 31 countries had become parties
to the 1954 International Convention and 17 had adopted the
amendments. On 18th May 1967, new and strengthened amendments
came into force, but the treaty does not begin to cope with the ocean
traffic, 40% of which consists of tankers.

Since ships will no longer have the right to discharge oil products
in vast zones, they will be obliged to have separators on board or to
use those in the harbours where they load or unload their cargoes.

This apparatus separates oil products suspended in the water which has been used to clean cargo tanks, takes them in special tanks to shore and discharges the clean water into the sea.

Shipbuilders must be able to dispose of waste products cheaply and without delay because tanker rotation must be rapid if a profit is to be made. The apparatus must, therefore, be installed in areas used by oil freight and equipped to function without delay. Standard Oil of New Jersey has issued 'don't dump' orders to cargo captains and developed a clean seas programme devised to prevent pollution.

The Convention with its amendments represents definite progress, if it is applied after ratification by all nations with large fleets of tankers. To ornithologists it has the definite merit of providing effective protection for continental plateaus bordering the countries and inland seas where most marine birds live, except forms like petrels that fly far from land.

But this Convention should be regarded as just one step farther towards the total prohibition of discharging oil products into the sea. A study of maps of the forbidden zones reveals that oil wastes can be deposited in the Atlantic between Europe and the Azores. Marine currents will pile up wastes near these islands, and pollution may have serious consequences.

The only satisfactory solution is a *complete* ban on depositing any oil product in the sea. The London Convention, however, is important because it created an opportunity for free discussion between shipbuilders and oil companies on one side, biologists, travel companies, administrators and politicians on the other. The Convention showed that it is possible to reach an agreement despite difficulties in international law inherent in any question relative to the high seas. This leads us to hope that in the near future oceans will no longer be a sewage disposal for products whose toxic nature is no longer questioned by anyone.

3 ATMOSPHERIC POLLUTIONS

Land and water are not the only elements man has poisoned. Industries deposit in the atmosphere tremendous quantities of gas and solid matter in the form of tiny particles that can remain in

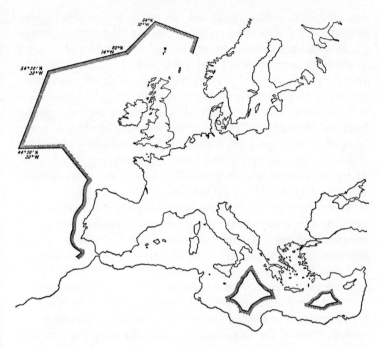

Fig. 40
Map showing zones where it is forbidden to dump oil products off the coast of western Europe and in the Mediterranean. From the documents of the International Conference on Oil Pollution of the Seas, 1962.

suspension and pass into the respiratory tracts of men and animals or settle after being carried considerable distances.

In the 17th century fires were forbidden when Parliament was in session, and this was before there were any factories in London. Evelyn in his *Fumifugium* (quoted by Landsberg, 1956) wrote in 1661: 'For when in all other places the Aer is most Serene and Pure, it is here Eclipsed with such a Cloud of Sulphure, as the Sun itself, which gives day to all the World besides, is hardly able to penetrate and impart it here; and the weary Traveller at many miles distance, sooner smells, than sees the City to which he repairs.' What would the same traveller say if he were arriving in the British capital, or any other great metropolis, to-day!

This problem has become serious enough to alarm public

opinion.[1] Both public health and the whole world of nature are involved, for this form of pollution entails a change in the atmosphere. Cities are covered by a grey pall of dust particles floating at altitudes between 4,500 and 8,200 feet. This layer absorbs a considerable part of the sun's rays causing a notable lack of sunshine; according to some writers, this may reach 20% in summer and 50% in winter. Measurements taken in Vienna between ground level and the cathedral towers, 230 feet in height, show that this layer of air intercepts 5·7% of the rays. The composition of the light is also changed; according to Maurain (*in* Landsberg, 1956), ultra-violet rays now account for only 0·3% of the energy of the sunshine in Paris, as against 3% in the suburbs.

Atmospheric pollution is produced by gases and solids in suspension. The former come chiefly from combustion, and by far the most important is carbon dioxide, which, far from preventing life, even stimulates plant growth. The era of fossil combustibles—coal and oil—has increased the amount of carbon dioxide in the atmosphere, as was proved by precise measurements taken during the last International Geophysical Year. The increase, estimated at 0·2% annually, amounts to some 10% since the beginning of the industrial era, if the CO_2 cycle is taken into consideration. This change has exerted far-reaching effects on the chemical balance of the globe. Although the current warming trend is a natural phenomenon, an example of climatic fluctuation, it is not impossible that industry has accelerated the warming-up process of the atmosphere and the oceans. This would be one of the most fundamental effects of man on our planet. (See *Implications of rising carbon dioxide content of the atmosphere*. The Conservation Foundation, New York 1963.)

Combustion also produces carbon monoxide, which is poisonous to animals. This gas may exert a considerable influence on city inhabitants because of the quantities involved. A thousand automobiles produce 3·2 tons of carbon monoxide a day, between 400 and 800 pounds of partially consumed hydrocarbon fumes and

[1] See Besson, 1931; Kratzer, 1937; Landsberg, 1956; the Proceedings, National Conference on Air Pollution. US Dept Health, Education and Welfare, Washington 1948, (Public Health Service, Publ. no 654), in addition to various specialized magazines such as *Air and Water Pollution* and the *Revue de la Pollution Atmosphérique*.

Imperial eagle: Guadalquivir Marismas, Spain. This bird is now
almost extinct except in Spain, where the population totals
only about a hundred birds

Korrigum hartebeest at a waterhole: Waza Reserve, Cameroons.
If properly managed, this antelope, which is still common,
could provide an appreciable amount of animal protein

between 100 and 300 pounds of nitrate derivatives. In Tokyo more than 800,000 cars compete for parking spaces in the city centre, and over 57 tons of soot and dust fall on each square mile of the city in an average month. It has been said that in the USA automobiles pour daily into the atmosphere a mass of pollution equal in weight to a line of cars stretching bumper to bumper from New York to Chicago. A recent advertisement in Philadelphia is headed 'Does your baby smoke?' The caption states that breathing the air in the Friendly City is equivalent to smoking eight cigarettes a day.

The products of carbon oxidation are, of course, not the only ones, for partial combustion of impurities in combustibles produces a number of others, chiefly ammonia and a series of derivatives of chlorine, fluorine, nitrate and sulphur. The latter are of particular importance to industry. A large thermal centre disposes of tons of sulphur products daily, especially in the form of sulphur dioxide, which oxidizes and is transformed into corrosive sulphuric acid.

In addition to these gaseous products, factories pour out large quantities of solids that remain for a time suspended in the air, where some of them form aerosols. The density of these centres of condensation, with a diameter of 0·01 to 0·1 μ, is 5 to 10 times larger in the city than in the nearby country, and the proportion of dusts with a diameter of 0·5 to 10 μ varies in the same ratio. Concentrations of 25 to 30 particles per 0·061 cubic inch (=1cm³) have been recorded whereas there were only 1 or 2 in nearby country. It is estimated that a large thermal centre disposes of 50 tons of dusts a day; these saturate the atmosphere and then settle within a radius of three miles or sometimes considerably farther. A large number of chemical bodies, from mineral salts to silica and sulphur derivatives, some of which are definitely toxic, appear in this form. The complexity of these particles, mingled with natural gases, is further increased by diverse chemical reactions that occur in the atmosphere under the influence of oxygen, ozone and solar rays.

In Pittsburgh, which was formerly considered the most polluted city in the world, measurements proved that an average of 610 tons of dusts were deposited annually on a single square mile. 5% of this deposit consisted of soot, 20% of iron oxide, 16% of silica and the rest chiefly of various metallic oxides.

The city atmosphere also contains a high percentage of live

germs. There are 0·3 microbes per cubic foot at Ballon d'Alsace in the Vosges Mountains, as against 25,000 on the Champs Elysées and 1·1 million in a Paris department store. This is an argument in favour of the wide open spaces. Dust collected in the lungs from atmospheric pollutions also encourages attacks of bacilli.

Aside from their influence on the climate and a perceptible decrease in sunshine, the products poured into the air—especially sulphur derivatives, various aldehydes and soots—cause serious irritations in the respiratory tract. Their effects can be lethal to people in a weakened condition, particularly those susceptible to respiratory or circulatory diseases. The large amount of carbon dioxide poured in the air may also cause city dwellers to contract anaemia, which lowers their resistance to other attacks.

Finally, these products contain a certain number of cancerous substances, notably polycyclic carbons. Benzopyrene has been found in concentrations 100 times higher than in the country. It is almost certain that cancer of the lungs is caused by inhaling such substances.

The influence of these polluted gases is especially harmful when air becomes stagnant over cities, especially in the case of thermal inversion. Lower layers of air are usually warmer than upper ones, but when the situation is reversed the mattress of air covering the ground is remarkably stable. Smog, a mixture of fog and particles in suspension, occurs in many highly industrialized cities, but it is noteworthy in London due to climatic factors and the vast number of factories. A crisis of exceptional gravity occurred there on 5th-8th December, 1952. Measurements showed that the concentration of sulphur dioxide in the air changed suddenly from 0·27–0·23 to 1·34 parts per million, considerably higher in some areas. Simultaneously the quantity of solids in suspension increased to 3 to 10 times the normal amount. It was estimated that 4000 deaths were caused by this smog, and a very large number of people were taken ill. London hospitals admitted four times the normal number of patients suffering from respiratory or circulatory diseases. In the Meuse Valley, Belgium, smog, which lasted from 1st December to 5th, 1930, caused numerous cardiovascular and respiratory troubles and ten times the normal death rate. Some sixty fatalities occurred in a 13-mile area along the river.

The New World is by no means free from smog. Donora, near Pittsburgh, a town of some 12,000 inhabitants, was covered with a dense pall of smog in October, 1948. About 42% of the population contracted cardiac and respiratory ailments. Ten point five per cent of the cases were serious, and a score of deaths was attributed to it. On 3rd August, 1967, the US Public Health Service released a list of 65 metropolitan areas with the most severe air pollution problems in the United States. New York is first, Chicago second and Philadelphia third.

But the city which suffered most was Los Angeles, where frequent temperature inversions, coupled with intense sun, increased the smog menace. Solar radiation caused photochemical reactions in nitrogen and sulphur oxides and started reactions producing irritating aldehydes, which remained at soil level because of meteorological conditions. Pollution caused more accidents here than in any other city, and the air remained contaminated, especially by automobile fumes, until the city waged a vigorous campaign which virtually eliminated atmospheric pollution.

Numerous examples attest the degree of atmospheric pollution above cities, especially industrial centres. Public health is severely affected, and the consequences are not as yet fully known. Even buildings are attacked by substances spread in the air, particularly acids. It has been noted that Cleopatra's Needle, in Central Park, New York, has suffered more damage since it was set up in 1880 than during the centuries since it was quarried by Thotmes III in 1600 BC. And during this time New Yorkers have breathed the air which was attacking the granite.

Nature also suffers from atmospheric pollutions. Recent studies have proved that when young seedlings are exposed to polluted air they become structurally malformed, develop abnormal superficial layers, chiefly of cork, and later produce cankers, turn brown and often die. Frequent instances of this have been observed in the United States. Several valleys in the French Alps were disfigured by industry. In Maurienne, in the narrow corridor between Modena and Aiguebelle, where metallurgical plants produce aluminium, a fluoride pollution is responsible for the degeneracy of coniferous forests. Fluorides produce cankers on the needles, which turn brown and fall, causing death of the trees, or at least retardation of their growth. Foresters found 16,565 dead trees in 1,730 acres. Up to 80% of the Norway pines were destroyed; Norway spruces are also very sensitive, while firs and larches seem more resistant.

Smelting gases have caused destruction of large forests in the United States. Thousands of tons of various substances are poured on fields and forests, poisoning them. The situation is all the more serious since many countries, particularly in western Europe, are now encouraging the construction of factories in areas which had remained rural. While these measures may prove socially useful, they are multiplying pollution centres. Several valleys in Normandy, for example, are being developed by industrialists who wanted to get away from crowded conditions in Paris.

The best methods of preventing air pollution are to condition furnaces carefully, to install apparatus which will recover harmful products, especially incompletely burned oil and sulphur products, and to remove particles from gases and other waste matter that are to be poured back into the air.

In January 1967 the United States Public Health Service reported that 7,300 communities had air pollution problems but only 130 had even nominal programmes to combat them. A huge national campaign is getting under way, and one very important item is the fume-suppressing equipment on 1968 motor cars, which is required by Federal law.

It is expected that $20 billion will be spent in the next six years, of which the US Federal Government will contribute $6 billion. The economic dimensions of air pollution control are suggested by Los Angeles County, the only place in the country which has developed a comprehensive control. In an area of 4,000 square miles the County Air Pollution Control District has an annual budget of about $3·5 million. In the past 20 years industry has spent $250 million on purchasing, installing and operating fume control hardware.

Another important measure is to arrange a maximum number of green areas in urban zones. Trees and carefully chosen plants protect city dwellers, because foliage not only retains particles suspended in the air but 'regenerates' the atmosphere. All plans for urbanization and construction of residential areas should reserve space for vegetation to preserve a little fresh air, as well as to provide 'recreation' facilities in the centre of the city. Atmospheric pollution upsets the natural balance by pouring large amounts of toxic substances on habitats. Hence the problem concerns conservationists as well as doctors. The atmosphere is not intended to serve as a depository for detritus which man has the technical skill to eliminate.

4 RADIOACTIVE POLLUTIONS

Since the last world war man has discovered he can pollute the whole world by strewing products of artificial nuclear fission. Aside from an atomic conflict, which would probably destroy humanity, the multiplication of radioactive substances presents many dangers for man and all living beings. Atomic scientists assure us that all precautions are being taken, that radioactivity has never passed the critical threshold, and we are forced to believe them.

Several important works have been devoted to the medical aspect of the nuclear problem, but little is known about the influence of radioactivity on nature. Even scientists can obtain scant information because certain phases of nuclear pollutions are 'military secrets'. Public opinion should be better informed about these questions, which are troublesome if only because of the mystery attached to them.

Radioactive products affect the air, the soil, and both fresh and salt water. The first source of pollution is to be found in atomic explosions. Following the formation of the atomic 'mushroom', a large quantity of gas and radioactive solids is liberated. These particles are carried away by winds and their fallout can contaminate large surfaces. At the time of an atomic explosion most particles are arranged along an axis in a relatively narrow strip determined by whatever winds are blowing. But the smallest particles may travel around the earth several times before dropping at some indeterminate point. Nuclear experiments in space, in the atmosphere and under water were forbidden by the Moscow Treaty, signed in August, 1963. If this measure is observed, it should prevent contamination by radioactive fallout.

The second source of pollution is the water used in atomic factories to cool the reactors; it can become radioactive and transport dangerous bodies when emptied back into the rivers. The third comes from atomic waste. The factories which produce, transform, or use radioactive products are faced with a growing volume of waste which they aim to dispose of in the best way possible. Highly radioactive products are deposited in expensive reservoirs, built for the purpose, and occasionally buried in galleries of disused mines. These reservoirs soon become inadequate, however. Another solution, which has been adopted by various countries, is to place the waste in sealed containers, surrounded by layers of radiation-absorbing material. These are then sunk in masses of concrete and buried in very deep ocean trenches. Atomic experts think this is the best way to dispose of these dangerous products, for the containers are solid, safe from any attack and, even if one of them were ripped open by chance, the depth of the abysses, which are like another world, would protect man from harm.

This is only partly true. The duration of the container is far below that of some of the radioactive bodies it contains. Iodine 129 lasts 20 million years, cesium 135 lasts 3 million years and zirconium D_3 1 million years. These bodies represent more than 10% of the products of fission of heavy elements, especially uranium 235 and plutonium 239. We may therefore wonder whether the containers are really capable of resisting sea water for a million years. Oceanographers have recently shown that marine currents can stir water in the abysses. Some scientists believe there is circulation between the depths and the surface. Furthermore, as living beings are capable of transporting substances along complex food chains, these dangerous bodies may eventually return to the surface. Although our generation should be safe, barring an accident, we cannot be so sure about the future.

Unless there should be an atomic war or a serious accident in an atomic factory, there is little risk at present from direct effects of atomic pollution. But the facts are much more complicated because of the biological concentration of radioactive bodies along food chains. As in the case of pesticides, these bodies pass into the simplest organisms, which concentrate them and then transmit them in dangerous amounts to their predators.

This phenomenon appears very clearly in the sea. It has long been known that aquatic animals are capable of concentrating substances highly diluted in the water. Some mollusks concentrate copper 4,300 times, fluoride 6,900 times; some crustaceans (copepods) concentrate silica 13,000 times; some fishes concentrate 2,500,000 times the phosphorus dissolved in sea water. Radioactive bodies are no exception, especially rare elements normally present in nature in infinitesimal amounts. Deposited in greater quantities as atomic detritus, they can cause serious contamination of the natural environment and accumulate in living organisms. Strontium 90, which is only produced by artificial nuclear fission, has a 25-year duration permitting accumulation in live organisms and concentration along food chains. Metabolizing like calcium, this element settles in bones and is liquidated very slowly. The same is true of some iodine isotopes (for example, iodine 129) which settle in the thyroid gland.

Large concentrations have been found in various aquatic plants. Tests made at Plymouth in England show that marine algae concentrate from 20 (*Ascophyllum nodosum*) to 40 times (*Fucus serratus*) the strontium 90 of sea water. In the USA the algae of the Columbia River, which receives discharges from the atomic factory at Hanford, have a radioactivity 1,000 times greater than water. The Clinch River, which gets discharges from the Oak Ridge factory, has plankton 10,000 times more radioactive than the water in which it lives. And freshwater bivalves concentrate radioactive iodine 100 times. Both freshwater and marine fishes, being at a high level in food chains, are from 20,000 to 30,000 times more radioactive than the surrounding water. Marine fishes can disperse radioactive products when they are on migration; this explains the atomic catastrophe which struck the Japanese fishermen of the 'Fukuryu Maru'.

Phenomena revealing this kind of concentration, notably with phosphorus, exist along food chains which have aquatic birds at the summit. In the Columbia River an isotope of this element (phosphorus 32) passed from a concentration of 1 in the water to 35 in aquatic invertebrates, to 7,500 in ducks and 200,000 in their eggs. The yolk, very rich in phosphorus, contains 2 million times as much as river water. During nuclear experiments in the Pacific it was reported that colonies of sea birds, especially certain terns, were completely destroyed, as the eggs were sterilized. We may wonder whether sterilization was caused by rays emitted at the moment of the explosion or whether it was due to an accumulation of radioactive bodies in the egg.

Procellariiformes—albatrosses, petrels and shearwaters—would eventually be highly sensitive to marine pollution from radioactive fallout or detritus. These birds are essentially plankton eaters, and we have seen that plankton is capable of concentrating various radioactive bodies in massive amounts. Ornithologists were concerned about atomic explosions in the Pacific, as they occurred on the migration routes of the short-tailed shearwater (*Puffinus tenuirostris*), which describes an immense curve over this whole ocean, from Tasmania to Bering Strait and California.

Although land food chains are less sensitive, we can observe similar concentrations in various iodine isotopes, although their short duration happily makes them less dangerous. Difficulties may be caused when cows feed in contaminated pastures. Their milk then contains a large number of radioactive bodies, especially strontium 90, which constitutes a serious menace to children. According to observations in Great Britain and the USA, part of the radioactive fallout is absorbed by plants at root level; another part falls on the plants themselves and is consumed by cattle. After several bad accidents occurred, measures were passed to prevent further disaster.

We shall not describe the effect of radioactive bodies on animals or man, merely note that the skin, eyes and genital glands are particularly sensitive. Observations have shown that increase in radioactivity in some North American lakes caused a change in the aquatic fauna, slower growth and decreased longevity. At Hiroshima the marine fauna, particularly mollusks, suffered severely from high mortality, destruction of tissue and regression of genital glands.

We must also point out the dangers of increased radioactivity on the genetic future of plant, animal and even human populations. The menace is a very real one because the chances of mutations increase with radioactivity, and unfortunate transformations could occur.

Up to the present, dangers due to radioactive pollutions are still potential. Neither man nor nature has had to suffer very much from atomic fissions, despite those who claim they are responsible for the scarcity of certain animals—and for bad weather during their holidays.

Some ornithologists have blamed the disappearance of various migrants, chiefly ducks and geese, on Russian atomic experiments in Nova Zembla, where birds were killed on their breeding grounds. Abnormalities in the moult of small waders nesting in these Arctic regions, such as redshanks (*Tringa totanus*), have been 'explained' by the effects of irradiation. Some were doubtless killed on the scene of the explosions, but the birds themselves do not appear to have become radioactive. (See Niethammer and Sauerbeck, *Bonn. Zool. Beitr.* 10: 316-323, 1961). It was recently discovered that caribou in Canada and Alaska have been contaminated by lichens which provide most of their food. These plants absorb almost all the radioactive fallout from nuclear explosions.

Risks are inherent in even the peaceful use of atomic energy, but as nuclear fission is man's greatest hope when other sources are exhausted, dangers from atomic pollution will increase even in normal circumstances. We cannot now withdraw from the atomic age. Fortunately man is gradually becoming aware of the menace of radioactivity, and the benefits are so tremendous it is worth taking pains to see that we do not 'poison' nature in such a way that other forms of pollution would seem child's play in comparison.

8 Artificial biological communities

Little causes, great effects. Nature's balance depends on a straw.
                    Roger Heim. *Un naturaliste autour du monde*

Man has carried plants and animals around the world to reconstitute natural communities of his homeland and to increase productivity in newly-settled areas. He has also introduced domestic animals which may upset the natural balance even more than animals liberated in the wild, since they are artificially protected from any real competition.

In addition to this deliberate transportation seeds and small animals were carried from place to place as the volume of interchange increased. We have known for a long time about the spectacular consequences of man's introduction of birds and mammals, but the introduction of microfauna, which has a fundamental role biologically, has been neglected.

Soils are characterized by a balance between millions of microscopic plants and animals; their fertility and stability depend on this. By transporting plants and the earth that goes with them, man unwittingly introduced foreign elements whose swarming has modified the soil balance. Parasitic worms and even earthworms play an important part in soil transformation and are among these introductions.

In their original milieu animals and plants occupy clearly determined ecological niches, where their populations are controlled by competition and predation. In a new biological association they may either disappear rapidly, being 'smothered' by the environment, or else they may become pests. In the long run their explosive success becomes catastrophic for natural habitats, native plants and animals, and often for the human economy.

The success of an introduced animal is explained in various ways. It may occupy a suitable ecological niche that is vacant; it may prove a more robust competitor than the native species; finally, it may prey on them. In most instances introduced species do not fill the ecological niche which it had been hoped they would occupy. They often change their mode of life, especially their diet. The raccoon-dog (*Nyctereutes procyonoides*), which was introduced from eastern Asia into Russia and Siberia, where it has become economically important for its fur, has changed its diet in certain parts of its new habitat. Originally it fed on fishes and crustaceans, but now preys on rodents, game birds and even poultry (see Bannikov, *Mammalia* 1964). It has thus become a threat to hunters, farmers and to the natural balance.

This transformation, which frequently relates to different ecological conditions, may also be caused by genetic modifications. As the number of introduced animals is relatively small, the hereditary patrimony is redistributed. These differences are sometimes even apparent in animal structure; for example, Corsican wild sheep or moufflon introduced into Czechoslovakia have differently shaped horns. The best example is the hare (*Lepus timidus*) of the Faroe Islands, imported from Norway in 1854-55. In less than a century it developed into a new subspecies (*seclusus*), easily recognizable in its smaller size, dental peculiarities, and in the fact that these hares no longer change their coat. (Degerbol, *Mammalia*, 1940, *in* Zoology of the Faroes, Vol. 3, Pt II, no 65).

Ancient attempts at acclimatization, frequently renewed in modern times, have contributed to the destruction of natural communities. A few plants have been beneficial to man, but the havoc wrought in many forms is widespread.

1 IMPORTED PLANTS

Since time immemorial man has transported cultivated plants, and these have contributed to the creation of artificial milieus. He has also modified natural habitats by acclimatizing wild plants. Numerous species familiar in the European and North American countryside seem to be native, yet they are only intruders introduced at various periods in the past. Man has thus fabricated whole communities. Aside from some high mountain or Arctic associations there is no natural plant association left in either Europe or

America. Clark (1956) states that plant associations in California consist chiefly of introduced species. We may wonder what would happen if the human race vanished and if plants were abandoned to the laws of natural balance. It is certain that native species would again become dominant in many cases, but it would take a very long time for primitive associations to become re-established, if indeed they ever succeeded in doing so.

Human influence is particularly evident in grasslands (Foury, Vernet, 1960). While the naturalist likes plants best adapted to local conditions, the soil specialist replaces natural associations by artificial ones with a higher yield. The list of grasslike or herblike species introduced in various parts of the world is a very long one. Of the forty leading grasses cultivated for fodder, 24 come from Eurasia, 8 from East Africa, 4 from South America and 4 from other parts of the world. Most of the Leguminoseae come from western Europe and the Mediterranean region. Although America has contributed only one important plant, field corn (maize), it has imported a number from Europe. Various meadow grasses (blue grass, *Poa*) and *Agrostis* (bent grass) are now part of the North American flora. Most of the fodder plants found to-day in Australia and New Zealand come from the Mediterranean region. Much more recently work has been started to acclimatize similar plants in tropical zones, and there is a tendency to create uniform pastures from Brazil to Africa and Indonesia. A good many weeds were introduced along with these plants, despite the most careful screening.

Forests, especially those in temperate zones, have been transformed by introduction of foreign species, artificial selection of native trees most useful to man, and modern methods of sylviculture. A great many trees have been transported around the world. Special mention should be made of eucalyptuses (*Myrtaceae*). Native to Australia, where they constitute the dominant element of the vegetation, they are now found in most warm and temperate zones (Penfold and Willis, 1961). Although the first seeds reached Paris in 1804, there were no eucalyptus groves in southern Europe and North Africa before 1857. The trees were sent to Chile in 1823, to South Africa in 1828, to India in 1843, to California in 1853 and to Argentina in 1857. Numerous species of the 500 comprising the genus are cultivated on about 3,500,000 acres through-

out the world. In Brazil alone, where the eucalyptus was introduced between 1855 and 1870, plantations cover 1,976,800 acres,
and number about 2,000 million trees, with 1,200 million in the
state of Sao Paulo. These groves are being enlarged by large international companies.

As the numerous species fill the requirements of various types of
soil and climate, the trees offer many advantages. They restore areas
destroyed by man, such as south-eastern Brazil, which was ravaged
by deforestation and bad agricultural methods. Since their growth
is rapid, they provide a considerable amount of wood in a short
time, although quality is mediocre in some species. Hence they are
important in the economy of deforested countries. A tropical
forest of native species provides a maximum of 8 tons of wood (dry
wood) per acre per year. Malay forests are more productive and
certain eucalyptus forests furnish 14 tons. But over the years reforestation with other trees is often more profitable, and to the
biologist these forests are deserts since they have no animal inhabitants.

Many other species have been transported by man. As North
America and Japan have more conifers than Europe, European foresters imported a whole series of species. Several of these have grown
better in their new home than native trees. Because they grow
rapidly, they have made it possible to re-establish or maintain a
plant cover in many parts of the world.

Introduction of trees often increases the productivity of fine wood,
just as pastures are improved by the introduction of new grasses.
Man has nevertheless deliberately destroyed certain plant associations by the introduction of foreign plants favoured at the expense
of native forms, and modern methods are very similar to those of
agriculture. Trees or crops for fodder are grown as if they were
cereals or beets. This results in the creation of artificial milieus
because introduced species usually dominate. The naturalist must
understand the necessity of transforming lands to obtain maximum
productivity. The economist, on the other hand, must admit the
necessity of preserving some natural communities. These parcels
of land must be protected against the intrusion of any foreign plant
which would upset the natural balance. It will take understanding
and good will on both sides to reconcile these opposing points of
view.

A large number of plant acclimatizations have had catastrophic results. In New Caledonia (Barrau and Devambez, 1957), the lantana (*Lantana camara*), an ornamental from tropical America, was planted with the idea that its spiny branches would restrain cattle. It soon spread over whole pastures, along with other plants that are equally prolific: *Acacia farnesiana*, the giant sensitive plant *Mimosa invisa*, imported in the thirties with the mistaken idea that it would be valuable for fodder, and the American guava (*Psidium guajava*). These plants invaded dry grazing lands on the western slope of the island. Although they help protect the soil against erosion, they have considerably reduced the pasture yield, to the detriment of more interesting native plants. The lantana, introduced in all tropical countries as an ornamental, has wrought havoc everywhere, especially in India and the Hawaiian Islands. Biological warfare by means of insects imported from its American homeland has helped to control the invasion. In Hawaii the lantana was chiefly disseminated by the mynah, also imported, which feeds on fruit. This is a curious alliance of two foreign elements against the natural balance of the islands.

The introduction of cactus (prickly pear) in Australia was even more catastrophic. A single stalk of *Opuntia inermis* was taken to New South Wales in 1839. By the end of the century this cactus covered 9 million acres, in 1920 about 59 million, and it continued to spread at the rate of 9 million acres a year. The best grazing lands were disappearing. In 1925 someone had the idea of importing from Uruguay and northern Argentina a small butterfly (*Cactoblastis cactorum*), whose caterpillar devours prickly pears, digging galleries through which bacteria and fungi enter. The result was spectacular, for the cactus disappeared as rapidly as it had spread. The victory of the caterpillar over the cactus was celebrated in a poem published in the *Cactus and Succulent Journal*.

> So abandoning disguises
> Cactoblastis chews away
> Till another problem rises
> To confront another day:
> When the pear pest in the past is
> Who will blast the cactoblastis?
>
> (quoted by Cansdale, 1952)

It seems that there is no need for anxiety about the eventual transfer of the insect to other plants, since it has such a highly specialized diet.

At least 20,000 plant species are cultivated. Since many of them can only live in greenhouses in certain climates, they have no chance to spread. Others, however, escape from 'captivity', compete with native species and tend to become real 'pests'. The best example is the water hyacinth (*Eichhornia crassipes*), which has been called the 'green plague'.

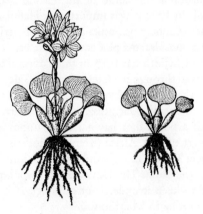

Fig. 41
Flowering stalk of water hyacinth,
Eichhornia crassipes.
From Robyns, 1955.

A monocotyledon of the family Pontederiaceae, it is a floating plant with blistered leaf stalks arranged in a rosette and with a slightly immersed rootstalk (*fig* 41). The flowers form large, very decorative purple or mauve-blue clusters. Multiplication is asexual and such plants benefit from these methods, which are less sensitive to environmental factors than sexual reproduction.

This plant came from tropical America, its centres of dispersion being Guyana and the borders of Brazil and Paraguay, and it was introduced into various warm areas as a pool ornament. A related species (*E. diversifolia*) lives in tropical Africa and Madagascar; it has never been a pest, since it seems to live in balance with its environment.

Introduced into Louisiana in 1884, the hyacinth spread to Florida and by 1888 had invaded the whole south from Virginia to California. It rapidly became a pest which even interfered with navigation on the Mississippi. It has been called the 'million dollar weed' because of the millions which have been spent to check it from spreading.

In 1894 the hyacinth was cultivated in the famous Bogor botanical garden (Buitenzorg); it then spread to Java, through Indonesia, the Philippines, Australia and some of the Pacific islands, including Fiji and Hawaii. In 1902 it was imported to Hanoi, from which it invaded the Indo-Chinese peninsula and India. It arrived in Ceylon in 1905 and was considered a pest two years later.

Although the hyacinth has been in the Congo since 1910, it did not begin to spread through the Congo basin and along its tributaries until recently (about 1952). Even at Leopoldville the great river carries masses of water hyacinths, while the narrower arms are choked to such a point that navigation is impossible. The plant is colonizing part of East Africa (Kenya, Rhodesia) and has penetrated the former French Congo and even the Cameroons. In 1958 it invaded the Nile basin. The United Arab Republic spends $1·7 million a year to keep it under control. Since 1959 it has been in the Sudan, from Juba to Khartoum.

The water hyacinth has thus invaded almost all tropical and subtropical areas of the Old World with amazing speed, thanks to its ability to reproduce by stolons. A plant can produce a new stolon in two weeks. In Louisiana it has been estimated that ten mother plants can produce 655,360 new plants in a growing season (March 15 to November 15), and in the tropics, of course, multiplication continues through the year.

This decorative plant, the delight of amateurs, has upset the natural balance by eliminating native aquatic forms. It hinders navigation and fishing and causes a reduction in fish populations by transforming spawning areas.

Various methods to combat the menace have been suggested (De Kimpe, 1957). Mechanical destruction, with crews of men pulling the hyacinths out of the water and throwing them on river banks or hauling them to crushing machines, was not satisfactory. A vast campaign of destruction by spraying with 2.4D (2·4 Dichlorophenoxyacetic acid) was then undertaken. By 1955 the

Néné (or Hawaiian) geese in captivity: the Wildfowl Trust, Slimbridge, Gloucestershire. Only breeding in captivity has saved this species from extinction

Arabian oryx preserved in captivity. Formerly found throughout much of the Middle East, it now inhabits only Saudi Arabia

water hyacinth was controlled and had been eliminated from some areas. The cost, however, is very high, and it is quite possible that some remaining plants may start a new invasion. After three years of experimentation scientists in Florida are convinced that manatees may help to solve the problem in inland waterways. One adult manatee will eat up to 100 pounds of hyacinths a day, clearing 100 cubic yards of water. The problem now is how to obtain enough of the animals since they have been hunted almost to extinction.

The hyacinth shows how an apparently inoffensive acclimatization can disturb the biological balance, modify native flora and fauna and upset the normal existence of the inhabitants. It should be an example to all those planning acclimatizations whose consequences cannot be predicted.

Finally, man has contributed to the formation of new 'species' by hybridizing native and imported plants. Although there are several cases in North America, the best example is *Spartina Townsendii*, a grasslike plant which flourishes in salt water; this is a natural hybrid between a European species (*Sp. maritima*) and a North American form (*Sp. alternifolia*) which was brought to Great Britain at the beginning of the 19th century. This hybrid, discovered in 1870, did not begin to spread until early in this century. It then advanced rapidly along the shore in salt marshes in England and northern France. Although not harmful to man, this spartina grass has changed a number of habitats by consolidating masses of moving mud. In certain areas it replaces fields of eel-grass (*Zostera*) mixed with algae (including *Enteromorpha*), which are favourite feeding grounds of barnacle geese (*Branta bernicla*). This spartina has been detrimental to these geese, whose numbers had already diminished, and to numerous ducks and small waders (Ranwell, 1962).

2 A HARMFUL MOLLUSK: THE ACHATINA OR GIANT AFRICAN SNAIL

Achatinas belong to a group of mollusks that are related to snails. Numerous species inhabit tropical regions of the Old World, particularly African rain-forests, while others occur in south-eastern Asia, the Malay Archipelago and Indonesia. One large species

(*Achatina fulica*), originally distributed across East Africa from Ethiopia to Mozambique, has a shell 5 inches and a body 8 inches in length (*fig* 42). It likes to climb trees, and the young mollusk feeds on tender shoots and buds. Although little damage has been observed in its native area, the mollusk has become a pest in tropical areas where it was introduced by man (Mead, 1961).

Fig. 42
East African giant snail, Achatina fulica.

These acclimatizations took place a long time ago. Although the achatina has been found on Madagascar since time immemorial, it is certainly not native to the island. The species first appeared outside Africa on Mauritius in 1803; about 1821 it was imported from Madagascar to Reunion Island by the governor, whose wife liked snail soup since it was supposed to cure tuberculosis. In 1847 W. H. Benson transported the mollusk from Mauritius to India, where he released it in the garden of the Bengal Asiatic Society.

Man then disseminated it throughout tropical regions of the Old World (*fig* 43). About 1840 it was seen in the Seychelles, in 1860 at the Comoro Islands, in 1900 in Ceylon, in Perak and the Malay Archipelago in 1928. Already the mollusk was causing damage, especially to tea and para-rubber plantations. In 1931 it appeared in southern China, in 1935 in Java, in 1936 in Sumatra and in 1937 in Siam.

The Japanese took the giant snail to the Marianas (Saipan and Tinian) in 1938 for culinary purposes, and it spread through the archipelago as plants were transported, reaching Guam in 1946. The snail also secured a foothold on many other islands of the Pacific and on Hawaii (1936), where, however, it does not seem widespread except on Oahu. It even appeared in certain parts of California in

1947—probably eggs or very small mollusks were stuck to military vehicles brought back from the Pacific after the war—but the Californian climate does not seem to agree with it.

This mollusk has swarmed through a broad area of the Old World tropics thanks to an extraordinary reproductive ability.

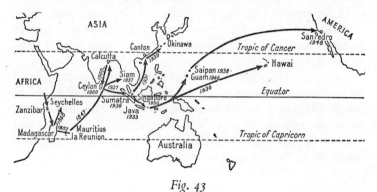

Fig. 43

Deliberate or accidental transportation and acclimatization of the giant snail, Achatina fulica. *From R. Tucker Abbott, 1949.*

After three years the potential progeny of a single mollusk is 8 billion individuals. In Ceylon 227 achatinas were found on the trunk of a single coconut palm. In Java one settler harvested over 400 every morning in a small garden. In the Marianas they are so numerous that tyres slip on crushed mollusks, causing car accidents.

In a curious fashion the achatina developed its tree-climbing propensities in every country it invaded. It attacks buds and shoots of whole series of cultivated plants, especially bananas, cacao trees, papayas, heveas, citrus fruit and cover plants, and causes catastrophic damage in the Malay Archipelago and the Marianas. Planters also accuse it of harvesting spores and germs of numerous plant diseases because of its broad foot.

The simplest method of combating achatinas is to collect them. In Singapore half a million adults and some 20 million eggs have been gathered, but the mollusk remained. Poisoned bait met with no better success. Biologists then tried another method. Since achatina populations seem balanced in Africa, scientific missions were dispatched to Kenya, where they discovered some of its enemies, particularly flesh-eating mollusks of the Streptaxidae family: *Gonaxis kibweziensis*, *G. quadrilateralis* and *Edentulina affinis*. These predatory mollusks were introduced on the island of Agiguan in the Marianas. In 1952, the *Gonaxis* already had destroyed 20% of the achatina populations, and some 60% in 1954. In some districts of Hawaii, the populations have decreased by 80%. These mollusks destroy the eggs and the young achatinas, and even attack adults up to 4 inches long. Thus it seems that the biological control of introduced mollusks is possible, at least under certain conditions (Petitjean, 1966).

Insects, including Diptera and Coleoptera, were also introduced on the Hawaiian Islands. Nevertheless acclimatization of predators can be dangerous. In the Marianas, as on the Hawaiian Islands, introduced animals often prefer native species to the achatina, and some of their prey are economically important. On the Marianas, for example, Partula snails are used for jewellery.

3 FISHES AND OTHER AQUATIC ANIMALS

Man has removed innumerable fishes from their area of natural distribution. Some of these attempts at acclimatization made it possible to solve food problems by supplying animal proteins to human populations. Others caused a serious modification of biological balances and harmed native species of greater economic value (Vibert and Lagler, 1961).

Acclimatization of various trout in mountain rivers of the Far East and East Africa, of salmon in New Zealand and shad (*Alosa sapidissima*) on the Pacific coast of North America, was successful because these species seemed 'preadapted' to their new habitats. They filled vacant ecological niches, did not eliminate native species, and there has been no exaggerated swarming (*fig* 44).

Another successful venture was the introduction into the Far East of Tilapia, a tropical African freshwater fish. This fish, now bred intensively in artificial ponds and rice fields, supplies animal proteins to tropical regions, and it has had almost no impact on natural communities. If it were in the wild, however, it might cause a considerable change in the natural balance because it has extraordinary reproductive powers. In other instances acclimatization

Fig. 44
Distribution of gambusias, Gambusia affinis, *throughout the world. The territory of origin is marked by hatching. Everywhere else this fish has been introduced by man to control the mosquitoes on which it feeds. Although this acclimatization has been generally beneficial, swarming of the fish has caused certain ruptures in balance. From Krumholz Ecol.*
Monog. *18, 1948.*

may lead to a swarming that produces dwarfism in the introduced species, elimination of native species through competition or predation, and even transformation of habitats.

The introduction of the French carp into North America almost caused a catastrophe. An original stock of 345 fishes was taken to the United States in 1876, raised and scattered over the country. This led to a huge population which spread at the expense of more interesting species, probably because carp are hardy. They modify original habitats by destroying aquatic vegetation and muddying the water. Some expanses have been entirely deprived of vegetation. The carp was also introduced into the Iguazu River in southeastern Brazil, where it aroused the wrath of fishermen who found that it had eliminated better fishes. This misfortune also occurred in South Africa (Bigalke, 1937).

Europe has also witnessed some disastrous acclimatizations. The catfish (*Ameiurus nebulosus*), introduced into France in 1870, is famous for its delicate meat but difficult to prepare for the table because of its sharp fins. The sun-perch (*Eupomotis gibbosus*), taken to France 14 years later, has replaced many more valuable species.

The Chinese crab (*Eriocheir sinensis*) (*fig* 45) was accidentally brought from the Far East in a vessel using water as ballast. First observed on a tributary of the Weser in northern Germany in 1912, this crab, which spends its life in fresh water but reproduces in brackish and salt water, began to spread in 1923, and is now swarming in a vast zone of the Baltic, in the Gironde basin and even in the Mediterranean. It has also gone inland along the Elbe and Moldau to Prague. This swarming seems to be related to the vacant ecological niche it occupies. As European freshwater fauna do not include any

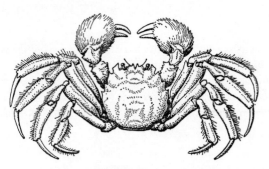

Fig. 45
Chinese crab, Eriocheir sinensis.
The shell can grow to 3.5 by 3 inches.

common crabs, and as some parasites cannot survive for ecological reasons, there are no limiting factors such as are found in the crab's original habitat (*fig* 46). This crab is so prolific that it has modified aquatic habitats by destroying submerged plants and competing with certain fishes for food. In Asia it feeds chiefly on worms and decomposed matter, but in Europe the crab preys on crayfish, insects, mollusks, even fishes. It hollows out banks and dikes, causing cave-ins and hindering fishing. It digs burrows and galleries reaching 31·5 inches in depth and 4·7 inches in diameter; up to 42 of them have been counted in an area of 50 cubic feet. No method of control has produced satisfactory results, despite vast numbers captured at dams and ditches when the crab was on migration. Two and a half million were collected on a river near Berlin in five

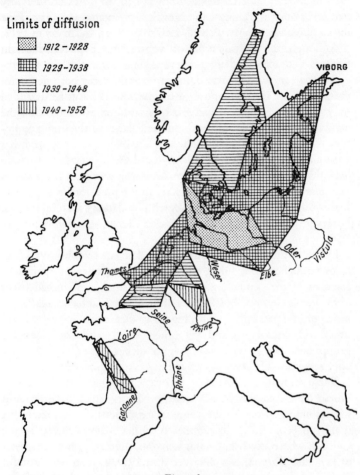

Limits of diffusion

1912 - 1928
1929 - 1938
1939 - 1948
1949 - 1958

VIBORG

Thames
Seine
Rhine
Loire
Garonne
Rhône
Weser
Elbe
Oder
Vistula

Fig. 46

Extension of the Chinese crab, Eriocheir sinensis, in Europe from 1912 to 1958. Although it has penetrated the Mediterranean, it seems to have disappeared in Sweden and Finland, where only a few isolated individuals have recently been observed. From Hoestlandt, 1959.

months; near Magdeburg 355 tons of crabs were collected in the Elbe in 1932. This crab has contributed to the destruction of the natural balance in the fresh waters of Europe and has wrought havoc in the human economy (André, 1947).

Although the introduction of vegetarian or plankton-eating fishes is not without danger, there is far greater risk when flesh-eating species are acclimatized, for some of them can become fearful predators. The introduction of a carnivorous fish can be defended only when an ecological niche is obviously empty and when the carnivore can have no influence on the balance of the prey populations. It is also justifiable if there is an overabundance of fishes without economic value or of introduced species that have become harmful. The introduction of the American blackbass (*Micropterus salmoides*) in Europe helped re-establish the predator-prey balance, as this fish limits catfish and sun-perch populations. Careful studies, however, should be made before such an acclimatization is authorized.

In the temperate and mountainous Andean regions rivers and lakes contained few fishes, apart from a number of species of catfishes of the genus *Trichomycterus* and small, soft-finned fishes of the genus *Orestias*(*fig* 47). Each of these was adapted to a different mode of life, particularly with regard to diet; some are vegetarian, others eat crustaceans and yet others small mollusks. They are groups occupying a series of ecological niches that remained empty after reduction of the stocks on the high Andean plateaus.

These animals are seriously threatened by the introduction of North American salmon and trout, predators which have brought several native species to the verge of extinction; this is a scientific, if not an economic, catastrophe. A similar case occurred in the Celebes, where a catfish, *Clarias batrachus*, previously unknown east of Java and Borneo, was discovered in 1939. A man had brought several of them from Java as a reminder of his youth. Actually it is a dangerous predator that feeds on spawn and may cause serious harm. The government has been unable to drive this species out of Celebes, where it now threatens valuable fishes (Schuster, 1952).

Man is occasionally indirectly responsible for the introduction of fishes. The best example is that of the lamprey (*Petromyzon marinus*) in the Great Lakes (East, 1949). This strange 'fish', a member of the Agnathes group of vertebrates, migrates from the sea where it

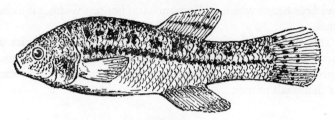

Fig. 47
Orestias agassizi *of Lake Titicaca. From Neveu-Lemaire,* Lacs des hauts
plateaux de l'Amérique du Sud, *Paris 1906.*

spends most of its life to the rivers where it spawns. Years ago
it became established in Lake Ontario and the Finger Lakes, but
Niagara Falls blocked its further extension. When the Welland
Canal was built in 1829, the lamprey entered Lake Erie. It reached
the Saint Clair River in 1930, Lakes Huron and Michigan in 1937,
and the western part of Lake Superior in 1946. This invasion then
became a real explosion. Lampreys multiplied rapidly in rivers
flowing towards the Great Lakes and soon began to ravage these
inland seas, where fishing is estimated as a 12 million-dollar industry.
Ninety per cent of the grey trout (*Salvelinus namaycush*) caught had
large wounds, for these predators attach themselves to their prey
and devour them alive. For every victim that survives their attacks,
hundreds and perhaps thousands die. The stock of trout and white-
fish (*Coregonus clupaeformis*) declined in catastrophic proportions
on account of a predation to which these populations were not
adapted. Total production of American waters in Lakes Huron and
Michigan has dropped from 8·6 million to less than 26,000 pounds of
trout, so a prosperous industry was ruined because man unwittingly
created migration routes for the predators.

This disaster led to the creation of the Sea Lamprey Committee
by the United States Fish and Wildlife Service, in collaboration
with similar Canadian groups. A vast campaign was undertaken
to combat the animal. Electrified fences stopped lampreys moving
towards their spawning grounds in the rivers; larvae were poisoned,
particularly by rotenones which often destroy all the fishes in an
area; special traps were used. Although lampreys are still present,
it is now thought that, after trying over 6,000 products, substances

have been found which will exterminate lampreys without injuring fishes.

This illustrates how such an apparently unimportant act as opening a canal can affect the natural balance and create a serious problem for protection of the natural wealth that provides a living for thousands of men.

4 TRANSPORTATION AND ACCLIMATIZATION OF INSECTS

Insects are obviously the dominant land animals at the present time. As some of them live with man, and others are attached to his crops and industries, it is not surprising that a number have been carried around the world.

Recently the quantity and variety of insects transported have greatly increased with more ships and improved travelling facilities, which enable living animals to arrive at their destination. On a rice-laden freighter from Calcutta and Rangoon to Cuba, no less than 42 species of insects and spiders, including bostrychids, meal-worms, snout-beetles and pyralises were found, despite repeated fumigations (Myers, 1934). The US Health Service discovered insects on board 28,852 of the 80,716 airplanes inspected between 1937 and 1947. This is enough to indicate how many are transported, and what a good opportunity they have to become established despite inspection, which is extremely inadequate in many countries and which, at best, can do no more than restrict the number of 'clandestine passengers and immigrants'. In 1961–62 inspectors of the US Agricultural Service intercepted 36,000 shipments containing dangerous insects, worms, mollusks and parasitic fungi. As among plants, man has created new arthropod communities harmful to native species and often to his own interests.

This impact on the fauna is especially marked in insular regions, where the natural balance has been upset. According to Zimmerman (1948), no less than 1,300 of the 5,000 species of insects on the Hawaiian Islands have been introduced by man. Most of these foreign elements arrived with food shipments or with plants; a relatively small number were brought voluntarily, chiefly for use in biological warfare. Many imported insects are responsible for the disappearance or massive decline of certain populations of native insects, principally at low and medium heights. One ant, *Pheidole megacephala*, which is present almost everywhere except on forested mountains, has killed most of the endemic insects. Among the Hymenoptera Eumenidae, millions of native *Odynerus* have practically vanished because introduced flies deprived them of the butterfly and moth caterpillars on which they feed. The battle seems especially one-sided between native and imported species, since the former require specific hosts and the latter are much more adaptable.

Predation and competition with introduced species, in addition to the destruction of habitats and native vegetation, are responsible for the marked decline of the insect fauna in the Hawaiian Islands. Mangenot (1963) notes that, when man came to this archipelago from Polynesia, the Hawaiian flora was 100% native, in most cases highly specialized and not competitive. To-day the flora is only 55% native, and many varieties are threatened. Almost half the species have been brought from America, Indo-Malaya and Europe. In other parts of the world as well, acclimatization has affected the balance of native insect populations and caused some species to disappear.

Numerous insects have taken advantage of the upset balance following land clearing and additional food supplies to swarm and cause serious damage to growing or stockpiled crops. Many harmful insects belong to introduced species. In 1939 Smith (US Dept. Agri. Techn. Bull.) noted that of the 183 species injurious to crops in the USA, 81 or 44% have been imported by man; they have no predators or natural competitors to limit their swarming.

The best European example is the Colorado beetle (*Leptinotarsa decemlineata*) which occurs from Colorado to Mexico. This parasite lived on wild species (including *Solanum rostratum*), in balance with its environment. When the West was settled and potatoes (*Solanum tuberosum*) were planted, the beetle transferred to the cultivated species. It then began to swarm, as the predators which had kept it under control did not move to the cultivated plant.

In 1859 the beetle began to move east. It reached the coast about 1874 and was thence transported across the Atlantic. In 1876 a first centre of European infestation was stopped in Germany; several later invasions were quelled, but in 1920 the beetle attacked the

Bordeaux region and then spread throughout France (1935) and the rest of Europe. Only the British Isles have been spared, thanks to their plant protection service. Expensive chemical warfare checked the beetle's damage but had little effect on the balance of the fauna. The history of this beetle shows how a plant imported from the New World by man, transformed in Europe by cultivation and then shipped back to America, has favoured the extension of a parasite outside its original habitat and throughout the entire area where the host plant is cultivated (Elton, 1958).

The list of acclimatized insect species is a very long one, but the mechanism of extension always follows the same general pattern. Irruption in a new environment is almost always followed by terrific swarming; the population can then become stabilized on a lower level, but without ceasing to pose problems requiring a costly struggle with insecticides, which also upset the natural balance.

Introduction of insects has medical repercussions as well. Man has involuntarily transported carriers of epidemics, the best known of which is doubtless malaria in north-eastern Brazil (Soper and Wilson, 1943). At the end of 1929 or early in 1930 a French sloop brought mail from Dakar to Natal. It had some stowaway passengers, several *Anopheles gambiae*, the mosquito which inhabits a good part of Africa and is one of the two chief carriers of malaria. Unlike other species of *Anopheles*, especially those which live in north-eastern Brazil, this form lives close to human habitations, and its larvae can develop in very small quantities of water. They have the same role that another mosquito (*Aedes aegypti*) plays with regard to yellow fever.

These *Anopheles* became acclimatized at once. By March 1930, 2,000 larvae were collected in Natal, and from there the mosquitoes spread throughout the suburbs. At the end of April malaria had become a serious problem. In January 1931, 10,000 cases were reported among the 12,000 inhabitants of a working-class suburb (Alecrim), and then the epidemic moved to other districts. Although malaria is endemic in north-eastern Brazil, it never attains the proportions of an epidemic. This was caused by the introduced mosquito, whose mode of life is altogether different from that of the native forms.

Between 1932 and 1937 malaria seemed to decline, for a quiet

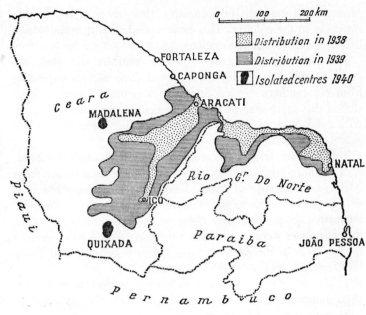

Fig. 48

Distribution of the African mosquito, Anopheles gambiae, *in north-eastern Brazil. This insect spread through the Jaguaribe, Assu, and Apodi valleys, where ecological conditions were particularly favourable; on the other hand, its progression west and south was handicapped by zones that did not favour its establishment. From Soper and Wilson, 1943.*

period followed the eradication of *Anopheles gambiae* in Natal. But the insect had meanwhile become established in other localities. In 1937 it was reported in part of the State of Ceara and in Rio Grande do Norte (*fig* 48). In 1938 a terrible epidemic hit the region; there were hundreds of thousands of cases, with an estimated number of over 20,000 deaths. Life was paralyzed in the contaminated regions, some of the poorest in the world, and the inhabitants were completely destitute. A Brazilian author (P. A. Sampaio) wrote: 'The mosquitoes advanced like hordes of Huns, leaving mourning and destruction in their wake.'

With aid from the Rockefeller Foundation, the Brazilian federal government organized a tremendous campaign, and the mosquito's progress was stopped. By November 1940, there were no more *Anopheles* in the country. This catastrophe had cost thousands of lives and over two million dollars.

The campaign protected the entire continent, for *Anopheles gambiae* could conceivably have spread over an area extending from the southern United States to Argentina. There is still a chance that there may be another epidemic, since traffic between Africa and America has increased, and it is difficult to check aeroplanes against insects.

Yellow fever arrived in South America with its chief carrier, another mosquito, *Aedes aegypti*. The disease probably came from Africa with convoys of slaves. Since these mosquitoes live near dwellings, they preserve yellow fever in urban tropical America; but native species, especially *Haemagogus*, have been infected, and they preserve a woodland form of the disease. This is very common in the forests of the Amazon basin and even beyond, since many monkeys serve as reservoirs for the virus.

This aspect of acclimatization must not be neglected, since accidental transportation of a stock of insect carriers may have serious consequences on public health.

5 THE STARLING AND OTHER AIRBORNE INVADERS

The common starling (*Sturnus vulgaris*) is spreading through the Palearctic region because it is adaptable, prolific and likes to live near man. It has been acclimatized in North America, South Africa, Australia and New Zealand, where it upset the balance among native bird populations and has done considerable harm to crops. It is almost impossible to eradicate it once it becomes a pest.

The starling's invasion of North America was spectacular (*fig* 49). After several unsuccessful attempts at acclimatization, 60 birds were set free in Central Park, New York, in 1890, and 40 more the next year. For six years the starling remained in the urban district. Then it spread across the north-eastern part of the country and began moving west and south. By 1926 it had reached the Mississippi Valley, where, as everywhere, a tremendous population explosion was followed by colonization of virgin areas by waves of birds.

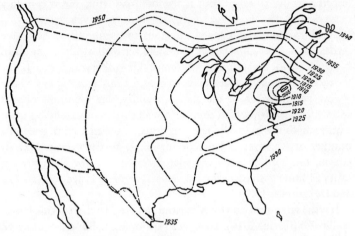

Fig. 49
Extension of the starling, Sturnus vulgaris, *in North America. The broken lines mark the approximate boundaries of its distribution at the dates indicated. After Wing, 1943.*

The starling has now invaded the whole continent. Since 1959 it has nested in California; there are starlings in northern Mexico, in Canada as far north as Hudson Bay, and recently they were observed in Alaska.

In some seventy-five years the bird has practically settled a continent. In 1943 its populations were estimated at about 50 million or about 1% of the whole resident bird population in the United States. And they all come from an initial stock of a hundred birds.

Cecil Rhodes took the starling to Cape Town, South Africa, in 1899, and from there it spread rapidly into neighbouring districts. Thirty-six birds were set free in Victoria, Australia, in 1863; they rapidly invaded all the inhabited areas with the exception of the western part of the continent. Seventeen birds were taken to New Zealand about 1862, and the following year new contingents were brought by acclimatization societies or private individuals. The starling has now invaded all of New Zealand, and even islands as remote as Kermadec and Macquarie.

As an insect-eater, the starling is useful, particularly during the nesting season when it consumes a large quantity of larvae and insects harmful to crops. But it also destroys fruit, and it can do a great deal of damage to orchards, vineyards, and even fields.

Starlings have also proved injurious to communities of native birds, for they occupy nesting sites and seize all available food. In New Zealand the number of pipits, kingfishers and tuis (*Prosthemadera novae-hollandiae*) has been considerably reduced as a result.

Another member of the starling family, the common mynah (*Acridotheres tristis*), which comes from a broad zone extending from Turkestan to the Indo-Chinese Peninsula, has been acclimatized in a number of warm areas from South Africa to the Pacific. Like its cousin, this bird may be considered responsible for the growing rarity of some native species, particularly in New Caledonia (Barrau and Devambez, 1957).

It is the same situation on Mauritius, where 23 avian species, largely Asiatic (Carié, 1916), have been introduced. Six red-whiskered bulbuls (*Pycnonotus jocosus*) were brought to the island in 1892. They multiplied so rapidly that within a period of eight years their descendants occupied an area 40 square miles in size. By 1910 the birds had invaded almost the whole island, and they are now found everywhere. In addition to damaging crops, these fruit-eating bulbuls attack native birds like the white-eyes (*Zosterops curvirostris*), which are now found only in dense forests.

6 THE RABBIT

The rabbit (*Oryctolagus cuniculus*), which seems so useful, is actually a pest. This rodent belonging to the order Lagomorpha, came from Spain and islands of the western Mediterranean. Even in antiquity the animal created economic problems. Strabo reported in 30 BC that Augustus had sent legionaries to help inhabitants of the Balearic Islands destroy rabbits ravaging their crops. It seems to have been brought to Italy and Greece about 230 BC, for classical authors refer only to the hare. During the Middle Ages it was introduced to central and northern Europe. It is not mentioned in England before the 13th century; furthermore, it could not have thrived outside the Mediterranean region until clearing and deforestation had created the open habitats it requires.

There are numerous historical proofs that rabbit populations increased rapidly, but the European invasion was only a first step, for, aside from rats and mice which have become man's habitual guests, the rabbit is undoubtedly the most widely distributed mammal in the world (*fig.* 50).

The first rabbits were taken to Australia in 1787, but they did not multiply. The present population stems from 24 wild individuals

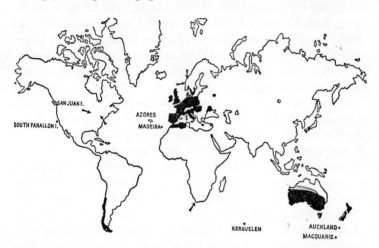

Fig. 50

Distribution of the rabbit, Oryctolagus cuniculus, *following introduction by man. The arrows show the site of restricted centres. The Siberian zone surrounded by stippling marks a place where the rabbit was introduced but seems to have disappeared. The hatched zone in Australia has only a scattered population.*

brought from England on the clipper *Lightning* and released near Geelong, Victoria, in 1859. They succeeded in colonizing two-thirds of the country, adapting themselves to all kinds of ecological conditions, including semi-desert, and they have become, both scientifically and economically, pest number one on the continent.

The rabbit was taken to New Zealand about 1864–67, and more animals were liberated there during the following decades. It began to swarm about 1874, since when it has invaded all appropriate habitats in South Island and a good part of North Island, where climatic and ecological factors are less favourable.

B.N.D.   Q

The domestic rabbit was introduced in the Chilean part of Tierra del Fuego about 1910. By 1947 it was spreading like a scourge across the South American continent, in Chile as well as Argentina. Despite the danger involved, the rodent was released on the San Juan Islands off the coast of Washington and California. There is now a possibility that it may be acclimatized on the continent under the misleading name of 'San Juan Rabbit', for some contingents have been sent to Ohio, Wisconsin and Pennsylvania. The rabbit has also been introduced on Robben Island, near Cape Town, South Africa. We hope that these experiments are not successful, for North America and Africa could be the scenes of invasions as disastrous as the one in Australia.

The rabbit was introduced on the subantarctic islands of Auckland, Macquarie and Kerguelen. On the latter domestic stocks liberated by the English expedition of the *Passage of Venus* in 1874 soon began swarming. These rodents are responsible for serious soil erosion and for the almost complete disappearance of the 'Kerguelen cabbage' (*Pringlea antiscorbutica*), a very characteristic cress now surviving only on islets and cliffs where the rabbit cannot reach it.

Though now found everywhere, it has been most disastrous in Australia and New Zealand, where its population 'explosions' have resulted in catastrophes of continental scope. This successful acclimatization is explained by ecological adaptability and an extraordinary reproductive ability. A female, which can breed at the age of 15 weeks, may bear 8 litters with an average of 6 young a year. But the rabbit's success is principally due to the fact that it irrupted in areas where there were no predators or strong competitors. Most native Australian mammals are marsupials incapable of contending against such a well-armed rival.

The size of the populations may be gauged from the fact that 428 million rabbit skins were exported from Australia between 1945 and 1949. In New Zealand 33,000 skins were exported in 1873; over a million in 1877; over 9 million in 1882, and about 17·6 million in 1945.

Since these rodents consume large quantities of grass-like plants, they compete with the sheep, which are one of the main agricultural resources of both countries. Seven to ten rabbits eat as much grass as one sheep, so the animals exported from New Zealand in 1945 were equal to 2 million sheep in consumptive power, but the sheep would have sold for more than £2 million, as against £1·3 million brought by the rabbits. This represents a net loss to the national economy of about £700,000, and here we are dealing with exported rabbits, not with the whole population, which costs New Zealand millions of pounds every year. The sale of rabbit skins and carcasses has been prohibited since 1st April, 1957. In southern Australia rabbits, because of their rapid reproductive rate, soon became the dominant animals, thereby restricting the amount of food available to sheep. Fifty-three million sheep were lost in the eleven drought years following 1896. Following the release of the Myxoma virus in 1950, the five-year average of the sheep population rose 19·5 million. In 1949 they numbered 108 million and in 1952 117,646,349.

The rabbit also destroys young trees and shrubs, for it likes bark. It is responsible for erosion because it impoverishes the soil, mining it with burrows, and it is the main cause of degrading habitats in both Australia and New Zealand. The rabbit has devastated every country where it has a large population. It transforms habitats, prevents new growth in forests and injures crops and pastures; in 1953 it was estimated that it had done more than £50 million of agricultural damage in Great Britain. It has also exerted a bad influence on the Australian fauna, upsetting the natural balance and eliminating all plant-eating marsupials.

Australia has tried a number of methods to eradicate this pest. Between 1883 and 1887 the government offered 917,000 Australian pounds in rewards for its destruction. Some measures, like the introduction of the European fox, were particularly unfortunate, for this animal multiplied rapidly and exterminated many native species.

There was also an attempt to check the rabbit's advance by the construction of some of the longest fences in the world. The one from Port Hedland on the Indian Ocean to Hopetown, on the southern coast, extends 1,345 miles and was intended to protect western Australia. Others were built in the eastern part of the continent to try to keep the animal from moving north. But 6,875 miles of fence did not restrain the rabbit, either because they were built too late or because the animal slipped through the holes.

Men have tried organizing battues, hunting with ferrets, smoking out, using poison gases and bait poisoned with phosphides, strychnine and arsenic (which killed many marsupials). The rabbit continued to thrive despite these efforts, which cost Australia and New Zealand a fortune. Between 1943 and 1945 about 170,000 New Zealand pounds were spent annually on these operations.

In 1950 the government tried to spread myxomatosis, an epidemic disease which had wiped out domestic rabbits in Brazil but is harmless to man. The Sanarelli virus is native among rabbits of the genus *Sylvilagus*, which are immune, although they may transmit it to rabbits of the genus *Oryctolagus*. Aragao suggested the idea of introducing the virus to Australia in 1934. After several unsuccessful attempts, the Australians contaminated a vast area with parasites and mosquitoes which transport the virus. The result was almost miraculous, for it is estimated that the disease killed 4/5 of the rabbits in south-eastern Australia.

Myxomatosis provided the first effective control of the rabbit. As it practically eliminated the animals from vast areas, their impact on nature can now be determined (see the reports of the 6th meeting of the IUCN, Edinburgh, 1956). Desert-like Australian regions have turned green, and agricultural production has increased steadily except for 1956–57, when wet conditions caused a reduction of the area sown to wheat. In 1964–65 there was a record of 34·7 million acres, 51% of which was under wheat. In Europe the landscape changed perceptibly, expecially in France, where degraded forests produced shrubs and various kinds of saplings.

During recent years the mortality rate, which was 99·5% in some cases, has dropped, as the virus weakened and rabbits developed strains capable of withstanding the disease. It is probable that a balance will develop between rabbits and the virus, which is now endemic in infected regions. The present measures of control should prove adequate, however, unless a strain of completely immune rabbits again besieges regions that are now vacant. The Australians also organize large-scale campaigns with poisoned bait, chiefly the famous '1080' (monofluoroacetate of sodium), which has produced excellent results.

7 MAMMALS AS MAN'S ACCOMPLICES

Since mammals are very important economically, there have been numerous attempts to acclimatize them in various parts of the world

De Vos, Manville and Van Gelder, 1956). No fewer than 200 species have been naturalized, with varying success. This has been done on a large scale even in natural reserves. In the USSR 115,000 animals, belonging to 32 species, were released between 1925 and 1948.

Some acclimatizations, like those of rats and mice, were accidental. These rodents have ravaged plant cover everywhere, while rats slaughtered most of the Pacific rails and marine birds on subantarctic islands. Furthermore, they have eliminated native competitors, such as the native rats on the Galapagos Islands (Brosset, 1963).

Other introductions, such as game or fur-bearing animals, were deliberate. There were also some domestic animals which, when acclimatized, became wild and upset natural balances. Although many acclimatizations have failed, in other instances the animals became pests. Results often differ widely from one place to another. The muskrat (*Ondatra zibethica*), a North American rodent with habits somewhat reminiscent of the beaver, was introduced to Europe in 1905 near Prague, and by 1914 there were some two million muskrats in Bohemia. The animal then invaded Bavaria, moving at a rate of some 30 to 45 miles a year, chiefly along waterways. In 1933 it occupied about 77,000 square miles in central Europe.

In 1930 the muskrat, which had been bred in France since 1920, appeared in a dozen centres scattered through the northern part of the country. Some animals died out at once, but others spread through Normandy, the Somme, the Ardennes and Alsace. At the present time this aquatic rodent occupies a broad area in northern France (*fig* 51); it is also an integral part of the mammalian fauna of Europe from France to Russia. In 1929 the muskrat was taken to the British Isles, where colonies became established from Scotland to southern England. A large-scale campaign to eradicate it was organized in 1937, and this is believed to have been successful. Finally, the muskrat was taken to Finland (1922), to Sweden (1944), and to the USSR, where, beginning in 1927, animals were liberated in both Russia and Siberia (Lavrov, 1960) (*fig* 52).

This rodent is now established from France to Kamchatka. In western Europe it is considered a pest because it undermines steep banks and dikes with its burrows. Furthermore, it seems to feed

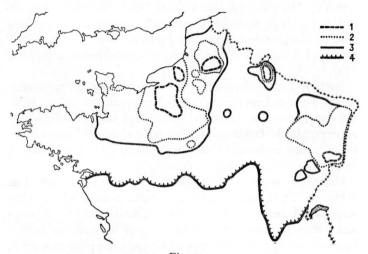

Fig. 51

Extension of the muskrat, Ondatra zibethica, *in France.*

1 territory occupied in 1932   3 territory occupied in 1954
2 territory occupied in 1951   4 territory occupied in 1963
From Dorst and Giban, 1954; brought up-to-date.

not only on plants but on animals. It is said to prey on fishes and freshwater crustaceans; but it does much more damage to fish populations by transforming habitats and clogging water expanses. This damage, which is not compensated by the sale of the fur, explains why people are spending large sums to prevent it from spreading in its new habitat. They have no hope of eradicating it.

In the USSR and Finland, on the other hand, the muskrat does not seem to have done any harm. Nature has been less affected by human intervention, and the prevailing balance is similar to that of the muskrat's original home. The animal, now a source of natural wealth, is bred by the Soviets, who collected some 649,000 skins in 1954.

The nutria (*Myocastor coypu*) is a large, semi-aquatic rodent found throughout South America from southern Brazil to Patagonia. In 1926 this fur-bearing mammal was taken to Europe, and it has now become established in the British Isles, France, the Netherlands, Denmark, Germany, Sweden, the USSR, even Japan. The animal

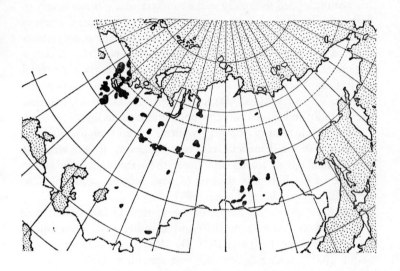

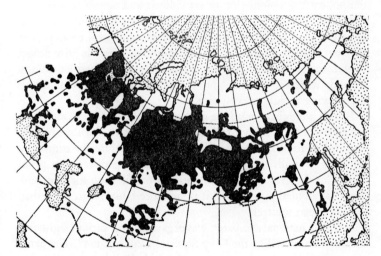

Fig. 52
Extension of the muskrat, Ondatra zibethica, *in the USSR.*
Above: territory occupied in 1936
Below: territory occupied in 1956
From Lavrov, 1960.

has not multiplied so rapidly as the muskrat, and it is not nearly so harmful. The nutria is even considered useful to fishermen, as it cuts down over-dense aquatic vegetation, cleans stagnant water surfaces covered with plants and increases productivity in ponds by accelerating mineralization of muds (Ehrlich, 1959). This activity is beneficial only if the population is small; too many animals destroy the habitat. When the nutria was introduced into Louisiana, it spread very rapidly and caused muskrat populations to decline.

The introduction of the grey squirrel (*Sciurus carolinensis*) into England had no beneficial results whatsoever. It has wrought serious damage in forests and upset the natural balance at the expense of the European squirrel (*Sciurus vulgaris*), which is now dwindling in numbers (Shorten, 1954).

The grey squirrel, a native of the eastern United States, was introduced in Cheshire in 1876 and in other parts of southern England between 1890 and 1929. By 1930 it occupied an area of about 10,000 square miles and was spreading rapidly, despite temporary regressions due to coccidiosis and severe winters. By 1945 the squirrel had invaded all of southern England, where its progress was halted only by broad rivers, ecological barriers such as moors and treeless swamps, and industrial areas. It now ranges over most of England, part of Scotland, and a broad expanse in Ireland, where it was introduced in 1913 (*fig* 53). The animal is multiplying rapidly everywhere.

British biologists regard the grey squirrel as a true pest, and some say that only the brown rat does more damage. All squirrels are harmful to forests, as they pull off bark and injure the cambium, inflicting wounds through which fungi causing disease can penetrate. But the grey squirrel has a special predilection for trees and, since its population is denser, it is far more injurious to them than the European squirrel.

In 1931 a national campaign was organized and various legislative measures enacted, like the Grey Squirrel Order of 1947. The battle was waged with shooting, traps, poisoned bait and nest destruction. It is unlikely, however, that more than a third of the squirrels are exterminated each year, and this will make it impossible to attempt to do more than keep the population under control.

The extension of the American squirrel through the British Isles has exerted a great influence on the balance of European squirrel

Kerguelen cabbage, *Pringlea antiscorbutica*: this cress, native to the Kerguelen Islands in the Indian Ocean, has been practically eradicated from all areas accessible to the rabbit

Below Rabbits round a water hole during a drought in Australia

Erosion of Australian pasture caused by the swarming of rabbits

Degradation of plant cover from overgrazing caused by the rabbit in Australia: on the left, the part protected by a fence and inaccessible to the rodent has a dense green carpet; on the right, it has completely disappeared

Effects of overgrazing caused by too large a herd of mule-deer:
Modoc National Forest, California

Herd of mule-deer

Above Erosion of river banks following the passage of a number of hippopotamuses in Queen Elizabeth National Park, Uganda
Below Herd of hippopotamuses on the Bank of the Rwindi River, Albert National Park

populations, which now seem to be disappearing (*fig* 54). Some say that the introduced species does not hesitate to kill the native squirrel, but these are doubtless isolated cases. Food competition is not a dominant factor, nor does the reproductive rate favour the intruder. But when two species manifest even slight ecological differences, the balance shifts in favour of the one that is better equipped for life. A different sensitivity to diseases, a better metabolization of food, a slight dominance in behaviour, and a greater speed in 'recuperating' after an unfavourable period explain such changes in balance.

The European squirrel seems better adapted to life in pine and yew forests than its American cousin. It has maintained its populations in Scotland, whereas the introduced species has spread most rapidly among the beech trees of the south. It is possible that a new balance will be established as evergreen forests are planted in England, as is the case in other European countries.

The grey squirrel was taken to Cape Town by Cecil Rhodes shortly after 1900. It now occupies an area covering 75 to 100 square miles, but the absence of seed-producing trees seems to restrict its distribution (Davis, 1950, *Proc. Zool. Soc. Lond.* 120: 265–68).

Some other mammals have been successfully acclimatized. The Sika deer (*Sika nippon*) was introduced in France and England, where it adapted itself to its environment and proved less destructive than the red deer. The latter, however, has suffered, and it might have been wiser to increase the number of the native species.

Turning to the carnivores, we find that the introduction of the mongoose in the Antilles caused havoc among the native fauna. The American mink (*Mustela vison*) did a considerable amount of damage when it escaped from breeding farms in Scandinavia and Iceland. In 1938 the mink and the raccoon (*Procyon lotor*) were taken to several islands off the Pacific coast of Canada, including Lanz Island and Cox Island, where they multiplied so rapidly that by 1950 they were preying on sea-bird colonies. If the mink were established on subantarctic islands, it would probably destroy the breeding colonies of sea birds, including penguins, which are their greatest treasure.

Finally, we should note that the introduction of mammals related to native forms may be followed by an unfortunate hybridization

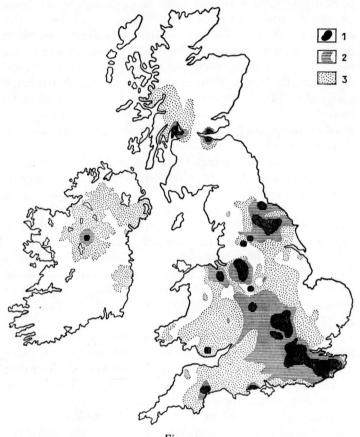

Fig. 53

Extension of the grey squirrel, Sciurus carolinensis, *in the British Isles.*
1 territory occupied about 1920   3 territory occupied in 1952
2 territory occupied in 1930   From Shorten, 1954, modified.

of the two. Beginning in 1901 the ibex (*Capra ibex*), the wild goat
(*Capra aegagrus*) and the Nubian ibex (*Capra nubiana*) were introduced into the Tatra Mountains. The resulting hybridization ruined
the entire population since the reproductive period was upset and
young were born in midwinter. In Czechoslovakia the Siberian
roe-deer (*Capreolus pygargus*) hybridized with the native roe-deer

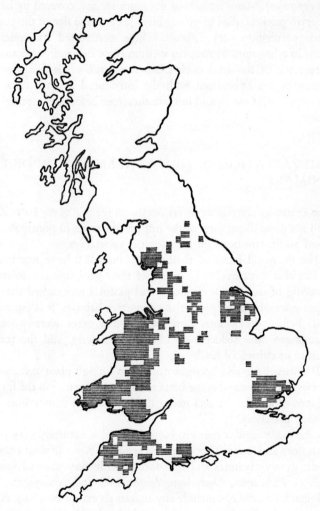

Fig. 54
Reduction of the territory of distribution of the European red squirrel,
Sciurus vulgaris, *in England (the map does not show its distribution in*
Scotland), according to the result of the 1945-1952 investigation. A
comparison with Figure 53 reveals that this species has almost disappeared
from the area inhabited by the grey squirrel. From Shorten, 1954, modified

(*C. capreolus*). Many females of the latter species, covered by larger Siberian prickets, died in giving birth because the size of the young made parturition very difficult. These unexpected consequences occur in other animal groups as well; in New Zealand, for example, pure stock of the wild duck (*Anas s. superciliosa*) is disappearing because it has hybridized with the introduced mallard duck (*A. platyrhynchos*). One should hesitate therefore before attempting any acclimatization.

8 DEVASTATION OF NEW ZEALAND BY IMPORTED ANIMALS

The examples considered so far deal with specific cases; New Zealand is a good illustration of the impact of a series of poorly understood acclimatizations on a biological association.

The flora and fauna of these islands include a large number of species that have evolved because of their geographical isolation. Clearing of land for agricultural and pastoral uses caused the disappearance of a large part of the primitive habitats. It is estimated that, before the Maoris came, 61 million acres were wooded. Forests are now reduced to 14·3 million acres, and the rest is pasture or cultivated land.

But men have also brought numerous foreign plant and animal species. New Zealand is the best example of a rupture in the fragile balance of an island fauna under the influence of competitors and foreign predators.

Like many insular regions, New Zealand is naturally very poor in its flora and fauna. There are two principal types of plant associations: grassy savannas and rain-forests with very unusual species such as *Podocarpus*, *Dacrydium*, *Metrosideros* and *Nothofagus*. The original fauna did not include any mammals except two bats. A rat (*Rattus exulans*) and a dog were brought by the Maoris from central Polynesia in the 14th century. The birds included some highly specialized flightless forms, the best known of which are *Dinornis* and the kiwi or *Apteryx*.

A region with so few animals was a temptation to those who wanted to introduce species from their distant homelands for sentimental reasons or who wished to add to the natural resources of the island (Clark, 1949; Wodzicki, 1950, 1961; Murphy, 1951; Elton, 1958; Howard, 1964).

In 1774 and 1777 Captain Cook introduced cabbages, beets, potatoes, goats, sheep and pigs to provide fresh food for ship crews. During the following century New Zealand became a colony, and settlers tried to introduce as many species as possible. This is apparent from the numerous acclimatization societies established at this time, as well as from legislative measures, such as the acts passed in 1861 by Nelson Provincial Council and the Colonial Parliament to encourage 'the importation of animals and plants, not indigenous to New Zealand, which may contribute to the pleasure and welfare of the inhabitants.' At the beginning of the 20th century, when conservationists first began to think about protecting the native fauna, the situation was already serious.

Up to 1950 attempts had been made to introduce some 53 species of mammals and 125 species of birds; 34 of the former and 31 of the latter were successful. Nearly half the mammals and 72% of the birds were acclimatized between 1860 and 1880, the majority of them from Europe.

Among the mammals that have been brought to New Zealand are 6 kangaroos, 1 opossum, the European hedgehog, stoat, weasel, ferret, rabbit, hare, thar, chamois, red deer, axis deer, sambar deer, American elk (wapiti), Sika deer, fallow-deer, the Virginia deer and the moose. We should add to this list the domestic animals that have become wild. Among the birds are the Canada goose, black swan, mallard, ring-neck pheasant, California partridge, Hungarian partridge, skylark, song thrush, blackbird, starling, mynah, rook, Australian magpie (*Gymnorhina hypoleuca*), sparrow, greenfinch, linnet, goldfinch and yellow-hammer.

This list enables us to envisage the extent of the devastation wrought by introduced species. As many ecological niches were vacant, there was a real 'explosion' of some animals. Competition and predation caused regression of native forms, especially of birds which dominated the biological associations.

Even the native rat (*Rattus exulans*) is being eliminated by *Rattus rattus* and *R. norvegicus*; it persists only on islets off the coast of New Zealand which its competitors have not reached. (See J. S. Watson, Proc. 9th Pac. Sc. Congr. 1957, Vol. 19: 15–17, 1961.)

The most spectacular extensions were made by large mammals.

In 1851 the red deer (*Cervus elaphus*) was introduced near Nelson on South Island. Later the species was released in a number of other areas (on North Island alone there were 155 acclimatizations in 55 places), so to-day it occurs almost everywhere in New Zealand (*fig* 55), although it is partial to man-made habitats with alternating forests, thickets and pastures. The fallow deer (*Dama dama*) has a more circumscribed distribution, but the populations are very large around the points where it was released. Six thousand were killed in an area of 19,770 acres. Deer hunting has increased with larger sales of meat to Europe.

The chamois (*Rupicapra rupicapra*) was imported from Austria in 1907 and again in 1913 (ten animals were freed on Mount Cook), and it has now spread all along the Alps of South Island. Among domestic animals that became wild the goat and pig were most successful, as they adapt themselves easily to a new habitat.

The Australian opossum (*Trichosurus vulpecula*) was brought to New Zealand in 1858. The animal multiplied very rapidly and to-day is found almost everywhere. Contrary to its behaviour in Australia, the opossum has killed forest trees in New Zealand by feeding on young saplings, and it is also destructive to orchards. Population increase may be measured by the number of skins a hunter with a shooting licence collected; the average rose from 163·8 in 1921–25 to 299·7 in 1935–40 and to 597·2 in 1940–45. Since then it has continued to rise. In some districts there are more than 1,500 animals per square mile.

These large populations of imported mammals have had a profound influence on the soil and plant cover. The opossum, being arboreal, destroys upper layers, while herbivores and the rabbit degrade lower ones. Forests have consequently regressed.

Until 1930 or thereabouts imported species were protected. Then bounties were offered for killing them. Teams were organized, and during the years following the Second World War professional hunters shot up to 40 deer apiece every day, a total of 2,000 in a single summer. Between 1932 and 1954, 512,384 deer were slaughtered by officially appointed hunters. If one adds the animals killed by private individuals and the skins exported, at least 1·4 million deer must have been shot during this period. The real figure is probably twice that size.

Opossum hunting is fully as intensive, for no less than 922,088

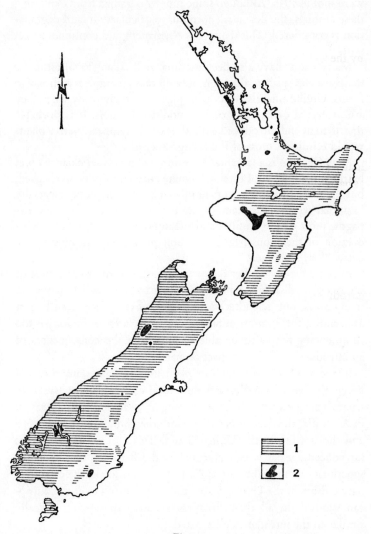

Fig. 55
Present distribution (1) of the red deer, Cervus elaphus, and (2) of the
fallow deer, Dama dama, introduced by man into New Zealand. Unlike
the red deer, the fallow deer remained in the vicinity of the points where
it was released and swarmed there. From Wodzicki, 1961.

were shot in 1945. Although some money is gained from exploiting these animals, the deficit is enormous, particularly if land degradation is considered. This damage is permanent and continues to get worse.

Many plants have also been acclimatized. Allan (1936) estimates there are 603 species, although only 48 really compete with native forms. Unlike animals, introduced plants can thrive only when they are protected or in more or less modified habitats. It is probable that if man and introduced animals should disappear, native plants would eliminate most of the foreign species.

New Zealand is a lamentable example of a natural balance upset by the introduction of foreign elements that multiplied unchecked, but the same situation occurs in other parts of the globe, especially in insular regions. Outstanding are the Hawaiian Islands, the Galapagos, most of the Antilles and subantarctic islands, where introduction of the mouse, rat and rabbit proved catastrophic to the native flora and fauna.

Imported species either die or swarm. In the latter case, most of them cause disaster. Amateur acclimatizations wreak havoc in many areas, but 'scientific' introduction of new forms can be just as harmful, for, in most instances, our knowledge of biology is too rudimentary for us to be able to anticipate the consequences of an introduction and its impact on nature.

Introduction of an animal or plant into a strange environment upsets the balance and creates new food chains. This is especially true when an ecological niche is vacant, as is the case with the rabbit in Australia, the deer in New Zealand, the Chinese crab in Europe and the starling in the United States. This also occurs when the introduced species is better armed in the battle of life, as in the superiority of the rabbit over Australian marsupials, the carp over native fishes in the United States, the grey squirrel over the European squirrel. In all these instances a native species, ecologically similar to the intruder, is eliminated.

At times man has tried to restore the balance by introducing a predatory species. This proved highly successful with insects but disastrous with vertebrates. The dog, which was taken to the Galapagos to destroy goats, killed young reptiles; the cat, introduced on some subantarctic islands to control rats and mice, ravaged bird colonies; the fox, imported to Australia to fight rabbits, slaughtered many marsupials.

Acclimatizations are thus followed by chain reactions which man cannot predict. Most catastrophes occurred on islands or in regions transformed by man. Elton (1958) gives a brilliant explanation of the ecological reasons for this. Insular systems are relatively simple since there is a natural reduction of food chains, and biological associations modified by man are so impoverished that they constitute veritable caricatures of the original.

A species multiplies in inverse proportion to the resistance of the environment, and the resistance of habitats naturally or artificially simplified is at a minimum. The way is then open for introduced species to swarm and become a pest. This is what occurred in New Zealand, which had no mammals, in the Antilles and on many island regions with greatly reduced faunas. In Europe and North America large areas had been transformed to the point where natural habitats were impoverished and extremely vulnerable. Introductions in complex environments, such as rain-forest, have scant opportunity to succeed. This is one more reason to conserve as many natural habitats as possible, since they have increased resistance to any foreign species introduced deliberately or involuntarily by man.

9 Pillage or rational exploitation of maritime resources

Man has taken advantage of marine resources since time immemorial. Salt water, one of the most productive natural environments, provides 12% of the animal proteins that man requires. Most of these resources come from the seas, which cover 71% of the globe, and from the mineral elements that include all simple bodies in the form of salts or free ions.

Life swarms in every part of salt water, although it attains its greatest concentration in the surface layers. The 'useful' stratum is, however, much deeper than on land. Marine plants, especially microscopic algae, descend to 60, sometimes to 300 feet, whereas the productive layer of the soil is only 15 to 20 inches.

The total amount of marine plants and animals is thus out of proportion with land ones. The waters form extraordinarily complex and flourishing biological associations with innumerable food chains running from microscopic algae and planktonic animals to giant fishes, squids and whales.

Furthermore, in spite of industrial methods, the catch is still relatively insignificant. According to the *Yearbook of Fishery Statistics*, published by the FAO in 1964, the Atlantic and North Pacific furnish 42% of the world total of 51,600,000 tons. Peru is now at the top with 20,130 million pounds (17·7% of the world total), Japan is next with 13,965 million pounds (12·3%), followed by China (mainland) in 1960 (the last year when figures are available) 12,346 million pounds, USSR 9.867 million pounds (9·7%), USA 5,816 million pounds (5·1%) and Norway 3,545 million pounds (3·1%). In 1960 the total catch unloaded (fish, crustaceans and mollusks) amounted to 113,757 million pounds.

Some sectors, such as part of the African coasts and seas in the southern hemisphere, are still barely affected by fishing. In numerous places, however, particularly near large cities, marine resources are being over-exploited. Improvement in fishing techniques and an increased demand for seafood are the responsible factors.

It is impossible to imagine that a marine species could be exterminated by human action, except in the case of such mammals as Steller's sea cow and some fur seals that have almost been destroyed. Fishes lay millions of eggs, an enormous proportion of which disappear even when the population is perfectly balanced. There is no danger of the breeding stock being exterminated, but there is a risk that individuals will be caught before attaining full growth, and the profitability of fisheries may be affected when pressure becomes too great.

As with all animals, the same quantity of food assures growth for the young, while maintaining life in adults without a perceptible gain in weight. According to some information, only 1% of food is utilized to increase the weight of 20-year old bass; the proportion rises to 25% in 4-year olds. If adults dominate, they take the food from the young, who perish. Catching adults thus increases the chance for survival of younger fish, and augments the total biomass of fish. So long as fishing does not exceed a certain point, populations actually benefit and productivity of areas that are fished is higher than that of 'virgin' districts. Some oceanographers have not hesitated to compare this to pruning fruit trees, which, by lopping off old branches and concentrating the sap in the more fertile ones, increases the yield.

Overfishing begins when immature individuals are taken (fig 56). It decreases productivity and consequently the volume of the catch. In one example, when 80% of different ages were caught, the resulting weight was 106,102 units; if only 50% were taken, this figure rose to 161,138 units because of the difference in size of the captured fish. This means that with less work (fishing 50% instead of 80%), the catch was half as large again, since the population average was on a higher level (Hardy, 1959).

Graham's classic diagram (1949) shows that if 30% of the fish stock is caught during a year, the weight is the same as if 90% was caught, because small individuals are eliminated (fig 57). If 90% is taken, the future of the population is endangered and the stock will soon be depleted. The best and most precise definition is that overfishing occurs whenever there is a combination of increased fishing and a smaller return.

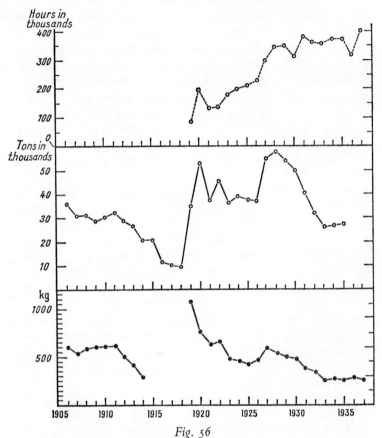

Fig. 56

An example of overfishing: haddock in Iceland seas. Above: following the development of cod-fishing (shown by the ascending curve indicating the duration of fishing operations), all fishes were overexploited; in the middle: fluctuations in tonnage of haddock unloaded; bottom: fluctuations in the capture per unit effort. Note how the catch declines perceptibly despite an increase in fishing; this is a statistical sign of overfishing. From Graham, 1956.

Fishing profits thus depend on some rather subtle notions about population dynamics. The stock of reproductors is usually quite important, and so is the number of small fishes, but it is not in man's best interest to capture any fish before it reaches *optimal* size

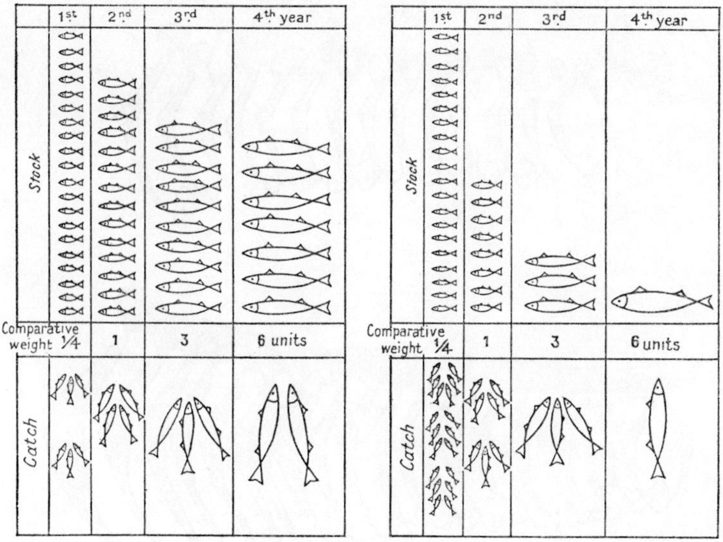

Fig. 57

Effect of fishing on the yield (taking into account the natural mortality, estimated at 5%.) On the left: fishing 30% of the stock annually; for the same total weight (26½ units), there are more large fishes, as they have had time to mature, and fewer small ones; on the right, fishing 90% of the stock; for the same total weight (26½ units) most of the catch consists of small fishes. This diagram shows that it is better to let the fishes attain a certain size, as they provide the same volume in yield with less effort. From E. S. Russell, in Graham, 1949.

(*fig* 58). This, however, does not mean *maximum* size, since population dynamics and the laws governing increase in weight must also be considered. Large fishes have a higher commercial value; hence pound for pound they bring more money to the fisherman. Postel gave me as an example of this the plaice: 2 individuals weighing slightly more than 1 lb. are worth more than 5 weighing about ½ lb., and these are worth more than 10 at ¼ lb.

Some specialists claim that commercial profits regulate fishing automatically. As populations decrease (*fig* 59), expenses rise, since boats have to fish in more distant waters and use more costly equipment. But this does not take into consideration the growing

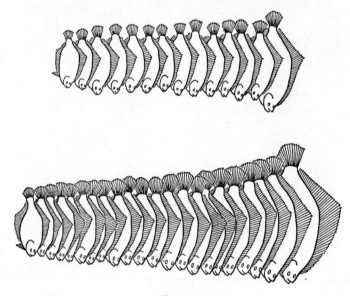

Fig. 58
Capture of plaice in 15 minutes' trawling in the North Sea.
Above: in 1938; below: in 1945. Note that the war enabled the stock to
regenerate and that the average size of the fishes has increased considerably.
From Graham, 1949.

demand for fish in the world market and the improvement in fishing techniques, which are responsible for overfishing in various parts of the world.

About 1880 the appearance of the steam trawler and, about 1894, production of more suitable trawls made it possible to fish in sectors farther and farther away from the coasts. The size of the vessels also increased; the average tonnage of English trawlers was 177 tons in 1906, 231 in 1926, 284 in 1937 and 410 in 1966. The vessels have also been greatly improved with electronic devices for detecting fish and refrigeration equipment which makes it possible to spend six months at sea.

As a general rule, the catch increases at first with improved apparatus; it then begins to drop, and the decline may be rapid.

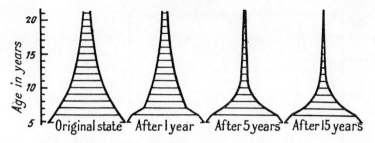

Fig. 59

Evolution of the age pyramid of a single fish population during some 15 years of exploitation. The disappearance of large individuals is due to overexploitation of older age classes. Decrease in the proportionate live weight is apparent from the graphs. From Huntsman, 1948.

In some cases laws have checked the evils of overfishing and a balance has been restored.

There are also many natural explanations for changes in population. Fishes, particularly during the spawning season, are closely tied to oceanographic conditions, particularly those governing temperature and salinity. But man should not add artificial destruction to causes outside human control.

1 HALIBUT FISHING

All around the Arctic Circle an excellent fish occurs—the halibut (*Hippoglossus hippoglossus*), largest of all the flat fishes. It may grow to a length of over 9 feet and weigh over 600 pounds, but growth is slow and the fish is slow to reach sexual maturity.

Atlantic populations have dwindled because of overfishing. There are doubtless some surviving in the waters between Greenland and Scandinavia, but the supply is not adequate for industrial fishing, except off the Norwegian coast where halibut are carefully protected.

Populations in the North Pacific would have met the same fate if Canada and the USA had not adopted protective measures. In 1888 1·5 million pounds were caught; this rose to 50 million in

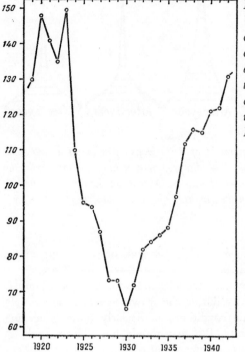

Fig. 60
Variations in yield
of halibut fisheries
on the Pacific
coast of North America,
translated by tonnages
of captures per
unit effort.
From Burkenroad, 1948.

1908, but catches soon began to drop. In one district on the Pacific coast the take per unit effort dropped from 320 pounds in 1915 to 143 in 1920 and to 79 in 1927. In 1927 the grand total was only one-third of the catch in 1915; the halibut population thus presented clear indications of overfishing (fig 60).

In 1923 the governments of Canada and the USA passed a law prohibiting fishing during the spawning period. Other agreements to regulate the industry were signed in 1930 and 1937 and completed in 1953. These measures soon took effect, for by 1931 global tonnage and individual catches again increased. The latter rose on the fishing banks west of Cape Spencer, southernmost Alaska, from 65 in 1930 to 86 in 1934, to 112 in 1937, to 121 in 1940 and to 151 in 1944.

Since 1931 the supply of halibut has increased. The annual catch was 51 million pounds in 1951; in 1960 it reached 71·9 million, but

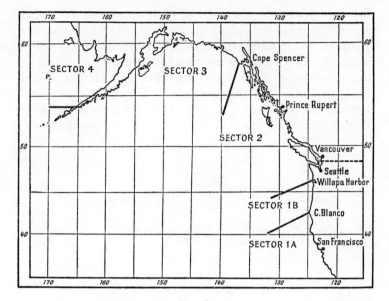

Fig. 61
Sectors to conserve halibut stocks defined in 1950 by the International
Pacific Halibut Commission on the Pacific coast. From Monod, 1956.

in 1965 it had dropped to 40 million. The International Pacific
Halibut Commission divided the Pacific into sectors within which
fishing is controlled, the catch limited and fishing seasons carefully
determined (*fig* 61). These measures are revised in accordance with
the size of the fish populations.

It is probable that the effects of overfishing were superimposed
on natural fluctuations in the halibut populations, for there are
certain discrepancies between variations in the catch and changes in
populations (Burkenroad, 1948). Nonetheless, the halibut is the
classic example of a marine resource which has been restored by
adequate measures after over-exploitation.

2 THE PROBLEM OF THE PACIFIC SARDINE

The Pacific sardine (*Sardinops caerulea*) may also be cited as an
example of over-exploitation of a marine animal (*fig* 62). This little

fish lives in enormous schools, which often number more than ten million individuals, along the coasts of North America, from Alaska to lower California. Although it lives in coastal waters, it may go out 350 miles when it spawns (Gates, 1960). Fishing for this sardine began at the close of the last century, the first cannery being established in California in 1899. The annual catch varied between 300 and 2,000 tons up to 1912. It increased during the First World War, levelled off and then again increased in an

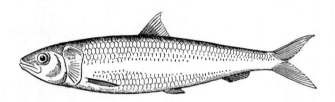

Fig. 62
Pacific sardine, Sardinops caerulea.

extraordinary fashion; in 1916–17 it reached 27,000 tons; in 1924–25, 174,000 tons, and no less than 800,000 tons were unloaded in American ports between British Columbia and San Diego during the fishing season in 1936–37. As these figures were maintained during the thirties and the first years of the following decade, the sardine led the whole New World in tonnage and came next to tuna and salmon in commercial value (over 10 million dollars annually). During this period of extraordinary prosperity sardines were also used to manufacture fish flour for cattle, and fertilizer.

Starting in the early forties the catch fluctuated, then began to drop (*fig* 63). In 1953–54, when only 4,460 tons were unloaded, vessels were dismantled and factories closed. The first symptoms of a decline in the population appeared in Canada, where the catch dropped from 34,000 tons during the 1945–46 season to less than 500 in 1947–48; then the northern part of the United States was hit, and finally California, the chief centre of the industry, in 1951. In 1965 the catch was only 2 million pounds, in contrast to 715 million fifteen years before.

Symptoms of overfishing were already apparent in 1941, as there were fewer adults and more immature sardines. But the effect

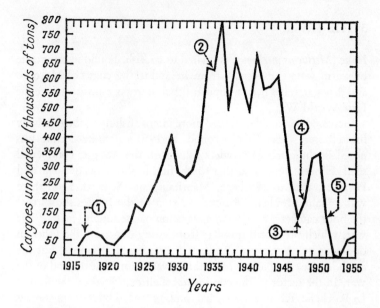

Fig. 63

Fluctuations in tonnages of Pacific sardines unloaded in American ports on the west coast.

 1 beginning of fisheries in British Columbia
 2 beginning of fisheries in Oregon and Washington
 3 abandonment of fisheries in British Columbia
 4 abandonment of fisheries in Oregon and Washington
 5 abandonment of fisheries in San Francisco

From California Department of Fish and Game, *Report, 1957.*

was still hidden by increased fishing and larger vessels in the fleet. Too many adults were taken and too many young before they had reached the age to reproduce.

To-day the pressure has diminished, and we may hope that stocks will be restored now that laws exist for the restriction of the fishing season and the establishment of reserves, where no fishing is permitted. But a prosperous industry was ruined, and fisheries in other parts of the world cornered the market when the California industry was handicapped.

3 THE HAKE

Hake (*Merlucius merlucius*) is related to codfish. Found in temperate or warm waters, especially from Ireland to the coasts of Morocco and Senegal, it has been a popular fish in Europe, especially since the First World War.

Increased demand has caused more intense fishing in the relatively limited area where hake is found. In 1910 a definite decline was noted in the catch of trawlers fishing on the Atlantic continental shelf. Fishermen went farther south, first to the coasts of Spain and Portugal, then to Morocco, Mauritania and Senegal. Soon there was a 'hake problem'. An examination of the figures shows that the poor catches were due to exhaustion of the supply (*fig* 64). The war, which prevented trawlers from going out, gave the fishes an opportunity to recover. At first there were fluctuations, but the catch increased rapidly when fishing was resumed at the end of the war. In the sector of the continental shelf exploited by the fleet at La Rochelle, the average annual catch unloaded by a steam trawler after a 12-day trip rose more than 21 tons between 1938 and 1946; with 23·3 tons as an average for 12 days at sea, the figure was over 13 tons more than before the war. The rate of increase in adults was greater than in the case of young hakes (3- to 6-year olds weighing less than two pounds), which indicates a maturing of the population (Letaconnoux, 1951).

This prosperity lasted only a short time. By 1949 the catch fell below the average of the past 30 years, so three years of over-exploitation had spoiled the gains made during the war. If fishermen had only increased the size of the meshes in their nets, the population would have remained at its high level.

In 1949 trawlers caught an average of only 14.4 tons per trip, or the same as during 1937–39 (14·7 tons). In 1948 the average annual catch was 8·9 tons and it dropped to 6·3 in 1949. In 1966 it was 6,395 pounds, gutted weight (M. J. Holden, Ministry of Agriculture, Fisheries and Food, Lowestoft, Suffolk.) Other fish populations also dwindled, indicating an exhaustion of the stock which had recuperated during the war.

Similar observations were made in the Atlantic south-west of the British Isles (Hickling, 1946). At Milford Haven, Wales, the

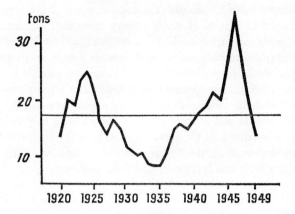

Fig. 64
Fluctuations of cargoes of hake unloaded at La Rochelle (total fishing in a 12-day span). The horizontal line shows the average cargo during the period. From Letaconnoux, 1951.

tonnage during 1941–43 was only 39% of what it had been before the war. After the end of the hostilities, there was a large increase, chiefly due to the bigger size of the hake. The number of haddock and rays also rose. In 1945 a 10,000-ton fleet caught two and a half times as many hake as a fleet three times its size had taken in 1932, but the stock was soon exhausted. There will be no improvement until legislation gives the populations time to increase and reach their maximal volume, and the catch must then be restricted.

4 THE HERRING PROBLEM

It was generally thought that surface fishes, especially herring (*Clupea harengus*), were less sensitive to overfishing than deep-water forms. Economically, the herring is the most important fish in the world; in fact, wars have been waged over the ownership of its fishing grounds. As with other fishes, there are very considerable fluctuations in its populations, chiefly due to variations in the rate of survival in the larval stage, but there seems to be overfishing, as Ancelin stated (1953), in southern sectors of the North Sea and the eastern part of the English Channel. A study of the abnormal replacement of classes of stock is very revealing. Furthermore, professional fishermen complain that the catch, although benefiting from improved techniques, is much smaller than it was after the war. The total dropped from 364 to 111 million pounds between 1950 and 1965. It thus appears that surface fishes are not protected from overfishing, despite their seasonal appearance and deep-sea character and the size of their schools. Trawl fishing may influence herring populations, as the areas are worked at the moment when eggs are deposited on the bottom. But it seems more likely that overfishing with nets is responsible for the decrease.

5 FISHING IN THE NORTH SEA

For a long time the North Sea has been visited by fleets of sea-going trawlers from twelve countries. This extensive fishing has seriously reduced populations. The tonnage of the haddock (*Gadus eglefinus*) when trawlers are out of English ports fell from 1,500 pounds per day in 1906 to 900 in 1914; it then rose to 3,100 in 1919 and dropped again to 900 in 1933 and to 400 in 1935. In the Netherlands the total catch of haddock dropped from 32,634 tons in 1915 to 355 in 1928. Simultaneously small fishes became more numerous, rising from 39% to 69% between 1923 and 1930. In the British Isles the proportions increased from 42·5% in 1913 to 81·7% in 1928; the figures are similar for codfish and plaice. From 1925 to 1938 and again since 1950, trawlers have had a very small catch.

The two world wars gave the populations an opportunity to recover (*fig* 65). The daily catch of English trawlers was about 2,000 pounds in 1906; it rose to 3,100 in 1919 and then dropped to an average of 1,300 between 1934 and 1937.

6 LIMITATIONS ON OVERFISHING

Although certain seas, such as the southern oceans bordering Australia, are not fished extensively, others are over-exploited with the ever-growing demand for seafood on the market.

Improved techniques make it possible to increase the volume of

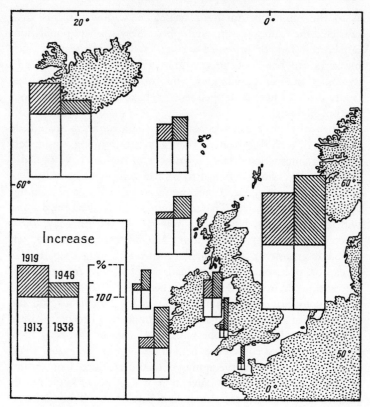

Fig. 65

Increase in fishing stocks in the North Sea and northeastern Atlantic, following the cessation of fishing during two world wars. The increase is indicated (by the hatched zone) as a percentage in relation to the tons unloaded the year before the hostilities (as explained in the framed diagram at the left). The surface of each graph is proportionate to the tonnage unloaded. The increase is very marked everywhere. From Graham, 1949.

the catch. Fishing on the high seas is as harmful as coastal fishing, which has destroyed a great number of young, especially flat fishes. Shrimp-net fishing is also deadly, since finely-meshed nets catch innumerable little fish of no commercial value.

On the recommendation of oceanographers and fisheries' experts, a number of measures have been put forward, such as regulations as to the minimum mesh of fishing nets. Governments have restricted the fishing season, established reserves where populations can be restored, or provided a rotation of fishing sectors. Such measures are based on precise knowledge of the ecology and dynamics of fish populations, and to this end oceanographic laboratories for pure or applied research have been set up in various parts of the world.

Other problems are of a legal nature. As the high seas are outside the limit of territorial waters, rules governing fishing are matters involving international law. A number of nations have signed a series of conventions designed to protect fish populations by forbidding fishing at certain times and in certain areas or prohibiting certain nets or mesh sizes. The first international convention, dealing with fishing in the North Sea, was signed on 6th May, 1882. Since then there have been about 150 bilateral agreements, ten regional agreements, and a smaller number relating to particular species or, occasionally, a combination of the two. A dozen 'big' conventions involving 42 states have been held (Gros, 1960).

The conventions governing fishing in the North Sea and the north-eastern Atlantic are particularly important because of their rich fish populations and the number of nations that send their fleets there. A first conference, held in London in November 1936, and March 1937, led to the signing of the International Convention of 23rd March, 1937. This Convention, which applies to the North Atlantic and adjacent seas, excluding part of the Baltic and the Mediterranean, determined the mesh size to be used in trawling these zones and the minimal size at which certain fishes might be sold.

In 1946 another conference was held in London to revise the 1937 Convention and to amend it in view of the evolution of the fish populations. The International Convention on Overfishing was signed on 5th April, 1948, by Belgium, Denmark, Eire, France, Great Britain, Iceland, the Republic of North Ireland, the Netherlands, Poland, Portugal, Spain and Sweden. Later the Federal German Republic (1954) and the USSR (1958) joined. This increased the size of the mesh, the size at which fishes could be sold, and added two species, namely whiting and dab. These regulations became effective in 1954. The Convention also foresaw the creation of a permanent commission to be charged with enforcement. At

Above Putting down poaching. A Kenya police plane spots the poachers and guards advance towards them *Below* Elephant skeletons scattered over a former poachers' camp in Kenya

Above Roan antelope in a snare set by poachers *Below* A band of poachers captured with their bows, poisoned arrows, and iron wire snares. These two photographs were taken on the border of Serengeti Park, Tanzania

England's suggestion, they discussed whether catches should be assigned according to the quota system, a method prevailing in this country since 1937. The plan was rejected, but it may be necessary in the future (*fig* 66).

Another international convention dealt with fishing zones in the north-west Atlantic (Washington, 8th February, 1949). This was designed to preserve haddock and codfish, the area's most important fishes. It was signed by Canada, Denmark, France, Great Britain,

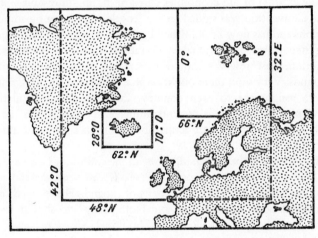

Fig. 66

Sectors defined by the Fisheries Convention of the Northeastern Atlantic London Convention (*1946*). From Monod, *1956*.

Iceland, Italy, Norway, Portugal, Spain, the United States. Later the German Federal Republic (1957) and the USSR (1958) signed it.

Similar conventions deal with other parts of the world. One was designed to protect halibut in the north-eastern Pacific. The Inter-American Tropical Tuna Commission regulated tuna fishing, particularly in the waters round the New World.

However, these measures did not obtain the desired results. So in 1959 a UN conference was held in Geneva which produced a 'Convention on fishing and the conservation of the biological resources in the high seas'. For the first time the necessity of conservation was emphasized, so as to preserve the dynamic balance essential for a constant optimal catch. This convention is also interesting from the point of view of international law. During the debates there was strong opposition between adherents of the old principles of international law, in particular the traditional one of the open sea, and those pleading for a preferential law that would favour nations bordered by the seas in question. An important place was thus established for the economic rights of the new countries, at the expense of old economies based on fishing in distant waters. The Convention was signed after a lengthy discussion by some 30 nations and has now been ratified by 25. Its application will mark a big step towards a rational exploitation of marine resources. In addition, vast reserves should be created to protect spawning grounds. Very soon there ought to be a rotation of districts, with a quota assignment to each country. Enforcement of regulations governing the high seas presents numerous problems, but the sea will only provide its best return if there is an agreement among men of good-will.

Fishes are also being raised, for example codfish in Norway, sole in France and plaice in Scotland. Plaice (*Pleuronectes platessa*) were also introduced along the east coasts of Jutland. This proved to be beneficial both economically and biologically and should be repeated in other parts of the North Sea (Postel, *Science et Nature*, no. 152, 1962). Some of these attempts go back to 1884, but the matter is still at an experimental stage. So too is the artificial introduction of marine species, such as the acclimatization in California of the shad (*Alosa sapidissima*) from the east coast of the United States. Some marine crustaceans have been acclimatized; a shrimp from the Far East (*Palaemon macrodactylus*) was put in San Francisco Bay about 1954, and this has developed into a profitable business (Newman, *Crustaceana*, 5: 119–32, 1963). These introductions may upset the natural balance. Furthermore, although man has conquered almost all the earth, on the seas he is still at the gathering stage.

7 WHALE HUNTING AND ITS REGULATION

Whalers now have equipment enabling them to capture the powerful and swift finbacks, which were long considered unobtainable, and modern whale factories can cut up 49 of them in 24 hours. Beginning in the northern hemisphere, the hunt spread to antarctic seas in 1905 (Budker, 1957). In 1925 the invention of the slip-way, a sloping ramp at the stern, made it possible to haul the whale to the flensing deck. The number of animals killed then followed a rapidly ascending curve, as these statistics show (from International Whaling statistics, Oslo, 1966):

1900	1,635
1905	4,592
1910	12,301
1915	18,320
1920	11,369
1925	23,253
1930	37,812
1935	39,311
1938	54,835
1951-52	49,794
1956-57	58,990
1961-62	66,090
1964-65	64,680 (32,563, or 50%, in Antarctica)

During the 1930–31 season 38 whale factories and 184 'catchers' hunted whales in Antarctica. In 1966–67 there were only 9 whale factories and 120 'catchers'.

Fluctuations in the number captured occurred because of overproduction. In 1932 the figure dropped from 43,129 (1931) to 12,988, and whaling companies began to realize the danger of depletion. Agreements were made between the great whaling countries, and companies began to set quotas for themselves. In 1932 Norway and Great Britain limited the catch, the hunting period and oil production. This Convention was renewed during succeeding years and Norway passed whaling laws to regulate its fleet. Even so some companies refused to co-operate.

In 1937 the first International Whaling Convention was signed in London by the countries chiefly interested—South Africa, Argentina, Australia, Germany, USA, Great Britain, Ireland, Norway, New Zealand. They fixed dates for opening and closing the hunt, set size limits and forbade hunting right- and grey whales. This Convention was renewed in 1938, with the addition of one important article: a reserve was created between Longitude 70°W and 160°W.

The whale population recovered during the Second World War, but there were fears of excessive hunting as soon as whaleboats were rebuilt. A meeting was held in London in 1944, at which the Blue Whale Unit (BWU) was introduced. As it was difficult to limit the take in species, it was decided to set a global limit in equivalencies, taking the amount of oil furnished by the largest, the blue whale, as a unit. This works out so that 1 blue whale=2 fin whales=2½ Megaptera ('humpbacks')=6 Rudolphi finbacks ('Sei'). For 1944 the hunt in the Antarctic was limited arbitrarily to 16,000 BWU. Before the war the average was about 24,000 BWU.

In November 1945, a whaling conference brought delegates of 12 nations to London. As there was a serious dearth of fats throughout the world, it was decided to hunt whales while limiting the catch so as not to spoil future hunting. An International Convention for Regulating Whale Hunting was signed by 19 nations in Washington on 2nd December, 1946. Its clauses prohibit the killing of a female with young. The catch is restricted, with a quota in BWU; dates for opening and closing the season are determined, reserves established between Longitude 70° and 160°W, and threatened species, especially right-whales, are protected. Furthermore, the Convention regulates hunting in certain zones. The whale factory may be used only south of Latitude 40°S and in part of the North Pacific. A permanent whaling commission was created, with the help of scientific committees, to enforce these clauses, penalizing whalers which do not observe the laws. Seventeen nations signed the Washington Convention: Australia, Brazil, Canada, Denmark, France, Great Britain, Iceland, Japan, Mexico, Netherlands, New Zealand, Norway, Panama, Republic of South Africa, Sweden, United States, USSR.

A large number of whales are still captured annually. In 1955–56 28,608 rorquals (14,874·3 BWU) were caught in the Antarctic;

to this should be added animals taken by stations on land, which are not affected by the limit imposed on whaling factories, and those captured in other parts of the world. The global figures in 1960–61 were about 50,000 whales (in 1950–51: 55,795), 70–80% of which were captured in the Antarctic. These numbers have now much decreased; only 28,211 whales were caught in Antarctica in 1964–65, due to depletion of stock.

According to studies made by the Discovery Committee, the rorquals of the Antarctic number between 142,000 and 340,000, with an average of about 220,000. Seventy-five per cent of these are finbacks, 15% blue whales and 10% humpbacks. If this is true, then there is overfishing of the blue whale and the finback. The blue whale is really in danger. Before 1937–38 it was the predominant species in the Antarctic, and from 1930 to 1933, for example, 80% of the whales captured were blue whales and 20% finbacks. This proportion has now been reversed, and in the last two seasons there have been only 5% of blue whales with 95% finbacks. The latter are now showing signs of depletion. The major concern of whaling countries is to find means of preserving their 'raw material'.

The five nations operating in the Antarctic (Japan, USSR, Norway, England, Netherlands) had already set their respective quotas in BWU. For the year 1962–63 only the Japanese caught the number to which they were entitled; the other countries were far below it. To-day only Norway, Japan and the USSR are sending catchers to the Antarctic.

For several years the Scientific Committee of the International Whaling Commission has been insisting that something be done. A committee of three specialists on population dynamics was organized in 1961. It met in Rome, then in Seattle, and presented a final report at the last session of the Commission. Its pessimistic conclusions confirm the warnings of the Scientific Committee of the Whaling Commission. The Committee of Three estimates that in 1963 there were only between 650 and 1,950 blue whales: a population so small that it would have grave difficulty recovering.

The BWU should be replaced by a limit *per species*. Unfortunately this is difficult to enforce, so, for the moment, the BWU is being retained. The quota of 10,000 units set for 1963 was reduced to 3,500 in 1966. This figure is still much too high on the basis of the report of the Committee of Three.

The Committee forbade the capture of blue whales in the region 'south of Latitude 40° South'—except in a strip north of Lat55°S and extending from 0° to Long80°E, the Kerguelen region.

The humpback, from now on, will be completely protected 'in all regions south of the Equator.' In other words, it is forbidden to harpoon *Megaptera* in the Antarctic and in tropical and subtropical waters of the southern hemisphere. This stops all whaling activity on the part of Australia and New Zealand. Sperm whales are now paying a frightful toll in warmer waters.

These three measures show that the Commission is making every effort to preserve the 'raw material' represented by the large whales. In June 1967, delegates attending the International Whaling Commission in London were told that only about 1,000 blue whales remain, as compared with 100,000 30 years ago. The killing of blue and humpbacked whales has been banned and the limit drastically reduced.

8 THE CRUSTACEAN PROBLEM

We shall mention crustaceans only briefly, although they too are dwindling because of overfishing. The various 'lobster wars' which have occurred, such as the one off the Brazilian coast, are an indication of the rarity of crayfish in certain zones. Fishermen are forced to seek other areas where they run into competition that is further complicated by legal disputes.

There are symptoms of overfishing in seas as remote as those around the subantarctic islands Saint Paul and Amsterdam, where a lobster (*Jasius lalandei*) is found (Paulian, 1957). The 1950–56 yields show that fishermen are having to work harder and harder to get the same results. It would be wise to restrict the catch, as the 'continental' shelf is limited and populations have been reduced. Lobster fishing should be forbidden for a year.

Similar decisions should be made in other parts of the world and minimal market size of fishes determined. Dimensions of lobster-pot meshes should be regulated.

9 THE MOLLUSK PROBLEM

Although oyster production in Europe has become an industrial enterprise quite independent of natural beds, in the USA one-third of the oysters come from these beds, which are exploited with no attempt to keep them productive. On the Atlantic coast overfishing has resulted in a considerable loss in annual production. But the chief devastation has been in French Oceania and the Tuamotu Islands, whose chief economic resources are mother-of-pearl, copra and phosphate (Ranson, 1962). Although pearl oysters of the Aviculidae family belong to several species, by far the most important is *Pinctada margaritifera*, which occurs from Tahiti to the Fiji Islands and New Caledonia. Related species are found in other areas, particularly Japan and the Indian Ocean, but the business of collecting them for their pearls has been abandoned. Their oval shell, blackish or greenish on the outside, has a layer of whitish nacre in the centre; this may be 11·8 inches in diameter and weigh up to 22 pounds.

In the lagoons of oceanic islands, where divers can reach the bottom, stocks of these oysters have been exhausted. Furthermore, the mollusks have only a slight chance of assuring the survival of their race. It is estimated that out of a million eggs deposited (a large female ejects twenty or thirty million) only between one and ten will produce mature individuals. Total extinction of the population will occur when the parent stock drops below a certain number. Tens of millions need to be concentrated in a rather small area to preserve populations, especially as the sexes are separate.

Polynesian divers literally exhausted most of the lagoons. As sales were irregular, the published figures about the export of 'nacres' gave only an approximate idea of the evolution of production. Information obtained at the lagoons is much more revealing; here are figures from the Tuamotus:

	ABOUT 1900 *pounds*	ABOUT 1940-50 *pounds*
Arutua	132,000	3,300
Kaukura	88,000–110,000	0
Manihi	176,000	10,313
Aratika	176,000–220,000	2,004
Hikueru	2,200,000	1,162,482
Takapoto	880,000	464,200

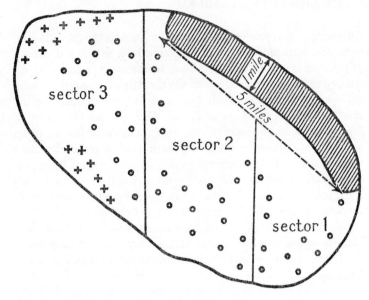

Fig. 67

Diagrammatic drawing of Hikueru Lagoon, Tuamotu Islands; the zones are arranged so as to obtain a rational exploitation of pearl oysters. The reserve where diving is forbidden is hatched. The three sectors where exploitation is to be rotated are marked. Collectors to encourage the settling of the larvae are indicated by crosses (wood faggots) and circles (stones). From Ranson, 1962.

To-day only six important centres of production remain; the other 35 have been practically exhausted. Although warnings were sounded in 1884, man continued to ravage these natural resources.

The best method of restoring the populations is to create natural reserves of full-size oysters in each lagoon. Fishing should never be permitted so larvae can scatter throughout the area. Supports in the form of stones or sticks should be placed where larvae can settle (*fig* 67). This method, the classic one employed for oyster culture, enriches depleted lagoons. Finally, sectors should be exploited according to a rotation system and no nacres less than 6 inches in diameter harvested. The general principles of rational exploitation can thus be applied to pearl oysters. If a reserve is constituted where

Fig. 68
Trochid, Trochus niloticus.

the species can multiply, the fecundity of the stock may reconstitute
the population.

In New Caledonia there is a similar problem with the trochid
(*Trochus niloticus*), another shellfish which yields a thick, resisting
nacre (Angot, 1959) (*fig* 68). Although there is a large population
on the reefy plateau, it has been over-exploited. When fishing began
in 1907, the trochid was harvested with shovels and rakes on the
reefs at low tide; by 1910–20 divers had to hunt for it. Although
the technique improved, production waned by 1930, a characteristic
sign of overfishing; 1,000 tons were exported annually until 1913,
790 in 1916, 622 in 1922, 389 in 1924 and 358 in 1928.

Despite vigorous warnings, exploitation continued until the
Second World War, with an annual average of 400 tons. When
markets were reorganized in 1946, there was overfishing again.
Between 1946 and 1948 the harvest dropped 1,221 tons (the high
figure is explained by the fact that fishing was interrupted during
the war) to less than 500 tons. After a stabilization from 1948 to
1953, on the basis of a yearly average of 500 tons, a tremendous
effort led to 880 tons in 1954, and then the figure dropped to 723
in 1955, and to 402 tons in 1956. More fishermen were exploiting
ever deeper zones, but they could not maintain the supply (*fig* 69),
and the trochid price spiralled.

To repair damage caused by overfishing, local authorities forbade
fishing for a year, beginning in September 1956, and stated that

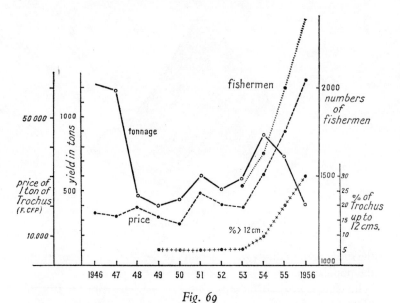

Fig. 69

Variations in yield of Trochus fishing in New Caledonia from 1946 to 1956. Notice the spectacular decline in tonnage in 1947-8. From 1953 to 1956 there was an intensification in fishing activities (chiefly an increase in the number of fishermen) but a decline in the yield. Increase in size of the shells, due to exploitation of deeper zones, also required greater effort. A comparison of these various curves reveals overfishing. From Angot, 1959.

no trochid could be sold unless it was at least 4 inches in diameter. Limiting the mollusk size is an excellent measure, for it will permit adults to repopulate reef surfaces from which they have almost vanished. This will ensure a constant income to communities of fishermen who have no other livelihood.

10 SEA TURTLES

Sea turtles have long been sought, especially for their eggs. Year after year they have come on shore to bury their eggs in the same places in the sand. Some species are killed for their shell; others, with a breastplate of a particular texture, are used for turtle soup. Although the animal may weigh 400 pounds, only 5 pounds can be used, and the rest is abandoned (Carr).

The various species have dwindled throughout the warm seas they inhabit (Hendrickson, 1961; Parsons, 1962). The leatherback turtle (*Dermochelys coriacea*), a giant weighing up to 1,500 pounds, is a living fossil whose shell is replaced by plates in the skin. To-day only some 2,000 remain, 85% of which lay their eggs on a beach $7\frac{1}{2}$ miles long in Malaya (Trenggann). It is estimated that the Trenggann population deposits about 850,000 eggs in 'nests' of a hundred each; the collector leaves only 4 or 5 of them, which is not enough to assure survival of the species, and for a time this turtle was considered extinct.

The green turtle (*Chelonia mydas*), which Archie Carr, the world specialist on sea turtles, calls 'the most useful reptile in the world', is also exploited for its eggs, especially in South-east Asia; this has caused production in the Sarawak colonies to drop from 2,184,095 in 1929–36 to 1,038,129 in 1955–61 (Harrisson, 1962). This species enjoys the sad privilege of being one of those used for soup. It is now in great danger, as are several other species, especially *Eretmochelys imbricata*, which furnishes tortoise shell as well as a substitute for the famous consommé. These sea turtles need protection. Several beaches where they lay their eggs have been made into reserves in Malaya, and Archie Carr has founded the Caribbean Conservation Corporation to save them from extinction. Every spring 100 baby green turtles born in Costa Rica are freed on Cape Sable and in other areas where rookeries once existed (1967).

11 THE DANGERS OF SPORT FISHING AND UNDER-WATER HUNTING

Sport fishing has developed during recent years, particularly in the warm waters bordering Florida and the West Indies. As one Florida visitor in four is a sport fisherman, construction of boats, manufacture of equipment and the hotel industry fully justify protection of the fishes.

Furthermore, underwater hunting has become a sport in every region where the sea is sufficiently clear and warm. Innumerable divers equipped with nets can help exterminate certain fishes, despite being restricted to a very narrow strip of shallow water.

The State of Florida has established the first sea park in the world (*fig* 70). A fringe of coral reefs along the Florida Keys off Key Largo, it is formed of various kinds of corals and inhabited by myriads of multicoloured fishes. Suppliers of curiosity shops were using explosives to tear off the corals, which are sold to tourists, and thus upsetting young fishes in their 'nursery'. In 1957 biologists took steps to preserve this natural treasure, and it was made into a reserve in 1960. Key Largo Coral Reef Preserve, also known as John Pennekamp Coral Reef State Park, is 21 nautical miles in length, 4 miles in width, and is carefully marked with buoys. This reserve is open to visitors for diving, but they are forbidden to do any harpooning or remove souvenirs. A programme of scientific research has been set up in this area. Other submarine reserves are in the Virgin Islands National Park, Buck Island, near St. Croix Island, at Dry Tortugas and Exuma Cay in the Bahamas. There are projects to set up protected zones in Phosphorescent Bay, Puerto Rico, and Bucco Reef, Tobago.

12 MARINE RESOURCES IN THE FUTURE

Overfishing is apparent in many parts of the globe, including some of the wealthiest. Depletion of fishing zones has caused 'fishing wars'; in recent years incidents have occurred between Russians and Americans on the Grand Banks of Newfoundland and in Alaska; between Icelanders and British off the coast of Iceland; between Americans, Japanese, Koreans and Russians in the North Pacific, and between Irish, Belgians and Dutch off the coast of Iceland. These reveal the bitterness of the struggle between nations, and the extent to which they are risking permanent depopulation of what were once the best fishing zones.

As human population increases, so does the demand for animal proteins, of which the oceans are the main source. Efforts must be made to increase the yield of fisheries while safeguarding the capital. On the whole, marine resources have not been fully exploited, with the exception of the North Sea, the Atlantic and the North Pacific. It would be possible to increase the global yield of the seas

Fig. 70
Site of sea park off the Florida coast.

by exploiting sectors along the coasts of Africa, South America and Australia. Tropical seas harbour numerous fishes that are practically untouched; the corals make trawling impossible, so new fishing methods, such as electric fishing, will have to be developed.

Research should be carried out on new species which may be used for human consumption. Ninety per cent of marine animals consist of invertebrates that are almost unexploited, save for some mollusks and crustaceans. The majority are doubtless inedible, but they should still be examined from the point of view of conversion into food.

Even among fishes, the percentage used for human consumption is very small. Only six percent are exploited, and only two percent regularly. In practice a dozen species are used commercially; if we can base our estimate on the catch, 33% consist of herring and sardines, 25% of cod and related species, 9% of mackerel and tunas, 3% of flat fishes, soles, dabs and turbots, and the rest of other species. We should consider exploiting some different types. This would present numerous difficulties, for the popular fish have large populations and are easy to catch. Fishing techniques would require modification, and consumers would have to be educated, but prejudices must be conquered if humanity is to survive.

Some people have advocated using plankton. Ecologically, this would eliminate a number of intermediate stages in food chains. It would also produce a higher return. It takes 10 pounds of plankton to make 1 pound of fish; in the North Sea 2 million tons of herring equal 50–60 million tons of plankton. Instead of utilizing the intermediary herring and sardine, man would consume his plankton food directly, thus deriving greater energy.

Plankton, consisting of innumerable species of algae and small invertebrates, is very rich in nutritive elements. However, numerous difficulties are involved in collecting these microscopic animals and vegetables. One hundred working hours were reckoned necessary to catch 58·6 tons of herring in the North Sea. To obtain the equivalent in plankton, 57·5 million tons of water would have to be filtered. Collecting one ton of plankton (dry weight) would cost between 5,000 and 8,500 dollars.

Should these problems be solved, there would still be the task of transforming the plankton into an edible product. There would be psychological obstacles as well, for people would shy away from it even if they were hungry. Despite a few successful experiments, it will be some time before man replaces surface fishes in the food chains.

The sea is very productive and capable of replacing, quite rapidly, the animals killed by man. It is one of the great sources of foodstuffs for to-morrow's world, and, if man exploits it reasonably, he may guarantee the marine harvests on which human survival will largely depend.

10 Man in Nature

We have raised the great problems relating to the preservation of nature in the modern world. We shall now attempt to formulate a philosophy of conservation and renewable resources designed to maintain a balance between man and his habitat. We have neglected emotional aspects of the subject to concentrate on preparing land for cultivation, a rational exploitation of natural resources and better crops.

As 'reserves' are being invaded, under the constant pressure of a growing population, the only way to save what remains of nature is by incorporating it into the realm of human activities. It will be said that man does not have the moral right to exterminate a plant or animal species. The real question, however, is whether it is in his interest to do so. Biologists have enough data to affirm that it would be a serious error to try to transform the world into an artificial system. Nature will never be saved against man. If powerful and legitimate human interests are opposed to the preservation of an original habitat, man will have the last word. But the problem to-day is to save man from himself. Man is a living being, not a machine; he needs a certain balance, as doctors and psychologists are emphasizing more and more. He will always depend on natural resources for food and many other items required in his daily life. He cannot, therefore, break the laws governing the products on which he depends. Man and the rest of creation form a single entity, despite appearances which are occasionally distorted by technocrats.

Modern engineers have rediscovered the value of a certain balance between nature and regions transformed by man. Man and all other living beings—grouped in balanced communities—form an entity which must be considered as such. This is the synthesis which we shall attempt to make as we mention some solutions capable of assuring man's happy development in a world that has preserved its primitive meaning.

1 THE GREAT DANGERS MENACING MAN AND NATURE IN THE MODERN WORLD

Most of these dangers are caused by the disproportion between a rapidly expanding human population and the vanishing natural resources that have been degraded by ruinous exploitation.

a: THE POPULATION EXPLOSION

It has taken 600,000 years for humanity to attain the three billion figure; if the present tendency continues, however, the population will double in 35 years. Man will doubtless find new resources; atomic energy will replace exhausted sources of energy. We shall perhaps succeed in the not too distant future in irrigating deserts; plans for the Sahara have been outlined; the Soviets intend to transform a vast area in central Asia. It is possible to consider changing the course of a great river or levelling a mountain. People are studying new resources for food, but it will be necessary to make human populations accept them. Virgin lands can be exploited, to the detriment of wild nature, and harvest yields considerably increased. The earth is thus capable of feeding the present population in spite of inadequate crops and a poor distribution, which is caused by political and economic factors. But by the time human hunger is appeased and decent living conditions assured, the world population will have increased again. The rates of increase are such that there is little hope of achieving a balance.

When the Industrial Revolution spurred a sudden growth of populations in Europe, a large fraction of the world's wealth was still intact. These reserves enabled western civilization to grow and then stabilize at a much higher level. Unfortunately, the circumstances are very different to-day, for now the whole world is involved. All our contemporaries have the perfectly legitimate desire to attain a standard of living comparable to that of the most privileged. But a large part of the global population ekes out a miserable existence on eroded lands, in communities with very high birth-rates. Few people are aware of the immense peril of over-population. It seems as if we have not as yet liberated ourselves

Harems of fur seals on the beaches of Saint Paul Island, Pribilof
Archipelago

'Old Faithful': the most famous geyser at Yellowstone, the oldest
National Park in the world

from complexes of solitude that preyed on our prehistoric ancestors. Lonely man believed his race was potentially a victim of some unforeseen disaster. Infant mortality was very high, epidemics ravaged western countries and famines brought deaths to tens of millions in the Far East. Numerous children were necessary because people knew that many of them were condemned to die.

Although circumstances have completely changed, the ancient myths persist. In North America a growing population is considered a sign of the expanding power of a still youthful country. Europe's population has been growing since the last world war. And the so-called underdeveloped countries are multiplying at a speed which is more worthy of rabbits than of intelligent human beings.

Political leaders preach the same dogmas. All over the world people are saying that a country with lots of children is strong and rich. Many politicians are hiding imperialistic ideas, both commercial and military in nature, under these noble statements. They are calculating in terms of 'human material' for peaceful or warlike uses. The expression 'arms race' is common, but it would be quite as true to speak of a population race. It was not long ago that fascist leaders encouraged their peoples to multiply so they could continue their aggressive policy.

Humanity, envisaged as an animal population, has succeeded in overcoming most of the obstacles to its swarming by applying the principles of hygiene and medicine, at the risk of multiplying hereditary diseases, which were formerly eliminated to a great extent by natural selection. Pasteur should not be blamed for his discoveries. Thanks to his wisdom, man has been able to lengthen the lifespan of every human being. He must now find a way of controlling exaggerated proliferation.

We can learn from the animals. It seems as if rodents will have a brilliant future when their litters follow one another at brief intervals and their populations increase in geometric progression. But symptoms of degeneration then appear. There are signs of a deep physiological disorder, which may be attributed to 'stress' caused by overpopulation. The stock then dwindles very rapidly, and there are few survivors to perpetuate the species. Overproduction is always a symptom of death. Some people think they have detected signs of degeneration in the human species and that they are caused by overproduction and a total absence of natural selection. But man is not a lemming or a rodent without a 'brain' and he owes it to himself to find other means of limiting this population explosion.

The methods are the same as those prevailing in animal societies. The first is colonization of new territories. But this is scarcely possible to-day, for the whole planet is divided into compartments. Although some countries have a small population, authorities jealously preserve the space for their own citizens. Furthermore, these solutions are only temporary, since human migrations, such as those of Europeans to America, show that irruption in a new environment triggers a tremendous swarming.

A second method is to increase the mortality rate. Some human societies eliminate old people, while others advocate slaughtering children when the food supply is inadequate. Needless to say, such procedures are impossible in an advanced society.

Although the third method, birth control, runs counter to many traditions, it is the only means of keeping the world population in reasonable bounds and of harnessing a slow expansion to economic development. A just limitation of human fecundity is no more unnatural than vaccination and treatment of diseases by antibiotics. Men who think they are motivated by principles of the highest morality condemn these methods. They would doubtless rather let a segment of humanity starve and risk bringing dire poverty to the rest of the world. If one day a war is fought for ecological reasons, they would doubtless consider it more moral than keeping human populations in harmony with their surroundings.

b: LAND WASTE

The other essential problem which must be solved is land waste. For thousands of years man has been transforming natural habitats and making serious mistakes in the process. A more intensified study of the phenomena involving the interrelations of human beings reveals that a certain number of laws govern the balance of the living world.

Each natural biological association is highly complex. A certain amount of energy falls on a piece of ground in the form of solar rays. This energy, the source of all life, is utilized by organisms, particularly plants on land and microscopic algae in the sea; following this purely vegetal primary productivity food chains develop which incorporate all living beings and in which energy derived from the sun passes through a large number of stages.

These food chains form well-articulated biological associations. The simplest are in the polar regions, where winter climate, lacking heat and light, is a highly important limiting factor. The most complicated are in humid intertropical regions, where flora and fauna are very rich. But every natural ecosystem is complex and in balance with the physical environment to which it is closely adapted.

Habitats created by man are extremely simplified. Transformation of a natural habitat into a cultivated field or pasture always involves reduction of the food chains. In certain instances man has come to these simplifications progressively. The primitive farmer lays out a small field, which is surrounded by natural habitats ready to reclaim the modified area as soon as he ceases to struggle against them. Until recent times the European farmer maintained a happy balance between hedge-bordered fields, interspersed with groves, and woods and marshes. A wise rotation of crops and practices thousands of years old keep the land very productive. 'Modern' farmers in most countries brutally transform original habitats and replace complex food chains by simplified ones in which man is the final and only beneficiary. Monoculture is the exaggeration and caricature of such a system, for it tends to direct all available energy into a single channel.

This has numerous consequences which ecologists place in two categories. First, the global harvest of an artificial environment is much smaller than that of natural environments because there is a terrific loss of solar energy. Instead of exploiting the thousand possibilities of a natural complex, man tries to concentrate energy in a single production. The productivity of habitats depends on their conversion cycle, that is, the processes of construction and demolition of living substances and the speed at which they are put back into circulation. Sir Julian Huxley said (1961), that the conversion cycle is the mechanism on which rests the circulation of energy among plants and animals of a single habitat; in other words, it is the metabolism of the ecological community belonging to this habitat. Conservation of a habitat requires that this circulation of energy be maintained and intensified. A single plant obviously cannot replace all those which live naturally in an area, and the number of cultivated plants is incredibly small in relation to those constituting the plant world.

It is the same story in the case of domestic animals. Man domesticated the cow, sheep, goat, horse, ass and a few birds, and he tends to substitute them for wild fauna everywhere. In the temperate zones he has been successful, for most of the animals came from these regions, so they simply passed from the wild to the domestic state and multiplied as man extended their habitat by transforming the natural environment.

As man moved to other parts of the world, he took his domestic animals with him. Accustomed to a certain diet, they did not find its equivalent in the tropics. Despite the efforts of zootechnicians to improve the cattle in warm climates, they will never be able to take advantage of all the resources offered, for example, by African savannas. While introduced bovines eat only part of the vegetation native animals are far more diversified. In the same region you find side by side vegetarians ranging from the elephant to the little duikers and passing through the gamut of antelopes, buffaloes, giraffes and gazelles. Since most animals were domesticated in the Neolithic Period, man has barely progressed since then.

Although our food requirements necessitate the radical transformation of part of the earth's surface, this does not imply that the whole world should be modified, for a second element now enters. Artificial habitats are subject to a much more rapid erosion than the more complex natural ones. Radical transformation of a natural habitat may seem highly profitable at first but it may eventually destroy the land.

It also appears that artificial habitats are infested by swarms of insects, rodents or birds. Elton (1958) gives a number of examples to show that areas where the natural balance has been maintained in temperate zones are rarely attacked by parasites. The situation is altogether different in arctic and mountain zones, where there may be a much greater fluctuation in animal populations. Thus it is in man's interest to preserve a partly natural balance in the zones he wishes to exploit.

The transformation of a vast district, where all wildlife has been abolished, and where the goal is to convert solar energy into wheat, rice or cotton, should be prohibited in most parts of the world. Excessive mechanization, suppression of mixed habitats, and monoculture are harmful to a high yield. The United States agricultural and soil conservation services are now advocating cultural methods which were called out of style a short time ago, and are encouraging the creation and maintenance of hedges, curtains of trees and fallow land to re-establish a certain ecological balance. Paradoxically, in many European countries habitats which made the continent wealthy are now being destroyed.

Even more serious is the fact that in recent times there has been an assumption that natural habitats could be transformed into artificial fields overnight. Thanks to bulldozers, shovels and mechanical cranes, a morning's work will clear an area of tropical forest that could not have been felled in a month by the old methods. A very rich natural environment is suddenly changed into an impoverished artificial one, subject to all the agents of degradation. Good clearing should be progressive to give the area time to adapt itself. The agricultural wealth of western Europe is due to the fact that it has taken centuries for this continent to reach its present state.

This is not all. It has been believed since the 19th century that any habitat, when transformed, will yield a substantial profit. Although certain zones have an agricultural use, marginal ones can be transformed only at the price of considerable investments or to the detriment of the soil's stability. Decrease of fertile soil and reduction of what remains as untouched capital deserve our attention at a time when world populations are caught in a demographic fever. And this is the very moment when cultivated fields are being exhausted by erosion. In February 1963, at the United Nations Conference on Science and Technology in Geneva, the academicians Gerosimov and Fedorov stated that 1,500 to 1,750 million acres, or half the cultivated land in the world, was eroded and that part of it was dead. These figures require no comment.

2 RATIONAL LAND USE
a: INTRODUCTORY COMMENTS

Man's top priority should be a complete sampling of all habitats. Once this is done, he can lay out the rest of the territory according to his needs and, especially, according to environmental factors. The world's surface will consist of highly diverse zones including:

1 natural reserves, where communities are preserved in their original state;
2 transformed zones devoted to urbanization, industry and agriculture;
3 between the two, a broad range of more or less transformed habitats that have preserved part of their primitive balance. These provide an income for man while assuring the survival of a large number of living beings.

These various zones, arranged in a mosaic according to the classification of the land, would reconstitute the primitive balance to some extent. Man is *in* nature, parts of which have been transformed for his benefit; but the very stability of these zones is guaranteed by maintaining a less man-made balance in neighbouring districts. We shall see how these different zones can be managed according to their classification and density.

b: CONSERVATION OF PRIMITIVE HABITATS

To naturalists the most important measure is setting up natura reserves under public control, where it is forbidden to modify habitats or to disturb the flora and fauna in any way. Nature is thus left to herself. These areas must be fairly large and surrounded by buffer zones such as national parks and hunting reserves or partial reserves, where human activities are restricted; otherwise man's influence would hinder the action of natural laws.

This proposal may seem surprising when human populations are growing so rapidly and 'land hunger' is omnipresent. But the measure is as necessary as the establishment of financial reserves set aside by industry for future emergencies. The reserve is justified both as a laboratory and as a conservatory where habitats are preserved in their primitive state. Just as museums have type specimens, plants or animals used to describe new species, so these habitat types should be chosen to represent all primitive environments from rainforest to desert and arctic tundra. It would be highly desirable to have several habitat types in a single reservation so that transition zones could also be preserved. A list should be drawn up so that the most gravely threatened can be established first.

These areas should be open only to administrators and qualified scientists. Even in the most carefully guarded parks tourists are responsible for a 'human erosion' which causes modification in habitats, even changes in animal behaviour. Creation of such a network of reserves will require careful planning and international co-operation under the auspices of a world organization, such as the International Union for the Conservation of Nature.

Although this measure is primarily intended to preserve samples of types of habitats, it is the only one which will assure survival of many living beings. While it is possible to save a certain number of large animals in relatively artificial conditions, including breeding in captivity, small animals and plants will never be saved unless the habitat to which they are closely linked is preserved. Conservation of nature concerns not only large mammals and birds but invertebrates and the most humble plants as well. It is in man's interest, and it is also his moral obligation, to assure the survival of all creatures now living, even though some seem at first glance to be useless or even 'harmful'. On the strictly material plane, we risk losing large profits if we exterminate species which may prove useful in the future, and this is as true of the tiniest micro-organisms as of the largest vertebrates.

Among mammals, domestic cattle in Canada have been improved by crossing the stock with American bison; as the hybrids, known as 'cattalos', are more resistant to cold, they make it possible to extend breeding areas and increase the economic potential of the country. If American bison had been exterminated, naturalists would not have been the only ones to regret it. Several African ungulates may also be domesticated or eventually crossed with domestic cattle; this would create new races with increased resistance to climate and disease. The eland, for example, has been bred for a long time in the USSR and in Africa.

Other examples may be cited among plants. In the USA several hybrids of native species and trees that are commercially valuable but susceptible to cold or parasites have increased wooded areas. In recent years similar crosses between cultivated and wild plants have increased the yield and the resistance of the former, as in the case of strawberry plants and tomatoes.

These natural reserves are thus not only sanctuaries but reservoirs from which man can draw new genetic combinations or stocks to restore degraded areas. Furthermore, they are natural laboratories.

The structure and evolution of biological communities cannot be studied experimentally, so long-term ecological studies are successfully undertaken only in these reserves. Research activity covers all the scientific disciplines, particularly ecological studies, which alone are capable of providing information about the natural evolution of habitats and their 'mechanisms'. These studies are of equal importance to the applied sciences, as they make it possible to compare the natural habitat with those transformed by man. An understanding of natural phenomena is an essential prerequisite to new techniques for clearing land, which must be closely adapted to local conditions. This is particularly true of tropical regions. Experimentation must never be allowed in these habitats, although it may take place in buffer zones.

Biologists are agreed that the preservation of habitat-samples is of the greatest importance, not only for pure research, which is limitless in view of our embryonic knowledge of biology, but also for practical application. Only a thorough knowledge of natural balances and the dynamics of original habitats can serve as a basis for rational land exploitation.

c: RATIONAL MANAGEMENT OF CULTIVATED LANDS

The first condition is that only lands with a definite agricultural potential should be converted into fields and pasture. Too often men have tried to utilize poor marginal soils, which have quickly become permanently degraded.

The second condition is wise management of the cultivated soil. In a few years bad cultivation can ruin soils which took centuries to form. They should be cultivated according to their relief, their nature, their structure and the climate to which they are subject. But these are technical questions we shall not discuss here.

d: MANAGEMENT AND RATIONAL USE OF MARGINAL ZONES

Marginal zones, corresponding roughly to Categories V-VII in the soil classification, are areas unsuitable for cultivation and have often been ruined by men who did not understand that they were intended neither for fields nor for pasture. The only way to fit them into the human economy is to utilize their often very important natural resources. But it is essential to maintain a natural balance, especially a plant cover capable of supporting the native wild fauna. These zones are vital for conservation.

It is possible that, thanks to the development of new techniques, man will be able to derive a more immediate profit from marginal zones. There are instances where he has succeeded in making almost unproductive lands fertile. These are additional reasons for keeping marginal zones in their natural state, so that their potentialities may be preserved.

The existence of a large forest cover is justified by increasing demand for wood products all over the world. Many marginal zones are well suited for forests; furthermore, these areas shelter a whole series of plants and a fauna ranging from mammals and birds to the most humble invertebrates.

Forest management has a very ancient history in western Europe, and some specialists in new countries have only rediscovered principles and methods that have been known for a long time. In France the first forest charter was promulgated by Louis XIV in 1669 at the instigation of Colbert. This masterpiece of legislation, based on sound ecological knowledge, contains almost all the laws in force to-day. Forests are part of a vast system of natural defence; they also constitute the best method of checking erosion, particularly in watersheds. Trees should never be felled in the upper basins of water-courses, even when agricultural pressure is strong. What happened in Central America and the Mediterranean region should serve as a lesson.

Marginal zones may be used in numerous other ways, including hunting, which some 'protectors' of nature call a barbaric survival. Although in civilized countries it is no longer needed to supply food, hunting gives man an opportunity to exercise his skill in outwitting and shooting game, and the interests of hunters coincide with those of 'protectors' of habitats.

Hunting should be strictly regulated in accordance with the supply. When a population is in balance with its environment, surplus individuals vanish every year through natural causes until the numbers are back to the carrying-capacity of the area. If man regulates his hunting in accordance with the populations, he is acting like a natural predator and he replaces, to a certain degree, other causes for reduction. An example of this is the mule-deer

(p. 303). Hunting should be considered a normal activity and a legitimate exploitation of a natural resource.

There are, however, serious problems in countries with large populations and many hunters. (For instance, there are 13,999,000 hunting licences (resident and non-resident) in the USA (1963)). Local nimrods do not always understand the restrictions imposed by biologists, who study the animals' ecological requirements. Hunting should not be considered as an evil but rather as a rational use of certain marginal zones, which are thus preserved from transformation. These zones can also be used to exploit large mammals for the production of protein foods, for tourist activities, and for the 'recreation' of urban populations.

i: Rational use of large terrestrial mammals
Reasons for managing the large fauna

Until recently it was thought that the only way of converting a plant cover into animal proteins was to turn it into grazing land. It is now apparent that large wild mammals often transform energy more efficiently than domestic cattle. In some cases it thus seems more logical to exploit the wild fauna than to replace it by domestic animals.

Many people believe that lands left fallow only satisfy 'friends of nature' a century behind the times. This is especially true in Africa, where the inhabitants think that all large terrains must be used for pasture. They regard large mammals as a 'waste' since part of Africa is deficient in proteins. In East Africa, for example, Albert National Park in the Congo has been threatened, ever since it was established, by shepherds from Rwanda, where there is over-grazing.

It is the same situation in Serengeti National Park, where the growing Masaï population created so much political and economic pressure that a large part of the Park had to be turned over to pasture. This is detrimental to the wild livestock, one of the most representative in Africa, because herbivores require large areas for their seasonal manoeuvres.

Africans consider the big beasts a survival of the past, like fetishes and folklore. As they were often deprived of hunting rights by the colonial powers, they associate the large fauna with colonization and feel it must be eliminated if Africa is to be a modern country.

Game has been methodically destroyed in much of Africa. The herbivores were accused of transmitting various diseases, particularly those affecting human beings and cattle. Preventive treatment, especially the destruction of tsetse flies, did not produce the desired results, and it seemed that there was no alternative but to destroy the virus reservoirs, that is the ungulates themselves. A campaign of systematic destruction of large mammals then began in East Africa. Between 1932 and 1954 some 500,000 animals were killed in Rhodesia alone as part of the tsetse control operations; 36,910 died in the year 1954. Other operations are in progress, even in the reserves.

Without being unduly pessimistic, we may predict that in a few years the only ungulates in Africa will be in parks and reserves. In 1950 Caldwell said that 'over most of this Protectorate (Uganda) game outside the reserves is almost finished' (*Oryx* 1: 173–86, 1951).

Although the fauna is most seriously menaced in Africa because of the political and economic evolution the situation is much the same elsewhere, and in all parts of the world the domain of the large mammals is threatened.

The best way of preserving wild fauna is not always to let populations develop at will. For a long time it was thought that the success of a reserve could be measured by the number of animals inhabiting it, but this can lead to very dangerous situations for animals and their habitat alike. Few reserves, including the national parks, are large enough to provide a natural balance.

The classic example is that of the black-tailed deer of the Kaibab Plateau near the Grand Canyon in northern Arizona (*fig* 71). In 1906 this area was made a national reserve and all hunting forbidden. At that time there were few deer, partly because of the hunters, but also because of the pumas, wolves, coyotes and lynx. When these predators were eliminated, the deer population at once increased; between 1906 and 1925 it rose from 4,000 to over 100,000 (Rasmussen, 1941), with overgrazing and habitat degradation as a consequence.

As plant cover was reduced, a period of famine began, especially during the winter. The starving animals succumbed to various diseases whose real cause was malnutrition. By 1930 there were only about 20,000 deer and by 1940 the number had dropped to 10,000. This shows that the conception of 'protection of nature', if too strictly applied, is contrary to the best interest of the animals. A territory can nourish only a certain number, the carrying-capacity being based on vegetation. When this capacity is exceeded, catastrophes follow.

An equally erroneous conception prevailed until very recent times with regard to maintaining large mammals in zones where hunting is permitted. Hunting is usually restricted to males and, since most large animals are polygamous, this does not diminish the reproductive capacity of the species. The hunting code considers it bad form to shoot a female. While this may be justified in areas where the population has dropped below a certain level, it is a serious mistake when hunting conditions are normal. The 'Buck Law', which forbids shooting does in a number of American States, has led to overpopulation and degradation of habitats. In a large portion of the western USA heavy mortality resulting from overpopulation has reduced the stocks, to the dismay of hunters. In March 1967, forest rangers shot several hundred elk in Yellowstone National Park to keep the animals from starving. Similar destruction of habitats occurred in some reserves where protective measures have led to a population exceeding the carrying-capacity. Bourlière and Verschuren (1960) have commented on the increase in numbers of elephants in Albert National Park, some of which have come from adjoining areas. In the plains south of Lake Edward the population has grown from about 150 in 1931 to 3,290 in 1959, or 4·4 individuals per square mile. The elephant frequently fells trees to get at the foliage, so a large population transforms the savanna from a wooded to a grassy area. This is detrimental to the primitive plant association that was in better balance with climatic conditions.

The psychological consequences of excessive protection should also be considered in relation to damage which may be wrought by too large a concentration of animals. The elephant on the Ivory Coast, the only large herd on the west coast of Africa, had been reduced to a minimum by overhunting about 1932. At that time the Bouna, Tai-Sassandra and other reserves were created, and elephants at once began to multiply. They soon invaded cultivated areas and did enough damage to arouse the ire of European planters

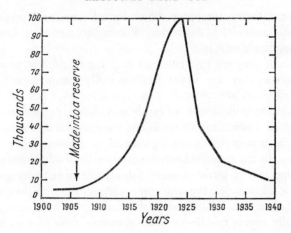

Fig. 71
Fluctuations in the population of mule-deer on Kaibab Plateau. From Rasmussen, 1941.

as well as African farmers. War was declared on the elephant, and to-day the animal there is becoming exceedingly rare.

Man has been determined to destroy predatory animals on the pretext that they are 'harmful'. Organized destruction of predators has led to total or partial extermination of some species, such as the black-footed ferret (*Mustela nigripes*) in North America and the Indian cheetah (*Acinonyx jubatus venaticus*). The former may be the rarest mammal in the USA to-day; only 90 were found during a seven-year survey, and some of them were counted twice. The cheetah is also threatened in Africa, like all spotted cats which are sought for their fur.

Predation is not necessarily a factor controlling the populations victimized. As predators eliminate diseased individuals and the old or infirm, they actually improve populations. Even if predation is a limiting factor, it is useful in that it prevents a numerical increase which upsets the biological balance.

In the western USA coyotes, wolves, pumas and lynx were destroyed because they were accused of killing lambs. This reduction led to a swarming of rodents, which ravaged the habitats. War was then waged on the rodents. The coyotes returned but as, in the meantime, the rodents had disappeared, the Canidae, deprived of some of their natural prey, inflicted much greater damage on the domestic animals. Maintenance of a balance between species is thus profitable to man.

Birds of prey are persecuted all over the world, yet, with rare exceptions, they are never fundamentally harmful, and their populations are always small, since they range over vast territories.

In aquatic milieus war on carnivorous fishes, particularly pike, has led to a swarming of undesirable species and an exaggerated multiplication of others, causing a dwarfism unfavourable to man's interests. In the Amazon basin the destruction of alligators led to a great increase of piranhas, small fish capable of devouring an ox in a few minutes. It is the same story when we examine the destruction of crocodiles. While it is true that their diet includes some fishes, especially among middle-aged adults, most of their prey are species without economic importance. This is the case with the Nile crocodile (H. B. Cott, *Trans. Zool. Soc. London*, 29, no. 14, 1961). These large reptiles therefore have an important place in the aquatic biological associations of warm regions. They are also hunted for their skin. All crocodilians are becoming rare, and the Nile crocodile has vanished from much of its habitat. Skin hunters are thus threatening a natural resource which would continue to yield good profits if the kill were kept proportionate to the size of the populations. The same is true of alligators in the southern United States.

Outside natural reserves, survival of the large fauna can be assured only if it is integrated in the huge ensembles now being planned. The notion of managing fauna goes back to Charlemagne and the decrees of medieval princes. These old texts, although unadorned with modern scientific terms, contain all the basic principles for rational administration of the fauna. In the past thirty years North American ecologists have developed a number of theories which combine protecting the animals with securing a profit from marginal zones. The principle consists in maintaining the largest number of animals compatible with the carrying-capacity, while slaughtering a maximal number annually. The principle applies to domestic cattle, for a farmer wants a maximum profit but realizes his pasture can support only a certain number of head.

This necessitates ecological research on every aspect of the problem, particularly the habitat's carrying-capacity and the structure and dynamics of animal populations.

Managing large fauna in temperate regions

The first modern data on this subject were obtained from North American Cervidae. As an example, the mule-deer (*Odocoileus hemionus californicus*) which live in the Jawbone district on the western slope of the Sierra Nevadas in California, number about 5,570, with an annual increase of 1,800 or 32% (Leopold *et al*, 1951). Only 7% are shot (400), and 2% are victims of predators; this means that 23% die from malnutrition. They could have been exploited by hunters instead of perishing miserably.

Although hunting and the annual slaughter of a certain number of animals would seem opposed to conservation, the contrary is true. A population is more productive when it is in balance with its surroundings. An abundant food supply favours reproduction by keeping does well during pregnancy. In a Utah forest, Costley (quoted by Longhurst *et al* 1952) found that in areas where there was an open season on doe the mortality among fawns was 25%, as against 42% in regions where only males were hunted. Population growth is clearly greater in zones where hunting pressure is greatest, as in the case of fish populations.

All large animals, including the American bison, resemble Cervidae in this respect. According to Fuller, the bison herd in Wood Buffalo National Park, Canada, which numbers between 14,000 and 16,500, is too large for its habitat. The same is true of Elk Island National Park in the province of Alberta. The southern part was enclosed shortly before 1950, and the following year 10 males and 65 females were placed there. By 1959 the population had grown to 520, and 110 animals had to be removed so as to prevent degradation of the habitat.

Constant increase in the size of bison herds led Canadian authorities to permit shooting 30 animals in 1959, the first time this had happened since 1893. Other animals, particularly pronghorns and wapitis, have been similarly exploited.

In the Old World the best example is the saiga antelope (*Saiga tatarica*) in the USSR (Bannikov, 1961). This formerly abundant species had dwindled to less than a thousand animals by 1920 and many people feared it would become extinct. Populations then

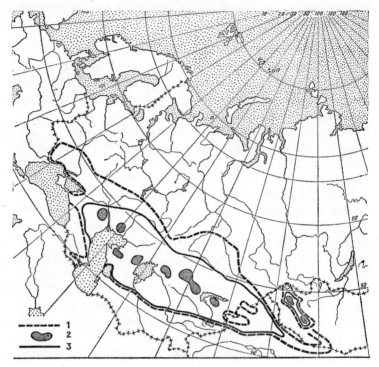

Fig. 72
Distribution of the saiga antelope, Saiga tatarica.
1 distribution in historic times   3 distribution today
2 reduction of the territory about 1920   From Bannikov, 1961.

increased until two million animals were scattered over a million square miles (*fig* 72). More than 500,000 saigas live on the right bank of the Volga. Since 1951, 300,000 have been shot annually, yielding 6000 tons of good meat, fat, leather and horn. Yet the population still seems to be increasing. This antelope, which, because of its mobility and regular migrations does not degrade its habitat, and which is capable of feeding on plants that cattle will not touch, provides a profit from zones that would otherwise be unproductive. Likewise, about 16,000 moose are shot every year in Sweden, without detriment to the stock.

European bison at liberty in Bialowieza Park, Poland: the species
has been saved by breeding in captivity

Left Bear cub, Yellowstone Park

Centre Rhinoceros put to sleep with a tranquillizer: the animal can then be transported to an area where the species has vanished

Below Lions in the Kruger Park. Visitors are forbidden to leave their cars or to feed the animals

Management of the large African fauna

The success of managing large animals in temperate regions led biologists to think that similar methods could produce interesting results in other countries as well. The question is particularly acute in Africa, which shelters the last surviving group of large mammals. Ungulates predominate, especially in the savannas. As the continent is in the midst of a political, economic and social evolution, it is essential to reconcile the imperatives of the protection of nature with the needs of a population more preoccupied with the present than the future. Rational game cropping might protect it better than a multiplication of reserves, whose borders are liable to be 'nibbled' away. Management would save it from human beings in whose language the same word designates the meat and the animal (such as *nyama* in Kiswahili), and it would provide them with the proteins so desperately needed in certain parts of the black continent.

A series of studies on the ungulates of the savannas, which have been made in East Africa and the eastern Congo since the last war, may serve as a basis for a rational utilization of African game.[1] These show that there can be an enormous density of game animals in open habitats. Bourlière and Verschuren (1960), for example, counted 203 animals, including 65 buffaloes and 104 Buffon cobs, per square mile in Albert National Park.

It is even more interesting to convert the number of animals into their weight, in other words, to determine the live weight of herbivores per surface unit by multiplying the number of individuals in each species by their average weight (biomass). This information, which is also used to estimate the value of pasture for feeding cattle,

---

[1] See also the reviews of the Manyara Conference, Tanzania (February, 1961) and those on the Arusha Symposium (September, 1961, Conservation of Nature and Natural Resources in modern African States). In Nairobi the General Assembly of the IUCN met in 1963 and a symposium on wildlife management and land use practices was held in the same city in 1967. There was also a Convention on Protection and Utilization of African Wildlife in Kampala in 1965. Dr N. J. van der Merwe, Secretary of the Committee for the Co-ordination of Nature Conservation in the Transvaal, writes (*in litt.*) that the Nature Conservation Co-ordinating Committee (NACOR) has been meeting annually since 1962 to discuss problems affecting wildlife management in Africa.

gives the nutritional capacity of a given habitat. Bourlière and Verschuren cite amounts of living matter varying from 43,190 to 116,723 pounds per square mile in the savannas of Albert National Park. The results of censuses covering 232 square miles lead to a record figure of 139,578 pounds of ungulates per square mile.

UNGULATES IN THE SAVANNAS OF THE CENTRAL SECTOR OF ALBERT NATIONAL PARK, ACCORDING TO 1959 CENSUSES COVERING AN AREA OF 232 SQUARE MILES.

Species	Average weight (lb.)	No. of animals	Average per sq. mile	Live weight per sq. mile
elephant	7,700	1,026	4·44	34,188
hippopotamus	3,080	4,800	20·77	63,971
buffalo	1,100	7,402	32·04	35,244
topi	286	1,199	5·19	1,484
waterbuck	330	760	3·29	1,086
Buffon cob	154	4,976	21·54	3,317
reed-buck	88	61	0·26	
bushbuck	110	53	0·22	
warthog	154	603	1·87	288
giant forest-hog	308	35	0·15	

139,578 lb/sqm

Some even higher densities have been observed. Petrides and Swank (1958) found that one square mile of Queen Elizabeth Park, Uganda, contained, on the average, 40 hippopotamuses, 7 elephants, 10 buffaloes, 8 waterbucks, 7 warthogs, 1·5 Buffon cob and 1·3 bushbuck, which corresponds to a live weight of 199,109 pounds per square mile. This is the record at present. These live weights are often much larger than those found in other parts of the world, especially on the Great Plains of North America.

A comparison with live weights of domestic herbivores is even more interesting if the natural habitats of wild ungulates are compared with those where domestic animals are now pastured. In the Congo to-day some natural pastures cannot support more than 31,000 pounds per square mile. In Kenya *Themeda* grassy savannas can carry cattle weighing 20,500 to 31,000 pounds per square mile; anything beyond this causes the habitat to show signs of degradation. Improved pastures can, of course, support larger amounts and, according to Bourlière and Verschuren, they can take up to 370,000 pounds per square mile. One should, however, examine the cost. Although such conditions may prevail in certain areas, the majority of African habitats would never be able to support such a live weight, even if they were transformed by man.

Natural African habitats can thus support as many wild as domestic animals and, in most cases, the live weight of native herbivores is the same in natural savannas as in pastures which have been improved at great expense.[1] The chief cause lies in the fact that the plant cover is better used. The total mass of wild herbivores, of which there are often from 10 to 20 species in the same district, utilizes the total mass of plants constituting the habitat. Grazing species such as zebras, gnus and hartebeest take the herblike plants; others, like impalas and many gazelles, feed on bushes, even thorny ones, while the elephant devours almost all plants, including the foliage of trees and plants rejected by other herbivores. It is ecological nonsense to replace an entire fauna by a single type of animal, for it leads to degradation of plant production. Furthermore, the part of the carcass useful for food is always proportionately larger among wild animals. Although it rarely exceeds 50% of live weight in cattle owned by Africans, it is as much as 58% in the eland and 63% in Grant's gazelle. The protein yield is also definitely larger in game which is low in fat, so it is easy to dry the meat (Ledger, *Conservation of Nature and Natural Resources in modern African States* N. S. Publ. no. 1 IUCN, 1963).

It appears with increasing clarity that the plant cover and soil characteristics in a good part of Africa are such that they cannot be changed without lowering their resistance. Moreover, human intervention requires financial investments for clearing land, creating water holes, fencing and spraying to remove insects, without counting maintenance—which young African states are poorly equipped to make. The best solution thus seems to be the preservation of natural biological associations, particularly those of large animals which are better adapted to their habitat than the domestic cattle that might take their place. They also have a natural resistance to a large number of tropical diseases and are better able to withstand high temperatures and drought.

---

[1] See L. M. Talbot and M. H. Talbot, *Trans. 28th N. Amer. Wildlife Nat. Res. Conf.* 1963: 465-476.

Rational use of the fauna consists in taking every year a number determined by ecological studies and based on population structure, productivity and rate of replacement. Hunters can eliminate the excess number of animals, but a better method involves organized cropping of the wild fauna regarded as 'cattle'. The major problem, which has not yet been solved, concerns the preservation and transportation of the meat. Unlike domestic cattle, which can easily be taken to abattoirs, wild animals have to be cut up on the spot and the meat transported from the 'bush' to the city dweller in good condition and as quickly as possible.

Some mammals can be kept in huge enclosures, where it is easy to capture them. A number of South African farms are now raising springboks commercially. In other instances it is possible at certain seasons to head the animals toward corrals, where they are sorted. The meat can also be dried at abattoirs, like the African biltong, and better procedures will doubtless be found to preserve it.

Several attempts to exploit wild game rationally are in progress in East Africa, particularly at Henderson ranch in Rhodesia, south-east of Bulawayo. A preliminary census was taken there and a study made of the structure of herbivore populations by age and sex. This information makes it possible to determine how many animals, especially impalas and zebras, can be slaughtered while keeping populations at a high level. This operation yields a profit estimated at £15,000 sterling, which is higher than that of regular cattle raising.

A similar utilization of the large wild fauna is in process in the Transvaal, South Africa (Riney, 1963). In 1959 no less than 3,593 tons of meat were sold by ranch owners, most of it from impalas which had become too numerous, kudus and gnus; the total revenue from this came to £194,530. Farmers in a specific area proved that 8,800 lb. of live weight of cattle per square mile degraded pastures and yielded an annual profit of £600, whereas 17,600 lb. of wild herbivores yielded £700 and preserved the habitat, which even regenerated in eroded areas.

A rational use of large African game would also suppress, or at least discourage, poaching. The main causes, aside from profit, are the 'meat hunger' of the inhabitants and an innate love of the hunt. Rationalization of the sport would eliminate some of the excuses for poaching, which would become a crime with no economic or psychological justification.

Management of the fauna would also make it possible to control the overpopulation of large mammals in several parts of Africa. It would avoid overgrazing and absorb the population excess, which causes degradation of habitats. In and near Queen Elizabeth National Park, Uganda, there are over 28,000 hippopotamuses in Lakes Edward and George. This is too many in view of the fact that the district is also inhabited by elephants, buffaloes, waterbucks, cobs and warthogs. As a hippopotamus takes about 400 pounds of plants (wet weight) every night, the habitat is suffering from serious degradation and erosion, especially severe gullying. Much of the soil is becoming bare, while plants are disappearing in favour of thorny bushes that hippopotamuses do not touch. The situation is different in Albert Park, where the population is equally dense, but where the habitat has remained in as good condition as when the zone was set aside as a reserve. Soil factors may partly explain this (see Curry-Lindahl, Expl. P. N. Albert and P. N. Kagera, IPNCRU Brussels, 1961).

It was suggested that the population be reduced to about 5,000 animals, a number corresponding approximately to the carrying-capacity of the habitat (Petrides and Swank, 1958). A thousand animals could be slaughtered each year without harming the population. These measures would assure the Africans a supply of excellent proteins. The same solution would also be helpful with elephants which have been multiplying in East Africa, especially in the Congo, Uganda and Kenya. Over-population causes profound transformation of habitats through deforestation. Fifty-five to fifty-nine per cent of the trees in the Murchison Falls National Park were destroyed between 1932 and 1956 (see also the spectacular photographs published by Bourlière and Verschuren, 1960, Pl XII). In most reserves elephant populations require control, for natural regulation does not take effect until the balance has already been badly upset.

Uncontrolled massacres, such as the traditional hunt of the lechwe (*Kobus leche*) in Rhodesia, must, of course, be avoided. Although these antelopes have regressed in part of their ancient habitat, they still live in large flocks in flooded plains and swampy areas, especially in the Kafue Flats. Inhabited districts show signs of overgrazing and there is high mortality during the dry season. Periodically the Africans had the habit of driving flocks of lechwe towards corrals, where several thousand were slaughtered. This hunt—known as *chila*—could be replaced by a more sensible exploitation which would assure the survival of this beautiful antelope, while providing a good profit for inhabitants of the flooded plains of the Kafue River. In December 1966, the lechwe was put under government protection as its numbers had been reduced from 17,000 to 4,000.

Management of the large African fauna may thus reconcile the interests of conservationists with those of economists eager to derive a profit from marginal zones. Any mistake could cause a decrease in the size of animal populations, but careful exploitation of the game should assure a supply of protein which would help the African diet.

Natural reserves and national parks are, of course, excepted, because no human intervention must interfere with the natural balance in these areas. Furthermore, the fauna cannot be treated in the same manner everywhere. There are fundamental differences between East and West Africa, caused by ecological conditions and densities in big game populations. As in all aspects of conservation, there are no general solutions: rather a multitude of individual cases. But if man is prudent, the fauna can be managed so as to assure its survival in a world which has been transformed in a man-orientated manner. This will solve the complicated problem of the coexistence of large mammals with an expanding human industry.

ii: Rational exploitation of populations of marine mammals and birds
Seals and walruses

Land mammals are not the only ones which man can protect while at the same time deriving a reasonable profit from them. The most striking case is that of the fur seals (*Callorhinus ursinus*) of the Pribilof Islands in the North Pacific (Kenyon, Scheffer and Chapman, 1954). These seals settle on the beaches in large herds during the summer and are now exploited for their fur. Their populations have suffered many vicissitudes, and at one point it was feared they would disappear or share the sad fate of other species, particularly those in the Antarctic.

When the Pribilof Islands were discovered in 1786–87, these seals had a population of 2·5 million, but the animals were slaughtered until scarcely a million remained in 1835. In 1868, when the United States obtained possession of the islands, 242,000 seals were killed, and the massacre continued until the end of the century. Hunting on the high seas was particularly devastating since no distinction of age or sex could be made. By 1897 the seal population had dropped to about 400,000 and by 1911 to 215,000, or less than one-tenth of the number that had inhabited the islands at the time of their discovery.

The United States Government then forbade all hunting at sea of seals and otters, and at once the seal population began to recover. In 1947 it was estimated at more than 1·5 million, despite the killing of a certain number determined by scientific studies based on the biological characteristics of the species (fig 73).

Population structure is based on polygamy. As is the case among many seals, breeding bulls come ashore first; they acquire a harem of females, which usually numbers between 80 and 90 but may contain 160 or more. (The average number of females in a harem increased from 42 in 1935 to 95 in 1947 as populations grew). As these harems are obtained by battling other males, there are a great many whose survival is not essential to the welfare of the species. These 'bachelors', ranging in age from one to seven, collect in large groups while waiting for the time when they will be old enough and strong enough to challenge the harem bulls. The present population is such that an average of 62,000 can be collected annually. The fur and by-products of these animals provide a good income for the island inhabitants. Since 1911 the US Fish and Wildlife Service has been administering this natural wealth and making scientific studies necessary to the welfare of the seals. The US also shares its profit with Canada, Japan and other countries in return for their work on sealing on the high seas.

The Cape fur seal (*Arctocephalus pusillus*) is also rationally exploited along South African coasts, but other southern populations, once abundant, have been reduced so much that their exploitation in the near future seems unlikely.

Guano birds

These birds provide another illustration of how man can derive profit from natural resources without upsetting the natural balance, but the essential in this case is not so much the management as the protection of the birds (Dorst, 1956). Representatives of the Pelecaniformes order, cormorants, boobies and pelicans, nest in enormous colonies on the northern coasts of Chile and Peru and deposit guano, a fertilizer famous for its nitrogenous products. Despite their tropical latitudes, these shores are bathed by the cold Humboldt Current, which is so rich in plankton and fishes that oceanographers speak of waves 'black with animals' and of 'plankton soup.' An anchovy (*Engraulis ringens*) is the cornerstone of this marine life with a population estimated at 10 thousand billion individuals or a mass of some 20 million tons. The marine birds which feed on the fishes and are the chief producers of guano are the guanay or Peruvian cormorant (*Phalacrocorax bougainvillii*), the variegated Peruvian booby (*Sula variegata*) and the brown pelican (*Pelecanus occidentalis thagus*). These highly gregarious birds form dense colonies on little islets near the coast. Cormorants may have three nests per square yard and, as each pair produces an average of two or three young, there are roughly twelve birds to a square yard. All of them deposit their excreta on the nesting sites, instead of scattering them as do other marine species. As they do not build nests, and as it never rains on the Peruvian coast, the deposits rapidly form a crust. By the 19th century these layers, which had been accumulating since ancient times, were in some places 125 feet deep.

Although this fertilizer was used in pre-Columbian times, the Incas had strict laws to protect the birds. Garcilasso de la Vega, in his 'History of the Incas,' published in 1604, records that 'in the time of the Inca kings they were so careful of the birds that, during the nesting season, no one was permitted, under penalty of death, to go to the islands for fear of frightening them or making them leave their nests, or to kill them on the islands or elsewhere.' Unfortunately a real 'guano fever' spread round the world in the 19th century. Whole fleets of ships came to collect this product, which was 'mined' by armies of Asiatic coolies. It is estimated that between 1851 and 1872 about 10 million tons were removed from the Chincha Islands, one of the largest nesting centres. Between 1848 and 1875 20 million tons were exported to North America and Europe.

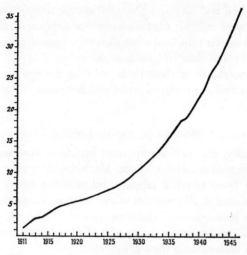

Fig. 73

Increase in the population of fur seals, Callorhinus ursinus, *on the Pribilof Islands since the application of protective measures and a rational exploitation of these seals. In ordinates, numbers in hundreds of thousands. From data published by Kenyon and Scheffer US Dept. Interior, Fish and Wildlife Service Special Sci. Report—Wildlife no. 12 1954.*

This feverish exploitation was accompanied by complete destruction of the nesting colonies. The harvest continued throughout the year, even during the breeding period, and workers did not hesitate to club birds to death for 'fun'. Eggs were also collected and shipped off in barrels for various industrial purposes.

This soon led to a reduction of the guano supply, and in 1909–1910 only 23,000 tons were collected. In the face of this dire threat to the national economy, the Peruvian Government confided the administration of the islands to the newly established Compañia Administradora del Guano, which forbade visitors completely. Soon the colonies began to recover, although the balance has doubtless changed since populations suffered in varying degrees. The most common birds to-day are those best adjusted to man; the Peruvian cormorant, now the predominant species with a population estimated at 15 million, produces 85% of the guano.

Two hundred and fifty-five thousand metric tons of the fertilizer were deposited in 1953; the following year deposits reached a peak of 300,000 metric tons, and since then they have declined. To-day the deposit is less than 100,000 tons annually.

The preservation of these birds provides a magnificent natural spectacle as well as a material profit which was almost lost by man's heedlessness.

iii: Nature and tourism to the rescue of human health

Paradoxically, one of the important problems man will have to solve in the next decades is leisure. Machines are freeing him more and more from physical labour, and working hours are being greatly reduced in all countries where a certain degree of technical ability has been attained. The time may not be far off when men will be able to devote the major part of their time to activities not connected with earning their daily bread.

There is no end to the number of amusements man invents to broaden his culture or occupy his time. Among these activities tourism plays a major role. The love of nature, born a century ago under the influence of the Romanticists, has continued to develop. It is motivated by a deeply-felt need, for civilized, western man leads an artificial life in cities of monstrous size. Most of his life is spent in houses, offices or workshops where the noise and aggressions of collective life fray his nerves. The increasing number of nervous diseases shows that men are in danger when they abandon a balanced natural environment, and this tendency can only become more pronounced as the population grows.

Man's reaction is to take advantage of every free minute to return to nature. Long lines of cars filling suburban roads on a Sunday show that city dwellers will spend hours travelling to reach a forest or river far from their factories. They make us realize the tremendous importance of 'green girdles' of forests and natural landscapes—the marginal areas—in the life of city residents. Suppression or transformation of these districts would be catastrophic in the eyes of the naturalist, as it would remove the last refuge of wildlife in industrialized countries. It would certainly result in serious psychic troubles for the inhabitants, who would find themselves cut off from all contact with a more healthy environment, where outdoor activities are still possible.

Another problem is touring during the increasingly long holidays. Travelling is becoming cheaper and easier. Tourist utilization of natural resources, if properly organized, makes it possible to preserve nature, to derive a profit from marginal zones, and to satisfy the growing need of human populations to enjoy landscapes with their wild flowers and animals.

For man likes to visit not only cathedrals and palaces but natural monuments. Some countries, as in tropical Africa, have little of historical or architectural importance, and a folklore that is rapidly losing its significance. Although there are spectacular waterfalls, and equatorial mountains covered with snow and luxuriant forests, the monotonous savannas have no tourist attractions other than the large animals inhabiting them. Sir Julian Huxley wrote that the sight of large animals evolving freely and without fear in their natural habitat is one of the most moving and exalting spectacles in the world; it is comparable to contemplating a noble edifice or hearing a great symphony. (*The protection of the large fauna and natural habitats in Central and East Africa*, UNESCO, Paris, 1961).

The survival of a fauna which provides the biologist with a thousand subjects for research may also be a source of considerable profit. So many tourists visit Victoria Falls that they may yield more revenue in their natural state than if they had been converted into a hydro-electric factory. Hunting safaris can also help a country to balance its finances.

Landscapes, habitats, the fauna and flora are natural resources whose importance man is apt to minimize. This form of tourism requires transport, hotels, trails, guides and publicity, but it is a mistake to assume that natural reserves can be maintained only by wealthy nations, for new countries can obtain a good income from tourists without making large investments and without ruining their soil by poor agricultural practices.

The national parks in the USA are a model in this respect. Thirty-three in number, they cover 13,461,228 acres and are primarily designed to preserve the grandeur of natural sites, with their flora and fauna. But they are also preserved 'for the profit, the satisfaction and the inspiration of the American people.' They are therefore well organized for tourists, with roads, trails and camp sites. A remarkable information service and abundant guides enable visitors to understand what they see—for example, geological history and physical geography of the regions—and to recognize plants and animals: in a word, to profit both spiritually and intellectually from nature. Bus services, garages and shops are provided for visitors who have the privilege of fishing and swimming in some reserves. The purpose of the parks is to put the public in contact with nature, while providing the essentials in comfort and preserving the natural resources. The National Park Service administers 9 historic parks, 83 National Monuments and various other classified areas, making a total of 192 reservations covering 26,446,477 acres.

These parks have been highly successful; in 1950 there were 37 million visitors, in 1966, 123 million, and in 1967 there were over 139 million. These visitors spent 24 million dollars in the national parks in 1950, which provided a three-million-dollar revenue; in 1965 their expenditures amounted to 131,610 million, which brought a revenue of 7,530 million dollars. To these expenditures should be added a number of others, like the purchase of certain taxed items, such as petrol, that are indirect sources of revenue. These figures show the importance of the national parks, which are considered good investments by local business men. For a moderate sum a national park assures a good income, provides work and becomes part of the country's development.

It is estimated that in the USA the need for parks will be tripled by the end of the century. Vast programmes are being projected, notably 'Mission 66', a ten-year plan started in 1956. This long-range programme to improve and expand the National Park System has invested $350,000,000 to meet the needs of a growing population.

Many other countries, especially the East African states, Kenya, Tanzania, and Uganda (Mathews, 1962), have realized that there is profit to be derived from exploiting their natural wealth. According to figures quoted by Lamprey (*The Natural Resources of East Africa*, Nairobi, 1962), tourists spent some £7 million every year in Kenya, providing the second largest source of revenue. This figure has risen steadily: in 1963, it was 9 million, in 1965, over 10 million, and in 1966, 106,500 tourists spent over 14 million dollars in Kenya. (From Mr Ruoro, UN delegate from Kenya). At least 80% of the 60,000 yearly visitors to East Africa are chiefly attracted by the fauna. Some come to hunt, and outfitting of safaris has become a prosperous activity in large cities. Many visitors, however, prefer to admire the landscapes or to photograph the animals.

We must remember that travel in Africa is still a luxury reserved for the few, but the price of such a trip from Europe or America is decreasing. Hotel accommodation should be improved and bus trips organized so that African travel will no longer be restricted to the wealthy. Furthermore, local travel will develop as a modern western civilization emerges. A schoolboy in a large African city has little more opportunity to see an elephant or a giraffe than his European counterpart. African tours should be encouraged, such as those in Nairobi National Park, Kenya.

The administrators of a national park or reserve must take steps to preserve nature against 'human erosion'. They must also prevent the construction of luxury hotels or artificial attractions for visitors come to enjoy a natural spectacle. Occasionally the number of tourists has to be limited in accordance with the size and type of habitats so that life in the park will not be upset.

A better understanding of the purposes, methods and results of conservation will aid in maintaining and defending the reserves. Many national parks therefore publish inexpensive booklets and organize lectures and guided tours. Publications of the National Parks in the USA cover every aspect of natural history from geology to the identification of common plants, birds and mammals; there are also some good ones in certain eastern European countries such as Poland and Czechoslovakia.

Even in 'underdeveloped' parts of the globe national parks are trying to educate the public and to preserve nature. The interest expressed by Indians in the Kaziranga Reserve in Assam, where Indian rhinoceroses are protected, and the growing interest of Africans in their reserves show that tourism, knowledge of nature and its conservation are three aspects of a single problem. Some private groups not only maintain reserves but educate the public. The Nature Conservancy now owns more than an acre for each of its many thousands of members, while the National Audubon Society of America, the Scouts, youth and camping groups create a state of mind and public opinion receptive to the idea of a balance between man and his environment.

e: THREATENED SPECIES SURVIVE IN CAPTIVITY

Breeding in captivity

It seems apparent that a certain number of species can survive only in partial or complete captivity. Their area of distribution is already, in some instances, greatly reduced and in danger of being transformed. We can regret the fact that the animal cannot be saved in its habitat, but placing it in captivity preserves the stock, even if it is only saved 'as a memory', in Professor V. van Straelen's phrase, since wild animals in artificial conditions may degenerate.

Some attempts made years ago have been successful (Appelman, 1959). The classic example is Père David's deer (*Elaphurus davidianus*), a species of Cervidae native to the plains of north-eastern China. This deer has not been seen in the wild since the Shang dynasty, but survivors were kept in an imperial park south of Peking, Non Hai-Tzu, where no strangers were permitted. Père David, who discovered it in 1865, sent several specimens to Paris the following year, and their descendants perpetuated the species. It vanished from China in 1894 when the flooding Hun Ho carried away the park walls and the deer escaped to be massacred by starving peasants. The last individuals were killed during the Boxer Rebellion in 1900. The species survived thanks to a herd at Woburn Abbey, the Duke of Bedford's estate, from which they were shipped to zoos all over the world. The population has increased from 64 in 1922 to over 300 in 1935 and 447 in 1966.

The same procedure made it possible to save the Przewalski horse, the last wild ancestor of the domestic species, only a few individuals of which still live wild on the borders of Mongolia and China (Bannikov, *Mammalia* 22: 152–60, 1958). On the other hand, the species is flourishing in zoological parks; according to the *Pedigree Book* published by the Prague Zoo (J. Volf), 90 horses (38 stallions and 52 mares) were in captivity on 1st January, 1963. Later that year there were over 110.

The Mesopotamian fallow deer (*Cervus (Dama) mesopotamicus*) was formerly widespread throughout the south-eastern Mediterranean region from Syria and Iran to Libya and the Sudan. It is now found only in forests bordering the Dez and Karcheh Rivers, in the province of Khuzistan, Iran. This remarkable deer, which has been hunted since time immemorial, may vanish in the wild because of hunting and deforestation of its last refuges. It is believed that the population has been reduced to between 200 and 400. Plans have been made to breed the deer in vast enclosures in south-western Iran, and it has already reproduced at Kronberg, Germany, in the Georg von Opel-Freigehege; this is the best guarantee of its survival (Haltenorth, *Säugetierkundl. Mitt.*, 9: 15–39, 1961).

Poland has done a magnificent piece of work in saving the European bison. In 1931 it had 30 of the 96 surviving animals (35 were in Germany). Despite the ravages of the war, the Polish stock, which exists in five breeding centres, the largest being the famous Bialowieza forest, has multiplied until it now numbers 150, or 40% of the livestock in the world. In 1952 the Poles set the bison free in the Bialowieza, where some 120 were living in 1966, and have offered breeding stock to numerous countries.

The Fauna Preservation Society of London recently organized a vast programme to safeguard the Arabian oryx (*Oryx leucoryx*), which is threatened because hunters pursue it in cars. In December 1960, 48 of these unfortunate antelopes were struck down. This oryx used to cover Arabia, Israel, Jordan and part of Iraq, but is now restricted to a narrow region in the Rub-al-Khali desert, in the southernmost part of central Arabia. Its population is now believed to be less than 100, several of which are in Griffith Park, Los Angeles. In April-May 1962, an expedition captured two males and a female for the zoological park in Phoenix, Arizona, where they have since bred.

Similar methods have preserved bird stocks that cannot survive in the wild. In 1925 the trumpeter swan (*Cygnus c. buccinator*) (*fig* 74) population numbered about a hundred. Protective measures and intensive breeding in captivity, begun in 1923, enabled the population to recover (Delacour, 1945), so that there were over 1,000 in 1966. In 1941, when the American Army proposed to install an artillery range in a zone where there were trumpeter swans, President Roosevelt wired the Secretary of War: 'The verdict is for the Trumpeter Swan and against the Army. The Army must find a different nesting place!'

The nene or Hawaiian goose of the Hawaiian Islands (*Branta sandvicensis*), a representative of a group widespread in cold and temperate regions of the northern hemisphere, declined in the past century from an estimated 25,000 to fewer than 40 in 1950. This was caused by hunting, particularly during the moulting season when the birds cannot fly, by predations of introduced mammals, and by transformation of the habitats. An attempt was made to breed the nene first in Hawaii and then, in 1952, at the famous Wildfowl Trust at Slimbridge, in England. This proved eminently successful, thanks to the technical skill and experience of the breeders. In January, 1964, the count was 389 birds, at least half of which were in captivity in England and Hawaii. The US Government has organized a huge programme to restore and preserve the species in Hawaii. In 1967, 84 goslings were taken from the nest as soon as they hatched. The nene was permitted to keep her third family, and domestic nenes are now being released to mate with the wild birds. The goose has thus been preserved from extinction. Other threatened species could also be bred in captivity and then returned to their original habitat. In 1963, the whooping crane had only 33 individuals in the wild and 7 in captivity. On 9th June, 1967, 2 whooping cranes were hatched in Laurel, Maryland; this brings the total to 52, of which 9 are in captivity. As this bird is extremely vulnerable on account of its long migrations across the entire North American continent, more attempts should be made to breed it in captivity. Several have already succeeded.

These measures should, of course, be used only as a last resort, for zoological parks menace the existence of wild fauna, especially rare species. Although some parks try to educate the public by showing animals in an attractive way and play an important role both in propaganda and in breeding rare species, others are prepared to encourage poaching to obtain specimens. They threaten the survival of species in the wild and often keep their captive guests in abominable living quarters.

The most flagrant example is the orangutan (*Pongo pygmaeus*), a large ape of Sumatra and Borneo. Although this primate is protected by law in Indonesia, zoological gardens offer such high prices for the animal that a smuggling organization is centred in Singapore; to-day this ape is one of the most menaced species in the world. Dennis, the first smuggled baby orangutan ever to come to the United States, arrived from London on 7th March, 1967. He probably travelled from Borneo or Sumatra to Singapore, thence to Bangkok and then by jet to Washington, where he was taken to the National Zoo.

Swamp in Corkscrew Swamp Sanctuary, Immokalee, Florida

Half Dome, a granite monolith 8156ft high in Yosemite National Park, USA

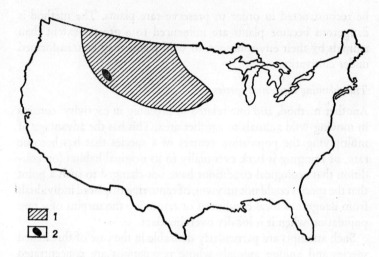

Fig. 74
Reduction of reproductive territory of the trumpeter swan, Cygnus cygnus
buccinator *in the USA (it also nests in Canada).*
1 Former breeding territory   2 Present breeding territory
From H. H. T. Jackson, 1943.

Growing demand for caged birds has also caused serious harm to
the wild avifauna because so many birds perish before reaching the
cages of the breeders.

Botanic gardens, like zoological parks, can preserve stocks of
species which could not be protected in the wild. That is the source
of the ginkgo (*Ginkgo biloba*), which was cultivated near Chinese
temples.

It is hoped that a Sicilian fir (*Abies nebrodensis*) may be preserved
by similar methods. In 1958 only 8 specimens of this tree remained
in the original habitat, and several of these had been seriously
harmed by grazing. Survival of the species is assured because
several nurseries have stalks that regularly bear fruit (Messeri, 1959).
A palm tree of the Marquesas (*Pelagodoxa Henryana*) is likewise
threatened in its homeland but grows under cultivation in Tahiti
and Florida (*fig* 75).

Artificial stations and even entire associations can as a last resort be reconstructed in order to preserve rare plants. The method is dangerous because plants are influenced to a greater extent than animals by their environment, so wild plants may be transformed under cultivation.

Transplanting threatened species

Another method, and one related to breeding in captivity, consists in moving wild animals to another area. This has the advantage of multiplying the population centres of a species that has become rare, of bringing it back eventually to its original habitat (on condition that ecological conditions have not changed to such a point that the species could not survive), of removing displaced individuals from dangerous local conditions or removing the surplus of a rare population when it is locally overabundant.

Such attempts are particularly desirable in the case of threatened species and among animals whose populations are concentrated in several places. Large mammals can now be captured and transported quite easily thanks to immobilizing or tranquillizing drugs injected with a syringe and a gun containing carbonic gas or powder. If this technique is properly employed, it is vastly superior to classic methods of capture such as pursuit by car and lassoing, for it saves the animals from a shock that often proves fatal to delicate species.

Transfers are made in Africa of the rhinoceros, which is disliked by farmers but may be protected in marginal zones. The most successful transfer has been with white rhinoceroses in Uganda. Their population had declined from 350 in 1955 to 80 in 1962 (Cave, *Oryx* 7: 26–29, 1963). The animals were taken from the district of West-Madi, west of the Nile, to Murchison Falls National Park, where the species, which had become rare in the northern part of its habitat, will be safer. Others that were captured in the Umfolosi Game Reserve of Natal were taken in August, 1962, to Rhodesia, where they used to live. Transplanting these rhinoceroses has the advantage of increasing population centres. It also avoids the overpopulation already apparent in Natal reserves, where, according to Colonel J. Vincent, there are 400 head too many. Overgrazing threatens the future of the species, but moving such large animals does pose numerous problems, if only on account of the expense involved.

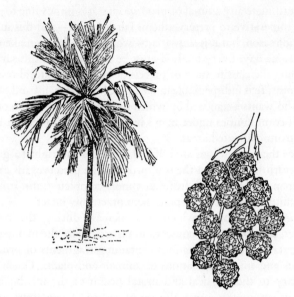

Fig. 75
Pelagodoxa Henryana *of the* Marquesas Islands *(the fruits may be our inches in diameter). This palm, restricted to low altitude rain-forests, has become very rare. Discovered in 1916 at Taipi Vai, Nukuhiva, only a few specimens remain. Its conservation in botanical gardens on Tahiti and in Florida constitutes its best chance for survival. From a photograph published in J. C. McCurrah* Palms *New York 1960.*

3 TOWARDS A RECONCILIATION OF MAN AND NATURE

The essential problems of conservation to-day are closely linked to those of man's survival. Although it is not our responsibility to state with philosophers that humanity has taken the wrong road, we can at least agree with biologists that man made a serious mistake in believing he can ignore his environment. We need to sign a new pact with nature, one which will permit us to live in harmony with it. Only thus can man and nature, twin aspects of the same problem, survive.

Man must realize first of all that he does not have the moral right to exterminate any animal or plant species. It is impossible to create these, imperative to preserve them. Furthermore—and this may be a sordid reason, but it is important—we shall be able to make use of them some day. Every method must be used to assure this survival, including the classification of parcels of ground in natural reserves. This measure is indispensable in the eyes of the naturalist and of anyone who wants a standard by which to gauge the evolution of biological communities under man's influence and who seeks a better yield from cultivated areas.

Once these conditions are fulfilled, man has the right to get the best return he can from the soil, provided he preserves his capital. This management varies from an almost complete transformation of primitive habitats to keeping them practically intact.

In industrial zones, which will increase during the coming decades, the problem of conservation is essentially the maintenance of a certain number of stations containing fragments of primitive habitats and small populations of animals and plants. Green areas necessary to the physical and moral health of the inhabitants of large urban centres must also be preserved. These zones are, of course, only distantly related to primitive habitats, but they shelter a flora and fauna which would have disappeared under other circumstances. Some large cities have made a remarkable effort in this direction. The City Council of Moscow, for example, is preserving an enormous forest girdle around the suburbs to please Sunday strollers and provide shelter for many kinds of animals.

Maintenance of forest and lakes permits the flora and fauna to live in harmony with man. In zones transformed for agriculture it is probable that only parcels of the original habitat can be preserved. Monoculture should be replaced by a polyculture more in keeping with the natural balance and which will take into account the potential of each parcel of ground. This balance makes it possible to preserve fragments of wildlife, while assuring man of sufficient living-space (see Nicholson, 1952).

Conditions are quite different in parts of the world that have not been greatly transformed. There are enormous areas which, to-day at least, could not be turned into fields or pastures without an investment far too great for the majority of the young States. Furthermore, these areas are, for the most part, in the intertropical zone where knowledge acquired in temperate climates does not really apply. It is premature to transform marginal zones, but they can be utilized for immediate profit, while preserving the capital. We must forget the idea that the only way to derive a profit from the earth's surface is by transforming habitats and replacing wild fauna by a few domestic plants and animals that have scarcely changed since man discovered them in Neolithic times.

Each region should be studied as a whole to ascertain its potential. Its use should be determined on the basis of climate, nature of the soil and biological needs. A committee of specialists, including economists, sociologists and biologists, should decide how zones are to be divided, and, in so far as possible, their plans should respect the diversity of the natural systems of the earth. This will prevent the construction of hydro-electric dams which soon become unproductive on account of silting and changing water-courses, and which despoil beautiful valleys for ever. It will prevent industrialization of zones with a very high agricultural productivity that are vanishing under houses and factories. It will prevent cultivation, after gigantic investments, of marginal zones, such as swamps and tropical savannas with a fragile soil. It will prevent poisoning of the planet by industrial waste and chemical products. It will also prevent the massacre of animals and destruction of plant associations, which will eventually be detrimental to humanity.

In the United States the importance of conservation was realized a long time ago, and no other country can rival the National Parks programme. It is also true that industrial and technical civilization has reached a higher point there than elsewhere, so that pressure on wildlife is especially strong. Nowhere else is there such a 'civilization of waste'. President Kennedy, in renewing the conservationist policies of Theodore Roosevelt, adopted a series of important measures, and President Johnson signed legislative acts to ensure the survival of wildlife, the maintenance of a natural balance, and victory in the battle against the multiple forms of pollution. The 'Wilderness Act' indicates that the American nation wishes to reconcile material progress with conservation of natural resources. Secretary Udall stated: 'For the first time, we are mature enough as a nation to have beauty as a part of our national purpose.'

Many nations which have adopted western civilization more recently have also understood this necessity. The new heads of government in Africa often show a comprehension of problems that one would like to find among politicians of older nations. This is also true in Asia, and Ceylon has developed the Gal Oya region in such a way that plantations exist alongside broad primitive habitats.

These vast plans integrating man in nature must, of course, be made by governments. But every one of us has a role to play in the protection or destruction of a parcel of ground. It is on this sum of individuals of good-will that depends the survival of nature, and perhaps of humanity.

The dodo, great auk, passenger pigeon, aurochs, quagga and many more humble animals have vanished for ever because of the misdeeds of men who thought they could be replaced by industrial products. Let us hope that these losses will be compensated by the extinction of *Homo faber* and '*technocraticus*'. It is time for *Homo sapiens* to dominate again, he who knows that only a just balance with nature can assure his legitimate subsistence and the spiritual and material happiness to which he aspires.

Postscript

We have tried to analyse the causes of the degradation of nature and to show by objective arguments that man is mistaken in trying to build a purely artificial world. As biologists we are convinced that the secret of the best utilization of natural resources lies in a harmony between man and his habitat.

Moreover, the world to-day is constantly changing. Men have always believed they were living at a turning-point in history. But there are points when history moves more rapidly just as, in a river, at certain places the current rushes and the water boils before it opens out into a calmer reach.

There is no doubt that we have been living in one of these pivotal periods since 1940, perhaps even since the close of the First World War. A new world is being created before our eyes. The energy at our disposal has already been increased tenfold, and will be increased as much again during the next few years. Methods of production, transportation, and communication are constantly accelerating. Even the form of our thoughts has changed. We live in a technical era in which the humanist has given way to the technocrat. A civilization on the human scale is being replaced by a civilization of machines and robots that may one day devour us.

Homo faber has a staunch faith in the future. To-morrow he will move mountains, change the course of rivers, gather harvests in the desert, go to the moon. And a terribly utilitarian concept has taken possession of us. We are interested only in what can be used now.

This confidence in our technical ability leads us to destroy everything that is still wild and to convert all men to the cult of the machine. Our ambition is to persuade pygmies, Papuans and Indians of the Amazon, to adopt 'western civilization', since we believe that the only pattern for life is that laid down by the inhabitants of Chicago,

London or Paris. We have firm faith in technical progress and in the need for making the whole world think as we do; the unitary tendency is evident.

But suppose man was mistaken in putting so much faith in his new toys? The civilization we are creating may lead only to ruin. Even if man follows the modern shepherds, he should not break all ties with the environment in which he was born. If the modern technical civilization proved to be a mistake, a new civilization could spring from what remains of primitive nature. Future historians would then describe the technical civilization of the 20th century as a huge cancer which almost destroyed humanity but which was discarded by remains of former, more brilliant civilizations and the scraps of nature with which they were in balance. We therefore urge everyone to take out some insurance with nature.

This is another argument for preserving natural stocks, which will assure the survival of our species in case the present course of humanity leads to destruction.

But the preservation of nature must be defended by other arguments than reason and our immediate interest. A man worthy of the name does not have to examine only the utilitarian aspect of things. In our daily behaviour we commit horrible blunders in the name of profit and of what is considered 'functional'. Nature should not be preserved merely because it constitutes the best safeguard for humanity but also because it is beautiful. For millions of years before man existed, a world that was similar to or different from ours displayed its splendour. The same natural laws prevailed, distributing mountains and glaciers, steppes and forests across continents. Man appeared like a worm in a fruit, like a moth in a ball of yarn, and he has chewed his habitat while secreting theories to justify his acts.

Whatever metaphysical position is adopted and whatever place is given to the human species, man has no right to destroy a species of plant or animal on the pretext that it is useless. We have no right to exterminate what we have not created. A humble plant, a tiny insect contains more marvels and greater mysteries than the most wonderful edifices we can construct.

Technocrats say that nature is useless, that it displaces cultivated fields, harbours parasites and prevents us from establishing man's domain based on commercial profit. Let us, therefore, suppress it, they say, as a trace of our past barbarism, so as to forget that we are descendants of cavemen.

But the Parthenon serves no useful purpose either; if we tore it down we could erect buildings to shelter an inadequately housed population. If Notre Dame de Paris is not completely useless, it is at least poorly located; by removing its towers and transepts traffic would be improved, and parking lots could be built where clerks might leave their cars before hurrying to the skyscrapers of to-morrow. We are abashed at the negligence and lack of imagination of technocrats who do not destroy monuments as anachronistic as the praetoriums of Roman forums, medieval cathedrals, the château of Versailles, and the temples of India or Central America; their only excuse for being is their beauty and harmony, and they lead men towards forms of thought and meditation which, fortunately, have nothing 'functional' about them.

And yet man, if he took the trouble, could rebuild the Parthenon ten times over. But he will never be able to recreate a single canyon, which was formed during thousands of years of patient erosion by sun, wind and water; he will never reconstitute the innumerable animals of African savannas, which emerged from an evolution that pursued its winding curves for millions of years before man began to appear among some minute Primates.

Man has enough objective reasons to safeguard nature. But in the last analysis it will only be saved by our hearts. It will only be saved if man loves it, simply because it is beautiful and we need beauty, in whatever form our background and training enable us to appreciate it. For that, too, is an integral part of the human soul.

Bibliography

This list of references incorporates only a small selection of the books and articles dealing with the problems of conservation of nature. A complete bibliography would fill a whole book, for a wealth of information exists in a wide range of literature touching on the most varied subjects. Here I have limited myself to listing those writings whose full bibliographical references are not given in the text. I have also included certain works of general interest.

ABBOTT, R. T. 1949. March of the Giant African Snail. *Natural History*, 58: 68-71
    1951. Operation Snailfolk. *Natural History*, 60: 280-5.
ABEYWICKRAMA, B.A. 1964. *Pre-industrial man in the tropical environment.*
    Pastoralism I.U.C.N. Ninth Technical Meeting. I.U.C.N. Publ. N.S. no. 4:
    50-9
ALEXANDER, P. 1965. *Atomic Radiation and Life.* London (Penguin Books).
ALLAN, H. H. 1936. Indigene versus Alien in the New Zealand Plant World.
    Ecology, 17: 187-93.
ALLEN, G. M. 1942. *Extinct and vanishing mammals of the Western hemisphere with
    the marine species of all the oceans.* Am. Com. Int. Wild Life Prot. S.P., no. 11.
ANCELIN, J. 1953. Peut-on parler d'un 'overfishing' du Hareng? *La Pêche
    maritime* 32, No. 903: 246-8.
ANDRÉ, M. 1947. L'envahissement du réseau hydrographique français par le Crabe
    chinois *Eriocheir sinensis*. H. M. Edw. *Eev. Scient.* 85: 33-8.
ANGOT, M. 1959. Evolution de la pêche du Troca *Trochus niloticus* L. en Nouvelle-
    Calédonie. Un exemple d' 'overfishing' avec ses causes et les remèdes apportés.
    Terre et Vie: 307-14.
ANONYMOUS. 1961. The Leathery Turtle or Luth. *Oryx*, 6: 116-25.
APPELMAN, F. J. 1959. *Zoological gardens and private collections can make an important
    contribution to the preservation of wild fauna.* Netherlands Com. Int. Nat.
    Protection (Amsterdam) Medd. 18: 15-31.
ARVILL, R. 1967. *Man and Environment. Crisis and the Strategy of Choice.* London
    (Penguin Books).
AUBRÉVILLE, A. 1947. The disappearance of the tropical forests of Africa.
    Unasylva, 1: 5-11.
    1949. *Climats, forêts et désertification de l'Afrique tropicale.* Paris (Soc. Ed. Geo.
    Mar. Colon.)
BAELS, H. 1946. Protection du cheptel marin. *La Pêche maritime*, 29 (no. 822),
    p. 193.
BANNIKOV, A. G. 1961. L'écologie de *Saiga tatarica* L. en Eurasie, sa distribution
    et son exploitation rationnelle. *Terre et Vie*: 77-85.
BARKER, R. J. 1958. Notes on some ecological effects of DDT sprayed on elms.
    J. Wildlife Mgt., 22 (3): 269-74.
BARRAU, J., and DEVAMBEZ, L. 1957. Quelques résultats inattendus de
    l'acclimatation en Nouvelle-Calédonie. *Terre et Vie*: 324-34.
BARTLETT, H. H. 1955. *Fire in relation to Primitive Agriculture and Grazing in the
    Tropics.* Annotated Bibliography. Ann Arbor (Univ. Michigan, Botanical
    Garden).
BAUER, L., and WEINITSCHKE, H. 1964. *Landschaftspflege und Naturschutz.*
    Iena (G. Fischer).
BENNETT, H. H. 1939. *Soil Conservation.* London (McGraw-Hill).
BESSON, L. 1931. L'altération du climat d'une grande ville. *Ann. Hygiène
    publique, industrielle et sociale*, 9 (8): 1-34.

BIGALKE, R. 1937. The naturalization of animals, with special reference to South Africa. *S. Afr. J. Sci.* 33: 46-63.

BLANC, M. 1958. Lutte contre l'onchocercose et protection pisicole en A.O.F. *Terre et Vie*: 112-27.

BOURLIÈRE, F. and VERSCHUREN, J. 1960. *Introduction à l'écologie des Ongulés au Parc national Albert.* Inst. P. N. Congo Belge, Brussels.

BROSSET, A. 1963. Statut actuel des Mammifères des îles Galapagos. *Mammalia*, 27: 323-38.

BROWN, A. W. A. 1960. *Ecological consequences of the development of resistance.* Report of the Eighth Technical Meeting. I.U.C.N., Warsaw-Cracow, 1960, R.T. 8//II3, 4p.

BUDKER, P. 1957. *Baleines et baleiniers.* Paris (Horizons de France).

BUGHER, J. C. 1956. Effects of Fission Material on Air, Soil and Living Species. In: *Man's Role in Changing the Face of The World.* Chicago (Univ. Chicago Press): 831-48.

BURKENROAD, M. D. 1948. Fluctuation in abundance of Pacific Halibut. *Bull. Bingham Ocean. Coll.* 11: 81-129.

CANSDALE, G. S. 1952. *Animals and man.* London (Hutchinson).

CARIÉ, P. 1916. L'acclimatation à l'île Maurice. Mammifères et Oiseaux. *Bull. Soc. nat. Acclim. France*, 63: 10-18, 37-46, 72-79, 107-110, 152-159, 191-198, 245-250, 355-363 (see also *ibid*: 1910, p.462).

CARSON, R. 1963. *Silent Spring.* London (Hamish Hamilton).

CHEVALIER, A. 1950. La décadence des sols et de la végétation en Afrique occidentale française et la protection de la nature. *Bois et forêts des tropiques*, no. 16: 335-53.

CLARK, A. H. 1949. *The invasion of New Zealand by people, plants and animals.* New Brunswick (Rutgers Univ. Press).
1956. The Impact of exotic invasion on the remaining New World Mid-latitude Grasslands. In: *Man's Role in Changing The Face of The Earth*, Chicago (Univ. Chicago Press): 737-62.

CLARK, C. 1963. Agricultural Productivity in relation to population. In: *Man and his Future*, London (Churchill): 23-35.

CLAUSEN, C. P. 1956. *Biological Control of Insect Pests in the Continental United States.* U.S. Dept. of Agriculture, Techn. Bull., no. 1139.

COLAS, R. 1962. *La pollution des eaux.* Paris (Presses universitaires de France).

COMMONER, B. 1966. *Science and Survival.* London (Victor Gollancz).

COUTURIER, M. 1962. *Le Bouquetin des Alpes.* Grenoble (published by the author).

CRAMP, S. 1963. Toxic chemicals and birds of prey. *Brit. Birds*, 56: 124-39.

CROKER, R. S. 1954. The sardine story—a tragedy. *Outdoor Calif.* 15 (1): 1 6-8

CUMBERLAND, K. B. 1962. Moas and men. New Zealand about AD 1250. *Geogr. Rev.* 52: 151-73.

DALE, T., and CARTER, V. G. 1955. *Topsoil and civilization*, Norman (Univ. Oklahoma Press).

DARBY, H. C. 1956. The clearing of the woodland in Europe. In: *Man's Role in Changing The Face of The Earth*, Chicago (Univ. Chicago Press): 183-216.

DARLING, F. F. 1960. *Wildlife in an African Territory.* London (Oxford University Press).

DARLING, F. FRASER, and MILTON, J. P. (Ed.) 1966. *Future environments of North America.* New York (Nat. Hist. Press).

DASMANN, R. F. 1959. *Environmental Conservation.* New York (John Wiley).
1964. *African Game Ranching.* Oxford (Pergamon Press).
1965. *The Destruction of California.* New York (Macmillan) and London (Collier-Macmillan).

DELACOUR, J. 1945. Le sauvetage du Cygne trompette *Cygnus cygnus buccinator.* *Oiseau R.F.O.*, 15: 40-8.

DETURK, C. 1962. *The economic value of a state park to an area.* I.U.C.N., Report of 1st World Conf. Nat. Parks (Seattle 1962).

DORST, J. 1956. L'exploitation du guano au Pérou. La protection de la nature au service de l'économie humaine. *Terre et Vie*: 49-63.

——— 1958. Le Cobe Lechwe en Rhodésie du Nord. *Terre et Vie*: 103-11.

——— 1958. Enquête sur le statut actuel des Ongulés dan l'Afrique au sud du Sahara. Introduction. *Mammalia*, 22: 357-70.

——— 1961. Le role du scientifique dans la conservation de la nature. *Experientia*, 17: 1-4.

——— 1961. The fate of wildlife in the Galapagos Islands. *Oryx*, 6: 53-9.

DORST, J., and GIBAN, J. 1954. Les Mammifères acclimatés en France depuis un siècle. *Terre et Vie*: 217-29.

DORST, J. and HOFFMANN, L. 1963. The importance of wetland habitat for European and Asiatic migrant waterfowl wintering in Africa. I.U.C.N., *Conservation of Nature and Nat. Res. in modern African States.* Publ. N.S. no. 1: 144-7.

DORST, J. and MILON, PH. 1964. Acclimatation et conservation de la Nature dans les îles subantarctiques françaises. In: *Biologie antarctique.* Paris (Herman): 579-88.

EAST, B. 1949. Is the lake trout doomed? *Nat. Hist.*, 58: 424-28.

EGLER, F. E. 1942. Indigene versus alien in the development of arid Hawaiian vegetation. *Ecology*, 23: 14-23.

EHRLICH, S. 1959. De l'intérêt de l'élevage du Ragondin en étangs de pisciculture. *Bull. Fr. Pisciculture*, 32 (194): 28-32.

ELLIS, M. M. 1937. Detection and measurement of stream pollution. *Bull. U.S. Bur. Fish.*, 48, no 22: 365-437.

ELTON, C. S. 1958. *The ecology of invasions by animals and plants.* London (Methuen) and New York (John Wiley).

ERICHSEN, J. J. R. 1964. *Fish and River Pollution.* London (Butterworths).

FONTAINE, M. 1956. Les océans et les dangers résultant de l'utilisation de l'énergie atomique. *J. Cons. int. expl. Mer.*, 21: 241-9.

FOSBERG, F. R. (Ed.). 1963. *Man's Place in the island ecosytem. A Symposium.* Honolulu (Bishop Museum Press).

FOURY, A. 1960. L'acclimatation des plantes prairiales. *In*: Colloque Etude. Prairies. Soc. Bot. France. Mémoires publiés par la revue *Fourrage* no. 4: 4-14.

FRIES, C. 1959. The fate of Arcadia. *Land use and human history in the Mediterranean region.* I.U.C.N. Seventh Technical Meeting. (Athens 1948), vol 1: 90-7. (One should also consult by the same author: *Vagentill Rom*, 1953 and *Romerska Vägar*, Stockholm 1957).

FULLER, W. A. 1961. The ecology and management of the American Bison. *Terre et Vie*: 286-304.

FUNAIOLI, V. and SIMONETTA, A. M. 1961. Statut actuel des Ongulés en Somalie. *Mammalia*, 25: 97-111.

FURON, R. 1947. *L'érosion du sol.* Paris (Payot).

GABRIELSON, I. N. 1959. *Wildlife Conservation.* New York (Macmillan).

GATES, D. B. 1960. Pacific Sardine. In:*California Ocean Fisheries Resources to the year 1960.* State of Calif. Dept. Fish and Game: 46-8. (See also *Biennial Reports*, California Dept. of Fish and Game, especially 1954 and 1957).

GEIER, P. W. and CLARK, L. R. 1960. *An ecological approach to pest control.* I.U.C.N. Report, Eighth Technical Meeting, Warsaw-Cracow, 1960; R.T. 8/II/7, 6p.

GILLET, H. 1960. Etude des pâturages du Ranch de l'Ouadi Rime (Tchad). *J. Agri. Trop. Bot. appl.* 7: 465-528; 615-708.

GOODMAN, G. T., EDWARDS, R. W., and LAMBERT, J. M. (Ed.). 1965. *Ecology and The Industrial Society.* Oxford (Blackwell). (Brit. Fcol. Soc. Symposium no. 5).

GRAHAM, E. H. 1944. *Natural Principles of Land Use*. New York (Oxford Univ. Press).

GRAHAM, M. 1949. *The Fish Gate*. London (Faber and Faber).

1956. Harvests of the Seas. In: *Man's Role in Changing The Face of The Earth*. Chicago (Univ. Chicago Press): 487-503.

GREENWAY, J. C. Jr. 1958. *Extinct and Vanishing Birds of the World*. Am. Com. for Int. Wildlife Prot. (New York) S.P. no. 13.

GRISON, P. and LHOSTE, J. 1960. *Aspects écologiques des traitements effectués sur des parasites autochtones ou importés*. I.U.C.N. Report. Eighth Technical Meeting, Warsaw-Cracow, 1960, R.T. 8/II/10, 6p.

GROS, A. 1960. La convention sur la pêche et la conservation des ressources biologiques de la haute mer. *Recueil Cours Acad. Droit Int.* (1959), 97: 1-89.

GRZIMEK, M. and GRZIMEK, B. 1960. Census of plains animals in the Serengeti National Park, Tanganyika. *J. Wildlife Manag.* 24: 27-37.

GUERRIN, A. 1957. *Humanité et subsistances*. Neuchâtel (Ed. Griffon).

GUILLOTEAU, J. 1949. La dégradation des sols dans les territoires d'outre-mer. Enquête en Afrique occidentale française et au Cameroun. *Bull. agr. Congo Belge*, 40: 1193-1242 (Conf. Afr. Sols, Goma, 1948: Comm. no. 74).

1950. La dégradation des sols tropicaux. *C.R. XXV session, Inst. Int. Sci. politiques et sociales appl. pays civilisations différentes* (1949): 83-135.

1958. Le problème des feux de brousse et des brûlis dans la mise en valeur et la conservation des sols en Afrique au sud du Sahara. *Terre et Vie*: 161-85.

HADEN-GUEST, S. WRIGHT, J. K., and TECLAFF, E. M. (ed.). 1956. *A world geography of forest resources*. New York (Ronald Press).

HARDY, A. 1959. *The Open Sea: Its Natural History*. Part II. *Fish and Fisheries*. London (Collins).

HARPER, F. 1945. *Extinct and vanishing mammals of the world*. Am. Com. Int. Wildlife Prot. (New York) S.P., no. 12.

HARRISSON, T. 1962. Present and future of the Green Turtle. *Oryx*, 6: 265-9.

HARROY, J. P. 1944. *Afrique, terre qui meurt*. Bruxelles (Hayez et Office int. de Librairie).

HARTHOORN, A. M. 1962. Translocation as a means of preserving wild animals. *Oryx*, 6: 215-27.

HAW, R. C. 1959. *The Conservation of Natural Resources*. London (Faber and Faber).

HAWKES, A. L. 1961. A review of the nature and extent of damage caused by oil pollution at sea. *Trans. 26th N. Amer. Wildlife and Nat. Res. Conf.*: 343-55.

HEICHELHEIM, F. M. 1956. Effects of classical Antiquity on the land. In: *Man's Role in Changing The Face of The Earth*. Chicago (Univ. Chicago Press): 165-82.

HEIM, R. 1952. *Destruction et protection de la nature*. Paris (Colin).

1961. *Equilibres de la nature et déséquilibre du monde*. Bordeaux (Imp. Bière).

HENDRICKSON, J. R. 1961. Conservation investigations on Malayan Turtles. *Malayan Nat. Journ.* Special issue: 214-23.

HICKLING, C. F. 1946. *The recovery of a deep sea fishery*. Min. Agr. Fish. Fish. Invest. Ser. II. 17, no. 1 (London), 59p.

HOESTLANDT, H. 1959. Répartition actuelle du Crabe chinois *Eriocheir sinensis* H. Milne Edwards en France. *Bull. Fr. Pisciculture*, 32 (194): 5-14.

HOLDGATE, M. W., and WACE, N. M., 1961. The influence of man on the floras and faunas of Southern Islands. *Polar Rec.*, 10: 475-93.

HOWARD, W. E. 1964a. Modification of New Zealand's flora by introduced mammals. *Proc. N.Z. Ecol. Soc.* no. 11: 59-62.

1964b. Introduced browsing mammals and habitat stability in New Zealand. *J. Wildlife Management*, 28: 421-9.

HUMBERT, H. 1927. La destruction d'une flore insulaire par le feu. Principaux aspects de la végétation à Madagascar. *Mém. Acad. Malgache*, 5.

1949. La dégradation des sols à Madagascar. *Bull. Agr. Congo Belge*, 40: 1141-62 (C.R. Conf. Agr. Sols, Goma 1948, Comm. no. 73)

HUNT, E. G., and BISCHOFF, A. I. 1960. Inimical effects on wildlife of periodic DDD applications to Clear Lake. *California Fish and Game*, 46: 91-106.

HUNTINGTON, E. 1915. *Civilization and Climate* (New Haven).

HUNTSMAN, A. G. 1948. Fishing and assessing populations. *Bull. Bingham Ocean Coll.* 9 (4): 5-31.

HUXLEY, J. 1961. *La protection de la grande faune et des habitats naturels en Afrique centrale et orientale*. Paris (Unesco).

HYAMS, E. 1952. *Soil and civilization*. London, New York.

ISE, J. 1961. *Our National Parks Policy. A Critical History*. Baltimore. (John Hopkins Press).

I.U.C.N. First International Technical Conference on the Protection of Nature. *Education and nature protection. General problems involving ecological research in the conservation of natural resources*. Lake Success. U.S.A. 1949 (1950).

Proc. and Papers of the (Second) Technical Meeting. *Rural landscape as a habitat for flora and fauna in densely populated countries. Management of nature reserves*. The Hague, Netherlands, 1951 (1952).

(Third) Technical Meeting. Amongst other themes: *Consequences of the use of fire for agriculture. Endemic species of small islands*. Caracas, 1952 (1954).

Fourth Technical Meeting. *Protection of Nature and Tourism. Protection of fauna and flora at high altitudes*. Salzburg 1953 (1954).

Hydro-Electricity and Nature Protection. Stating the Case. (Theme 1 of the Third Technical Meeting, Caracas, 1952). Vol. II. Coll. U.I.P.N. 'Pro Natura', Paris 1955.

Proc. and Papers of the Fifth Technical Meeting: *Arctic fauna. Insecticides, herbicides and consequences of the application*. Copenhagen 1954 (1956).

Consequences of Myxomatosis. Theme II of the Sixth Technical Meeting, Edinburgh 1956 (in *Terre et Vie*, 1956: 121-290).

Sixth Technical Meeting: *Management problems of nature reserves. Rehabilitation of areas devastated by man. Relationship of ecology to landscape planning*. Edinburgh 1956 (1957).

Seventh Technical Meeting. Vol. I. Erosion and civilizations (1959). Vol. II. Soil and water conservation (1960). Vol. III. Soil and water conservation (unpublished). Vol. IV. Soil and water conservation (1960). Vol. V. Rare Animals and Plants of the Mediterranean region (1959). Athens 1958.

Eighth Technical Meeting: *The management of wild grazing animals in temperate zones and its relation to land use* (in *Terre et Vie*, 1961: 181-358). *The ecological effects of biological and chemical control of undesirable plants and animals*. Warsaw-Cracow, 1960.

Conservation of Nature and Natural Resources in Modern African States. IUCN Publ. N.S. no. 1 (Symposium, Arusha, 1961) 1963.

First World Conference on National Parks. (Seattle, 1962). Washington (U.S. Dept. of Interior, Nat. Park Service). (IUCN Publ. N.S. no. 2) 1964.

Ninth Technical Meeting: *The Ecology of Man in Tropical Environment* (IUCN Publ. N.S. no. 4) Nairobi, 1963 (1964).

Proceedings of the MAR Conference, Les Saintes Maries de la Mer, 1962 I. *The Conservation and Management of Temperate Marshes, Bogs and other Wetlands* (IUCN Publ. N.S. no. 3) 1964. II. *List of European and North African Wetlands of International Importance*. (IUCN Publ. N.S. no. 5) 1965.

A Review of the Recent Knowledge on the Relationship between the Tsetse Fly and its Vertebrate Hosts. (P. E. GLOVER) (IUCN Publ. N.S. no. 6) 1965.

Tenth Technical Meeting: *Towards a New Relationship of Man and Nature in Temperate Lands*. I. *Ecological Impact of Recreation and Tourism upon Temperate Environments*. (IUCN Publ. N.S. no. 7) 1967. II. *Town and Country Planning Problems* (IUCN Publ. N.S. no. 8) 1967. III. *Changes due to introduced species* (IUCN Publ. N.S. no. 9) 1967. Lucerne 1966.

BIBLIOGRAPHY

335

Liste des Nations Unies des Parcs Nationaux et Réserves analogues. (J. P. HARROY 1967.
Conservation in Tropical South-East Asia. (Proc. Conf. Conservation Nature Nat. Res. Bangkok, 1965.) (IUCN Publ. N.S. no. 10) 1968.
JACKS, G. V., and WHYTE, R. O. 1939. *The rape of the earth. A world survey of soil erosion.*
JACKSON, H. H. T. 1943. Conserving endangered wildlife species. *Trans. Wisconsin Acad. Sci. Arts Letters,* 35: 61-89.
JANZEN, D. H. 1960. *Problems with fish and pesticides in the United States.* I.U.C.N. Report, Eighth Technical Meeting, Warsaw-Cracow 1960, R.T. 8/II/IV, 6p.
JEANNIN, I. 1947. *L'Eléphant d'Afrique.* Paris (Payot).
JEFFREYS, M. D. W. 1951. Feux de brousse. *Bull. I.F.A.N.,* 13: 682-710.
JOUANIN, C. 1959. Les émeus de l'expédition Baudin. *Oiseau et R.F.O.,* 29: 169-203.
KENYON, K. W., SCHEFFER, V. B. and CHAPMAN, D. G. 1954. *A population study of the Alaska fur-seal herd.* U.S. Dept. Interior. Fish and Wildlife Service. Sp. Sci. Rep., Wildlife no. 12, 77p.
KIMPE, P. DE. 1957. Le contrôle de la Jacinthe d'eau. *Bull. Agric. Congo Belge,* 48: 105-51.
KLEIN, L. 1962. *River pollution. I. Chemical analysis. II. Causes and effects.* London (Butterworths).
KNIPLING, E. F. 1960. The eradication of the Screw-worm fly. *Scient. Amer.,* 203 (4): 54-61.
KRATZER, A. 1937. Das Stadtklima. *Die Wissenschaft,* vol. 40.
KUENEN, D. J. 1960. *The ecological effects of chemical and biological control of undesirable plants and insects. General introduction.* I.U.C.N. Report, Eighth Technical Meeting, Warsaw-Cracow, 1960, R.T. 8/II/R.G., 6p.
KUHNHOLTZ-LORDAT, G. 1938. *La terre incendiée,* Montpellier (Lab. Botanique, Ecole nationale d'agriculture).
1958. *L'écran vert.* Mém. Mus. nat. Hist. Nat. N.S. B.9. Paris.
LANDSBERG, H. E. 1956. The climate of towns. In: *Man's Role in Changing The Face of The Earth.* Chicago (Univ. Chicago Press): 584-606.
LAVROV, N. P. 1960. *Acclimatization of Muskrats in the USSR.* Translation of Russian Game Rep., vol. 7.
LAWS, R. M. 1960. Problems of Whale Conservation. *Trans. 28th North Amer. Wildlife Conf.:* 304-19.
LEOPOLD, A. S. 1947. Status of Mexican big-game herds. *Trans. 12th North Amer. Wildlife Conf.:* 437-48.
LEOPOLD, A. S., RINEY, T., MCCAIN, R., and TEVIS, L. 1951. *The Jawbone Deer Herd.* State of Calif. Dept. Nat. Res. Fish and Game. Game Bull. no. 4.
LETACONNOUX, R. 1951. Considérations sur l'exploitation du stock de Merlu depuis 1937. Rev. Trav. Off. Sci. Tech. *Pêches Marit.,* 16: 72-89.
LEVI, H. W. 1952. Evaluation of Wildlife Importations. *Scient. Monthly,* 74: 315-22.
L'HARDY, J. P. 1962. Le rôle du mazout dans la destruction des oiseaux marins sur le littoral du Finistère. *Penn ar Bed,* no. 29: 187-91.
LINNARD, W. 1963. The Saiga. *Oryx,* 7: 30-3.
LOCKIE, J. D. and RATCLIFFE, D. A. 1964. Insecticides and Scottish Golden Eagles. *Brit. Birds,* 57: 89-102.
LONGHURST, W. M., LEOPOLD, A. S., and DASMANN, R. F. 1952. *A survey of California Deer Herds.* State of Calif. Fish and Game. Game Bull. no. 6.
MALIN, J. C. 1956. The grassland of North America: its occupance and the challenge of continuous reappraisals. In: *Man's Role in Changing The Face of The Earth.* Chicago (Univ. Chicago Press): 360-66.
MALLET, L. 1961. Recherche des hydrocarbures polybenzéniques du type benzo-3.4 pyrène dans la faune des milieux marins (Manche, Atlantique et Méditerranée). *C.R. Acad. Sci.* 253: 168-70.

MANGENOT, G. 1964. *Impact de l'homme sur le milieu tropical.* Espèces introduites. I.U.C.N. Ninth Technical Meeting, Nairobi. I.U.C.N. Publ. N.S. no. 4: 253-60.

MARSH, G. P. 1864. *Man and Nature.* London (Sampson Low, Son and Marston). 1874. *The Earth as Modified by Human Action.* New York (Scribner, Armstrong & Co.).

MARTY, J. P. 1955. Les Antilopes d'Afrique sont-elles menacées par l'industrie des peaux? *Mammalia,* 19: 344-6.

MATHEWS, D. O. 1962. *Some economic aspects of National Parks and Reserves in relation to tourism.* I.U.C.N. Reports, 1st World Conf. Nat. Parks (Seattle 1962).

MEAD, A. R. 1961. *The Giant African Snail: a problem of economic malacology.* Chicago (Univ. Chicago Press).

MEGGITT, M. J. 1963. *Aboriginal food-gatherers of tropical Australia.* I.U.C.N. Report, 9th Technical Meeting, Nairobi R.T. 9/I/4, 9 p.

MELLANBY, K. 1967. *Pesticides and Pollution.* London (Collins).

MESSERI, A. 1959. Notes sur l'*Abies nebrodensis* (Lojac) Mattei. I.U.C.N. 7th Technical Meeting, Athens 1958, 5: 130-4.

METCALF, C. L., and FLINT, W. P. 1951. *Destructive and useful insects: their habits and control.* New York (McGraw Hill).

MILLER, R. R. 1961. Man and the changing fish fauna of the American Southwest. *Pap. Michigan Acad. Sci. Arts Lett.* 46: 365-404. 1963. Is our native underwater life worth saving? *Nat. Parks Mag.* 37, no. 188: 4-9.

MITCHEL, B. L., and UYS, J. M. C. 1961. The problem of the Lechwe *Kobus leche* on the Kafue Flats. *Oryx* 6: 171-83.

MONOD, TH. 1956. La protection de la faune marine. *Le grand livre de la mer et des poissons.* Monaco (Union eur. Editions): 319-27. 1959. *Parts respectives de l'homme et des phénomènes naturels dans la dégradation du paysage et le déclin des civilisations à travers le monde méditerranéen* lato sensu, *avec les déserts ou semi-déserts adjacents, au cours des derniers millénaires.* I.U.C.N. Seventh Technical Meeting, Athens 1958, 1: 31-69.

MOORE, N. W. (ed.) 1966. *Pesticides in the environment and their effects on wildlife.* Oxford (Blackwell). Suppl. *J. Applied Ecology* 3.

MURPHY, R. C. 1951. The impact of man upon Nature in New Zealand. *Proc. Amer. Philos. Soc.* 95: 569-82.

MYERS, J. G. 1934. The arthropod fauna of a rice-ship, trading from Burma to the West Indies. *J. Anim. Ecol.* 3: 146-9.

NARR, K. J. 1956. Early food-producing populations. In: *Man's Role in Changing The Face of The World.* Chicago (Univ. Chicago Press): 134-51.

NICHOLSON, E. M. 1952. *General introduction. Le paysage rural considéré comme milieu naturel de la flore et de la faune dans les pays densément peuplés.* I.U.C.N. 2nd Technical Meeting, The Hague (1951): 54-7.

NIETHAMMER, G. 1963. *Die Einbürgerung von Säugetieren und Vögeln in Europa.* Hamburg and Berlin (Parey).

OLSON, T. A., and BURGESS, F. F. (ed.). 1967. *Pollution and marine ecology.* New York and London (Interscience).

OSBORN, F. 1948. *Our Plundered Planet.* Boston (Little, Brown & Co.).

PARSONS, J. J. 1962. *The Green Turtle and Man.* Gainesville (Univ. Florida Press).

PATTERSON, N. A. 1956. *Changes caused by spray of chemicals in the fauna of apple orchards in Nova Scotia.* I.U.C.N. Report, 5th Technical Meeting, Copenhagen, 1955: 123-6.

PAULIAN, P. 1957. La pêche autour des îles Saint-Paul et Amsterdam et son avenir. *Terre et Vie:* 267-82.

PENFOLD, A. R., and WILLIS, J. L. 1961. *The Eucalypts.* London (Leonard Hill)

PETITJEAN, M. 1966. Le contrôle biologique des mollusques nuisibles. *Année biol.* 5: 271-95.

PETRIDES, G. A. 1956. Big game densities and range carrying capacities in East Africa. *Trans. 21st North Amer. Wildlife Conf.*: 525-37.

1961. The management of wild hoofed animals in the United States in relation to land use. *Terre et Vie*: 181-202.

PETRIDES, G. A., and SWANK, W. G. 1958. Management of the big game resource in Uganda, East Africa. *Trans. 23rd North Amer. Wildlife Conf.*: 461-77.

PHILLIPS, J. 1959. *Agriculture and ecology in Africa*. London (Faber and Faber).

PICKETT, A. D. 1960. *The ecological effects of chemical control practices on Arthropod populations in apple orchards in Nova Scotia, Canada.* I.U.C.N., Reports of the Eighth Technical Meeting, Warsaw-Cracow 1960: R.T. 8/II/6, 5p.

RANSON, G. 1962. *Missions dans le Pacifique.* Paris (Lechevalier) (see also *Préliminaires à un rapport sur l'huître perlière dans les E.F.O.*, Paris, unpublished).

RANWELL, D. S. 1962. *Conservation and management of estuarine marsh in relation to Spartina marsh in the British Isles.* I.U.C.N., Report. Projet MAR.

RASMUSSEN, D. I. 1941. Biotic communities of the Kaibab Plateau. *Ecol. Monographs*, 11: 229-75.

RIDLEY, H. N. 1930. *The dispersal of Plants throughout the World.* Ashford, Kent (L. Reeve & Co.).

RINEY, T. 1963. *Utilization of wildlife in the Transvaal.* I.U.C.N. Conservation of Nature and Nat. Res. in Modern African States. Publ. N.S. no. 1: 303-5.

ROBYNS, W. 1955 Le genre *Eichhornia*, spécialement *E. crassipes* (Jacinthe d'eau) au Congo belge. *Bull. Séances Acad. Roy. Sci. colon. N.S.* 1: 1116-37.

RUDD, R. L. 1960. *The ecological consequences of chemicals in pest control, particularly as regards their effects on mammals.* I.U.C.N. Report of the Eighth Technical Meeting, Warsaw-Cracow 1960, R.T. 8/II/11, 8 p.

RUDD, R. L., and GENELLY, R. E. 1956. *Pesticides: their use and toxicity in relation to wildlife.* State of California. Fish and Game, Game Bull. no. 7, 209p.

RUSSELL, R. S. 1959. *The biological consequences of the pollution of the environment with fission products.* I.U.C.N. 7th Technical Meeting, Athens, 1958, I: 236-54.

SCHORGER, A. W. 1943. The Prairie Chicken and Sharp-tailed Grouse in early Wisconsin. *Trans. Wisconsin Acad. Sc. Arts. Lett.* 35: 1-59.

SCHUSTER, W. H. 1952. Provisional survey of the introduction and transplantation of fish throughout the Indo-Pacific region. *Proc. Indo-Pacif. Fish. Coun.* 3 (2) 3: 184-96.

SEARS, P. B. 1967. *Deserts on the March.* Norman (Univ. Oklahoma Press) 3rd ed.

SHANTZ, H. C. 1948. An estimate of the shrinkage of Africa's tropical forests. *Unasylva*, 2: 66-7.

SHORTEN, M. 1954. *Squirrels.* London (Collins).

SILLANS, R. 1958. *Les savanes de l'Afrique centrale.* Paris (Lechevalier).

SIMON, N. 1962. *Between the Sunlight and the Thunder. The wild life of Kenya.* London (Collins).

1963. *The Galana River Game management scheme.* I.U.C.N. Cons. Nature Nat. Res. in Modern Afr. States. Publ. N.S. no. 1: 325-8.

SMITH, J. E. (ed.). 1968. *'Torrey Canyon' Pollution and Marine Life.* Cambridge (Cambridge Univ. Press).

SOPER, F. L., and WILSON, D. B. 1943. *Anopheles gambiae in Brazil, 1930 to 1940.* New York (Rockefeller Foundation).

STEWART, O. C. 1956. Fire as the first great force employed by Man. In: *Man's Role in Changing The Face of The Earth.* Chicago (Chicago Univ. Press): 115-33.

TALBOT, L. M. 1959-60. A look at threatened species. *Oryx*, 5: 153-293.

TENDRON, G. 1958. Les pollutions chimiques des mers, des estuaires et des côtes. *C.R. Acad. Agri. France.* 44: 582-8.

1962. La pollution des mers par les hydrocarbures et la contamination de la flore et de la faune marines. *Penn ar Bed*, 29: 173-82.

THOMAS, H. F. 1957. The Starling in the Sunraysia district, Victoria. *Emu*, 57: 31-48, 131-44, 151-80, 269-84, 325-37.

THOMAS, W. L. (ed.). 1956. *Man's Role in Changing The Face of The Earth*. Chicago (Univ. Chicago Press).

THOMPSON, W. F. 1950. *The effect of Fishing on Stocks of Halibut in the Pacific*. Publ. Fish. Res. Inst. Univ. Washington. Seattle 1.

1952. Condition of Stocks of Halibut in the Pacific. Cons. Perm. Int. Expl. Mer. *Journ. du Conseil*, 18: 141-66.

THOMPSON, W. F. and FREEMAN, N. L. 1930. History of the Pacific Halibut fishery. *Rep. Intern. Fish. Comm.*, no. 5: 3-61.

THOMSON, G. M. 1922. *The naturalization of Animals and Plants in New Zealand*. Cambridge (Cambridge Univ. Press).

TRICART, J. 1962. *L'épiderme de la terre*. Paris (Masson).

TURNBULL, C. M. 1963. *Forest hunters and gatherers: the Mbuti pygmies*. I.U.C.N. Report of 9th Technical Meeting, Nairobi, R.T. 9/I/5, 7p (see also by the same author: *The Forest People*, New York 1961).

UNESCO. 1963. *Enquête sur les ressources naturelles du continent africain*. Paris (Unesco).

UVAROV, B. 1963. Influence du développement agricole sur les pullulations d'insectes. *Phytoma*, January 1963: 19-22.

VASSEROT, J. 1962. La pollution des animaux marins comestibles par des hydrocarbures cancérigènes. *Penn ar Bed*, no. 29: 183-6.

VERNET, A. 1960. Plantes spontanées et plantes cultivées. *In* Colloque Etude Prairies, Soc. Bot. France. Mémoires publiés par la revue *Fourrages*, no. 4: 15-25.

VIBERT, R. and LAGLER, K. F. 1961. Pêches continentales. *Biologie et aménagement* Paris (Dunod).

VIVIER, P. 1951. Poissons et Crustacés d'eau douce acclimatés en France en eaux libres depuis le début du siècle. *Terre et Vie*: 57-82.

VOGT, W. 1948. *Rond to Survival*. New York (W. Sloane Ass.).

VOS, A. DE, MANVILLE, R. H. and VAN GELDER, R. G. 1956. Introduced mammals and their influence on native biota. *Zoologica*, 41: 163-96.

WALFORD, L. A. 195 *Living resources of the sea: opportunities for research and expansion*. New York (The Ronald Press Co.).

WALLACE, G. J. 1959. Insecticides and birds. *Audubon Mag.* 61 (1): 10-12, 35.)

WASAWO, D. P. S. 1963. *Some problems of Uganda swamps*. I.U.C.N. Report of the Ninth Technical Meeting, Nairobi 1963. 9/II/14, 10 p.

WESTHOFF, V., and ZONDERWIJK, P. 1960. *The effects of herbicides on the wild flora and vegetation in the Netherlands*. I.U.C.N. Report of the 8th Technical Meeting, Warsaw-Cracow 1960. R.T. 8/II/8, 6 p.

WILLIAMS, G. R. 1962. Extinction and the Land and Freshwater-inhabiting Birds of New Zealand. *Notornis*, 10: 15-32.

WING, L. 1943. Spread of the Starling and English Sparrow. *Auk*, 60: 74-87.

WODZICKI, K. A. 1950. Introduced mammals of New Zealand. An ecological and economic survey. *Dept. Sci. Ind. Res.*, (New Zeal.) *Bull.* 98: 1-255.

WOLSTENHOLME, G. (ed.). 1963. *Man and His Future*. London (Churchill).

WORTHINGTON, E. B. 1961. *The Wild Resources of East and Central Africa*. London (H.M. Stationery Office) 26 p. (Colonial office, no. 352).

ZIMMERMAN, E. C. 1948. *Insects of Hawaii. Vol. I. Introduction*. Honolulu (Univ. Hawaii Press).

ZOBELL, C. E. 1962. The occurrence, effects and fate of oil polluting the sea. *Int. Conf. Water Pollution Res.* 3 (48): 1-27.

Index

Numbers in italics refer to text-figures and maps.